SOCIETY FOR NEW TESTAMENT STUDIES
MONOGRAPH SERIES
General Editor: R. McL. Wilson, F.B.A.
Associate Editor: M. E. Thrall

41

RIGHTEOUSNESS IN MATTHEW AND HIS WORLD OF THOUGHT

Righteousness in Matthew and his world of thought

BENNO PRZYBYLSKI
Research Assistant Professor
Department of Religious Studies
McMaster University

CAMBRIDGE UNIVERSITY PRESS

CAMBRIDGE

LONDON   NEW YORK   NEW ROCHELLE

MELBOURNE   SYDNEY

Published by the Press Syndicate of the University of Cambridge
The Pitt Building, Trumpington Street, Cambridge CB2 1RP
32 East 57th Street, New York, NY 10022, USA
296 Beaconsfield Parade, Middle Park, Melbourne 3206, Australia

First published 1980

⒟ Typeset by H Charlesworth & Co Ltd, Huddersfield
Printed in Great Britain
by Redwood Burn Ltd
Trowbridge & Esher

British Library cataloguing in publication data
Przybylski, Benno
Righteousness in Matthew and his world of thought. –
(Society for New Testament Studies. Monograph
series; 41).
1. Bible. New Testament. Matthew 2. God –
Righteousness – Biblical teaching 3. Dead Sea
scrolls 4. God – Righteousness – History of
doctrines 5. Tannaim
I. Title II. Series
234'.1   BS2575.5   79-41371
ISBN 0 521 22566 3

In memory of my father
Rev. Adolf Przybylski

CONTENTS

PREFACE

I am grateful to Professor E. P. Sanders for initiating me into the complex world of Rabbinic thought and making me aware of the intricacies of relating this knowledge to the study of the New Testament. While following his research on the relationship between Paul and Palestinian Judaism, my interest in the application of this type of criticism to the Gospel of Matthew was kindled. After various general investigations, my research began to focus on the relationship between the Matthaean concept of righteousness and that of the Tannaitic literature and the Dead Sea Scrolls.

My exhaustive analysis of the righteousness terminology in the Tannaitic literature and the Dead Sea Scrolls led to the unmistakable conclusion that the concept of righteousness is not to be equated with the soteriological system inherent in this literature. For the overall view of the intrinsic soteriology of Palestinian Judaism, I am, however, indebted to the work of Professor Sanders. On the other hand, the distinction between righteousness and soteriology in the Gospel of Matthew is based entirely on my own research.

Under the supervision of Professor Sanders this study was submitted to McMaster University as a doctoral dissertation and the degree of Doctor of Philosophy was granted in 1975.

The financial support provided by the Canada Council throughout my doctoral studies is deeply appreciated. I am particularly indebted for the grant which made it possible for me to engage in a year of research in Israel. At the Hebrew University of Jerusalem it was especially Professor D. Flusser who stimulated my thinking. Life in Israel presented numerous diversions which mitigated the painstaking work involved in word studies.

The present form of this study represents a major revision of the original doctoral dissertation. For their constructive suggestions concerning both form and content of this revised monograph I would like to thank my colleagues at McMaster University, Drs E. P. Sanders, B. F. Meyer, A. I. Baumgarten and A. M. Cooper. The suggestions by Professor R. McL.

Wilson, the editor of the SNTS Monograph Series, and by the appointed reader have also been most helpful and are appreciated.

Since this study deals primarily with unpointed Hebrew texts, a simplified method of transliteration has been adopted in most cases, that is, one in which there is no ambiguity concerning the identity of Hebrew consonants, while the numerous vowel points are represented by the appropriate English vowels without further distinguishing marks. In a few cases, i.e. especially when quoting unpointed terms in secondary literature, it seemed more appropriate to use solely consonants in transliteration.

For proofreading and sharing in the typing I would like to thank Miss Marlene Przybylski and Ms Phyllis Koetting.

For the laborious task of typing the bulk of this manuscript and helping in numerous other aspects of the preparation of this monograph I am deeply grateful to Brigitte, my wife. Above all, however, I am thankful for her encouragement and sincere interest in my research.

ABBREVIATIONS

AThD	Acta Theologica Danica
ATR	*Anglican Theological Review*
B.	Babylonian Talmud
BA	*Biblical Archeologist*
BASOR	*Bulletin of the American Schools of Oriental Research*
BEvTh	Beiträge zur evangelischen Theologie
BibSac	*Bibliotheca Sacra*
BNTC	Black's New Testament Commentaries
BThB	*Biblical Theology Bulletin*
BZ	*Biblische Zeitschrift*
CD	Damascus Document
DJD	*Discoveries in the Judaean Desert*
EQ	*Evangelical Quarterly*
ET	English translation
EvTh	*Evangelische Theologie*
FRLANT	Forschungen zur Religion und Literatur des Alten und Neuen Testaments
HbzNT	Handbuch zum Neuen Testament
HTR	*Harvard Theological Review*
HUCA	*Hebrew Union College Annual*
ICC	International Critical Commentary
IDB	*Interpreter's Dictionary of the Bible*
IEJ	*Israel Exploration Journal*
JBL	*Journal of Biblical Literature*
JJS	*Journal of Jewish Studies*
JQR	*Jewish Quarterly Review*
JSS	*Journal of Semitic Studies*
JStJ	*Journal for the Study of Judaism*
JThS	*Journal of Theological Studies*
KerDog	*Kerygma und Dogma*
LXX	Septuagint

Mek.	Mekilta de-Rabbi Ishmael
MS.	Manuscript
MSS.	Manuscripts
NCB	New Century Bible
NF	Neue Folge
NovTest	*Novum Testamentum*
NT	New Testament
NTAb	Neutestamentliche Abhandlungen
NTD	Das Neue Testament Deutsch
NTS	*New Testament Studies*
OSt	*Oudtestamentische Studiën*
OT	Old Testament
P.	Palestinian Talmud
1QH	Thanksgiving Hymns
1QM	War Scroll
1QpHab	Habakkuk Commentary
1QpMic	Micah Commentary
1QS	Manual of Discipline
1QSa	Rule Annexe
1QSb	Book of Blessings
4QFl	Florilegium
4QPatr	Patriarchal Blessings
4QpNah	Commentary on Nahum
4QpPs37	Commentary on Ps 37
4QSl(39)	Angelic Liturgy
4QTest	Testimonia
R.	Rabbi
RB	*Revue Biblique*
RevExp	*Review and Expositor*
RQ	*Revue de Qumran*
RSV	Revised Standard Version
SBT	Studies in Biblical Theology
Sifre Deut	Sifre on Deuteronomy
Sifre Num	Sifre on Numbers
SNTS	Society for New Testament Studies
SPB	Studia Post Biblica
StANT	Studien zum Alten und Neuen Testament
StTDJ	Studies on the Texts of the Desert of Judah
StTh	*Studia Theologica*
StUNT	Studien zur Umwelt des Neuen Testaments
Suppl.	Supplements

T.	Tosefta
TDNT	*Theological Dictionary of the New Testament*
ThA	Theologische Arbeiten
ThLZ	*Theologische Literaturzeitung*
ThZ	*Theologische Zeitschrift*
TU	*Texte und Untersuchungen*
VigChr	*Vigiliae Christianae*
VT	*Vetus Testamentum*
WMANT	Wissenschaftliche Monographien zum Alten und Neuen Testament
ZAW	*Zeitschrift für die Alttestamentliche Wissenschaft*
ZNW	*Zeitschrift für die Neutestamentliche Wissenschaft*
ZThK	*Zeitschrift für Theologie und Kirche*

1

THE PROBLEM OF THE MEANING AND SIGNIFICANCE OF THE MATTHAEAN CONCEPT OF RIGHTEOUSNESS

1 The state of the question

The controversy regarding the meaning of the Matthaean concept of righteousness has revolved primarily around the following question: Does the term 'righteousness' (*dikaiosynē*) refer to God's gift to man or God's demand upon man? This question has basically been answered in four different ways; that is, two diametrically opposed positions and two mediating views have been presented.

The positions of G. Strecker[1] and M. J. Fiedler[2] are representative of the diametrically opposed views. Strecker asserts that in all seven *dikaiosynē*-passages, righteousness refers to *Rechtschaffenheit*.[3] It is always seen as a demand upon man; never as the gift of God.

Fiedler, on the other hand, claims that in all seven *dikaiosynē*-passages in the Gospel of Matthew, righteousness is both the eschatological gift and the demand of God. The gift, however, precedes the demand. Accordingly, Fiedler views righteousness essentially as the gift of God.[4]

The two other views are essentially attempts at finding a mediating position between the two extreme views just expressed. These two mediating views are similar insofar as they both acknowledge that the term *dikaiosynē* does not have the same meaning in each occurrence. In some cases it refers to the gift of God while in others it refers to the demand made upon man. The point of contention between these two views stems from the relative importance assigned to these two aspects of righteousness.

In one mediating view greater significance is assigned to those passages in which *dikaiosynē* is interpreted as referring to the gift of God. For example, J. A. Ziesler comes to the conclusion that in Mt 5:20 righteousness refers to the demand made upon man while in 5:6 it refers to God's gift. With respect to the significance of these passages he concludes: 'It is probably no accident that 5.6 precedes 5.20: human righteousness is inadequate, and what is needed is not only a more thoroughgoing kind, but one which comes as God's gift to those who long for it.'[5] This view differs only minimally from the extreme position taken by Fiedler. While the interpretation of some passages differs, the end result is identical. Essentially the significance of the Matthaean concept of righteousness is seen in the fact that it refers to the gift of God.

The second mediating view does not gravitate toward either of the extreme positions. Such commentators as E. Schweizer[6] and E. Lohmeyer,[7] for example, treat each *dikaiosynē*-passage on its own merit. Some passages are seen as reflecting the meaning of righteousness as the gift of God; others, the demand made upon man. No attempt is made to subordinate one meaning to the other. The tacit assumption appears to be that Matthew simply does not use the term *dikaiosynē* consistently.

Despite wide disagreement as to the meaning of the Matthaean concept of righteousness, there is a scholarly consensus that this is an important concept in the Gospel of Matthew.[8] It is especially argued that the concept of righteousness plays a crucial role in determining the Matthaean view of the nature of salvation. Actually, irrespective of their views as to the meaning of the Matthaean concept of righteousness, scholars claim that the relative degree of agreement and disagreement between the Matthaean and Pauline concepts of righteousness is directly reflected in their respective views of the nature of salvation. The conceptual language employed in the scholarly discussion of the relationship between the Matthaean and Pauline views of salvation is that of righteousness by faith as the gift of God and/or righteousness by works as man's ability to meet the demand of God.

According to Fiedler's interpretation, the Matthaean and Pauline concepts of righteousness are essentially in agreement; both Matthew and Paul view righteousness as *Heilsgabe*.[9] It should be noted that in his introduction Fiedler shows obvious satisfaction in being able to claim that Matthew holds a Pauline understanding of righteousness.[10]

Exegetes who hold the view that not all *dikaiosynē*-passages in the Gospel of Matthew refer to righteousness as the gift of God, but who at the same time claim that the Matthaean and Pauline views of salvation are compatible, are confronted by a problem. This difficulty is generally solved by subordinating the demand to the gift. Kertelge, for example, argues that although the Jewish understanding of righteousness in terms of works still seems to be visible in the Gospel of Matthew, it is in fact fundamentally, i.e. christologically, broken.[11]

Scholars who do not subordinate one aspect of the Matthaean teaching regarding righteousness to the other, or who claim that righteousness refers solely to the demand of God upon man, acknowledge that the Matthaean view of salvation differs from the Pauline one. For example, P. Stuhlmacher points out that owing to the imbalance between the aspects of righteousness as gift and demand, it is impossible for Matthew to give expression to a view of salvation which is *sola gratia.* [12]

2 The method of the present study

The present study takes for granted that the final redaction of the Gospel of Matthew did not take place in an intellectual vacuum. By employing the concept of righteousness, Matthew intended to communicate a specific message to a particular audience. Since the Gospel of Matthew does not identify its audience, the exact nature of the audience may in fact never be known with any degree of certainty. It is plausible, however, that through a study of background literature the general intellectual milieu can be identified in which the Matthaean concept of righteousness is intelligible. Once such relevant literature has been found it can then be utilized to corroborate and in some instances even to clarify Matthaean usage.

Why is there wide scholarly disagreement regarding the meaning of the concept of righteousness in the Gospel of Matthew? It will be argued in the present study that the absence of consensus is largely due to the fact that scholars have misjudged what in fact constitutes the appropriate background literature for the Gospel of Matthew. After all, when an incompatible background literature is posited as governing Matthaean usage, it is to be expected that various views would result on how to harmonize conflicting types of usage. Specifically, it will be demonstrated that the Matthaean concept of righteousness does not become intelligible when viewed in terms of Pauline usage or in terms of undifferentiated Old Testament usage.

It will be argued that scholars who have used Pauline thought as the basis for their interpretation of the Matthaean concept of righteousness have essentially imposed a mode of thought foreign to the Gospel of Matthew. The Pauline categories of righteousness by faith versus righteousness by works are not applicable to the Gospel of Matthew. In comparison to the Pauline literature, the concept of righteousness has an entirely different function in the Gospel of Matthew.

The situation with respect to the use of the Old Testament as pertinent background material for understanding the Matthaean concept of righteousness is more complex than in the case of the Pauline literature. Since passages from the Old Testament are quoted in the Gospel of Matthew, it is obvious that the Old Testament forms part of the relevant background literature for this gospel. However, before Old Testament usage with respect to the righteousness terminology can be viewed as governing Matthaean usage, it has to be demonstrated that there was in fact such a direct influence; that is, in view of the significant time lag between the composition of the various Old Testament writings and the time of the final redaction of the Gospel of Matthew, it cannot be taken for granted that there had been no development in the usage of the righteousness terminology.

The present study will demonstrate that the influence of Old Testament thought upon the Matthaean redaction is primarily of an indirect nature. This conclusion is based on the two following findings. (1) The Dead Sea Scrolls and the Tannaitic literature clearly show that there was in fact a significant development in the usage of the righteousness terminology from Old Testament times to the period of the composition of these bodies of literature. (2) The Dead Sea Scrolls and the Tannaitic literature in fact provide an intellectual milieu in which the Matthaean concept of righteousness is intelligible. Indeed, these two bodies of literature are invaluable for the purpose of corroborating and clarifying Matthaean usage of the righteousness terminology.

This does not mean that the Old Testament is dispensable as far as the study of the background literature is concerned. On the contrary, the usage of the Dead Sea Scrolls, the Tannaitic literature and the Gospel of Matthew is more readily understood when its proper relationship to the Old Testament is brought into focus. After all, the Old Testament provides the point of departure for the development in the usage of the righteousness terminology exemplified in the later literature.

At this point the reader may be concerned with a number of methodological questions pertaining to the use of the Dead Sea Scrolls and Tannaitic literature as background literature for the Gospel of Matthew. Can it be demonstrated that the relevant passages in the Tannaitic literature are pre-Matthaean? What geographical implications are involved in positing these bodies of literature as background material for the Gospel of Matthew? Is a detailed analysis of the concept of righteousness in the Dead Sea Scrolls and the Tannaitic literature not simply duplication of previous work?

Let us deal with these possible objections. It should be noted first of all that in this study the background literature is not investigated with the intention of identifying literary sources of which Matthew was necessarily aware. Rather, the primary purpose in the discussion of the background literature is to gain a general perspective, that is, to identify the general intellectual milieu in which the Matthaean concept of righteousness is intelligible.

With respect to the dating of the background literature the present approach attempts to avoid the following pitfall. Often, when it has been shown that a body of literature predates a specific writing, the meaning of specific terms and concepts in the former is imposed upon the latter. The possibility is lost sight of that the meaning of a term can change in even a relatively short time or that at any one time specific terms can have divergent meanings and/or functions in contemporaneous systems of thought.

In the present study the meaning and function of terms and concepts found in the Dead Sea Scrolls and the Tannaitic literature are not simply imposed on the Gospel of Matthew. Rather, every attempt is made to discuss the meaning and function of terms and concepts in the Gospel of Matthew on the basis of the gospel itself. Once this process has been completed, the background literature is used for the purpose of corroboration; that is, the plausibility of the Matthaean usage is established on the basis of corresponding usage in other bodies of literature.

Once such correspondence of meaning and function has been demonstrated between two bodies of literature, then, and only then, are ambiguous passages interpreted in terms of the usage in the background literature. Care is taken, however, to utilize this procedure rarely and only in dealing with concepts of relatively minor significance.

With respect to the question of dating, this study therefore does not stand or fall on the basis of previous results as to the chronological relationship among the Dead Sea Scrolls, Tannaitic literature and the Gospel of Matthew. Instead, by demonstrating that the concept of righteousness in the Gospel of Matthew *in fact* becomes intelligible when viewed against the backdrop of the thought expressed in these two bodies of literature, new evidence is provided for the dating of these ideas. Specifically, with respect to the Tannaitic literature it becomes obvious that certain concepts predate the Gospel of Matthew even though the specific sayings in which these concepts are embedded may not do so.

These qualifications made, it should be noted that the Dead Sea Scrolls and the Tannaitic literature are not so far removed in time from the final redaction of the Gospel of Matthew as to warrant skepticism. The question of dating will be discussed in more detail in the introductions to the respective chapters dealing with these bodies of literature.

With reference to the geographical relationship between the Gospel of Matthew and the Dead Sea Scrolls and Tannaitic literature it is important to note that the two latter bodies of literature can be classified as being Jewish-Palestinian. This does not imply that all non-Jewish-Palestinian writings are necessarily irrelevant to this investigation. Yet the fact that these Jewish-Palestinian writings are adequate to provide the background against which the Matthaean concept of righteousness becomes intelligible must be taken into account in the continuing debate concerning the Jewish-Christian versus the Gentile-Christian character of the Gospel of Matthew.[13] For example, a major weakness in Strecker's study is that he has not systematically considered the meaning of the concept of righteousness in the Jewish-Palestinian writings.

Even if it is granted that the Dead Sea Scrolls and the Tannaitic literature are important for understanding the concept of righteousness in the Gospel of Matthew, is a new study of the righteousness terminology in these two bodies of literature warranted? The answer to this question is a definite yes. It is specifically these writings which have received very haphazard treatment in previous research.

For example, Ziesler and Fiedler are foremost among the scholars who have attempted to deal with all possible materials which might elucidate the meaning of the concept of righteousness in the New Testament. Their treatment of the Dead Sea Scrolls and the Rabbinic literature, however, is the weak point in their investigations.

In dealing with the Dead Sea Scrolls they have failed to grasp significant variations in the use of the righteousness terminology that exist among the various writings. In this study special attention will be focussed on these variations.[14]

In dealing with the Rabbinic literature the investigations of Ziesler and Fiedler have two major flaws. Like many other New Testament scholars, Ziesler and Fiedler have failed to apply the same critical methods of evaluation to Rabbinic texts as they have applied to early Christian texts. For example, sayings from the fifth- and sixth-century Talmuds have been applied indiscriminately to New Testament times. As a partial remedy to this situation, the present study will focus exclusively on the Tannaitic literature rather than on the Rabbinic literature as a whole. This focus is desirable, since it introduces a reasonable restriction on the time span to be covered. As was noted above, more precise dating of usage within the Tannaitic period is not strictly necessary, nor is it, at the present stage of research, possible.

The second flaw in Ziesler's and Fiedler's treatment of the Rabbinic literature is that they simply have not treated the vast majority of the most significant passages dealing with the concept of righteousness in the Tannaitic literature. Ziesler acknowledges that because of the 'sheer vastness of the material'[15] he has simply attempted 'to indicate the range of meanings without pretending to thoroughness'.[16] As a matter of fact, Ziesler has made a more exhaustive analysis of only two samples: Genesis Rabbah and the Targum Onkelos.

The choice of these two particular writings is unfortunate. Genesis Rabbah was compiled very late, probably no earlier than the Palestinian Talmud.[17] Although Targum Onkelos may possibly date from the second or third century A.D., its usefulness to the investigation at hand is limited. Since it is an Aramaic translation of the Pentateuch it is very limited in its ability to express Rabbinic thought.

Ziesler's acknowledged lack of thoroughness is especially evident with respect to the Tannaitic midrashim. For example, in Sifre on Deuteronomy there are a total of seventeen relevant passages containing a total of 41 occurrences of the nouns *tsedeq* and *tsedaqah*. Ziesler refers to only one of these passages and even this one reference is not discussed in the section dealing with the Rabbinic writings[18] but is merely referred to incidentally as one of the passages which Bultmann cites.[19] Ziesler makes no reference whatsoever to Sifre on Numbers and Sifra. Consequently, Ziesler's study is of little value as a word study of the righteousness terminology with respect to the Tannaitic literature.

Fiedler's analysis of the meaning of righteousness in the oldest Rabbinic literature[20] is beset with even greater problems than that of Ziesler. Fiedler, like Ziesler, treats only relatively few passages, but even the passages he does treat are not gleaned directly from the Rabbinic literature but indirectly from Strack and Billerbeck.[21]

In contrast to these studies, the present study intends to be exhaustive. All references to the nouns *tsedeq* and *tsedaqah* in the Tannaitic literature will be discussed.[22]

In addition to the nouns *tsedeq* and *tsedaqah*, this study will also deal with the adjective *tsaddiq* in the background literature. Fiedler dealt only with the nouns and not the adjective.[23] This omission has had negative consequences. Having looked only at *righteousness* and not at *the righteous*, Fiedler has failed to grasp the full significance of the use of the Matthaean concept of righteousness.

Ziesler has treated not only the noun and adjective but also the verb. Since Ziesler's aim is to deal with the meaning of righteousness in Paul, where the verb plays a significant role, this is indeed necessary. On the other hand, in the Gospel of Matthew, the verb does not play a significant role.[24] It does not form an integral part of the Matthaean concept of righteousness. As the study of the background materials is not an end in itself but is undertaken for the purpose of comparison, the verb related to the root *ts-d-q* has not been included in this investigation.

In the study of the Gospel of Matthew it is imperative that stress be placed not only on determining the meaning of the righteousness terminology but on determining the overall significance of the use of the concept of righteousness in the gospel. In order to provide a valid basis of comparison, the twofold approach of determining specific meanings of various terms and their overall significance or function will also be applied to the study of the background literature. This approach has largely been neglected; that is, previous studies have concentrated on meaning rather than on relative significance.

It is for these reasons that approximately half of this study is devoted to the investigation of the meaning and significance of the terms *tsedeq*, *tsedaqah* and *tsaddiq* in the Dead Sea Scrolls and the Tannaitic literature. After all, while these sources appear to be the most important for under-standing Matthew's concept of righteousness, they have in the past been the sources least often and least adequately examined.

3 The Old Testament as the point of departure

Having clarified the rationale behind the treatment of the Dead Sea Scrolls and the Tannaitic literature, let us now consider the appropriate treatment of the Old Testament. As was noted above, for the purpose of the present study the Old Testament essentially has significance as a point of departure; that is, the usage of the righteousness terminology in the Dead Sea Scrolls, the Tannaitic literature and the Gospel of Matthew should be viewed as the end-product of a process of development that had Old Testament usage as its point of departure. Since this process of development was marked by both continuity and discontinuity, it is clear that the Old Testament *per se* has only a very limited direct relevance as background literature for the Matthaean concept of righteousness. At this point it should also be noted that in contrast to the rather inadequate treatment of the Dead Sea Scrolls and the Tannaitic literature, there have been a number of comprehensive and insightful studies of the righteousness terminology of the Old Testament.[25] When these observations are taken in conjunction with the methodological principle that the study of the background literature is not an end in itself but should be undertaken for the purpose of providing a basis of comparison with the Gospel of Matthew, it becomes evident that a new, detailed analysis of all aspects of the concept of righteousness in the Old Testament is not essential in the context of the present study.

What is essential is a general outline of those aspects of Old Testament usage which are pivotal for gaining insight into the primary points of con-tinuity and discontinuity between this usage and that of the Dead Sea Scrolls, the Tannaitic literature and the Gospel of Matthew. In addition to this general outline, detailed discussions will be limited to those Old Testament passages which are quoted or presupposed in the bodies of literature under discussion. These discussions will be found in relevant contexts in the following chapters. The general outline, on the other hand, will follow immediately so as to serve as a convenient reference point for the discussion of the righteousness terminology in the Dead Sea Scrolls, Tannaitic literature and Gospel of Matthew. Since the following remarks are not innovative but based primarily on the research of others, it seems appro-priate to include them in this introductory chapter.

The following description of the Old Testament righteousness terminology is restricted to the relevant Hebrew terms. The Greek translation equivalents in the LXX already show signs of a development from the earlier usage in the Hebrew Old Testament. The relevance of Septuagintal usage for the understanding of the Matthaean concept of righteousness will be discussed in sections 1 and 3 of chapter 5.

Let us begin our discussion of the Old Testament righteousness terminology by summarizing Ziesler's analysis of the nouns *tsedeq* and *tsedaqah* and the adjective *tsaddiq*.[26] According to Ziesler's count there are 115 cases of *tsedeq*, 158 of *tsedaqah* and 208 of *tsaddiq* in the Kittel edition of the Hebrew Old Testament.[27] Ziesler discusses this total of 481 cases from the perspective of man's activity, God's activity and the righteousness of things.

With respect to man's activity or behaviour, Ziesler draws attention to the following categories of meaning: 'legal activity' in the sense of 'the activities of judging and establishing justice in the community, as against the *status* of being in the right' (14 cases each of *tsedeq* and *tsedaqah*, none of *tsaddiq*);[28] 'governing, ruling activity ... with the emphasis less on legal than on administrative functions' (3 cases of *tsedeq*, 10 of *tsedaqah*, 5 of *tsaddiq*);[29] 'general or undefined ethical uprightness' in the sense of 'the opposite of a word for "wickedness, evil, wicked" or as general terms for doing what is right in God's eyes, being faithful to him, not in some "spiritual" sense, but in the conduct of life and society' (22 cases of *tsedeq*, 56 of *tsedaqah*, 108 of *tsaddiq*);[30] 'referring to the life of the covenant people' not with primary reference 'to the perfect moral uprightness of the people, but essentially to their keeping the covenant' (one case of *tsedeq*, none of *tsedaqah*, 51 of *tsaddiq*);[31] 'obedience to the law' (one case of *tsedeq*, 5 of *tsedaqah*, one of *tsaddiq*);[32] 'gracious activity, reflecting God's own', approximating the 'meaning of "almsgiving" or "benevolence" for *tsedaqah* among the Rabbis' (one case each of *tsedeq*, *tsedaqah* and *tsaddiq*);[33] 'good speaking, telling the truth' (4 cases of *tsedeq*, 2 of *tsedaqah*, one of *tsaddiq*);[34] 'man's forensic or relational righteousness' having 'to do with man as not guilty before, or in a right relationship to, a human or divine tribunal, or else in a right relationship that is not specifically forensic' (3 cases of *tsedeq*, 5 of *tsedaqah*, 19 of *tsaddiq*).[35]

With respect to God's activity, Ziesler draws attention to the following categories of meaning: 'legal activity' in the sense of 'judging and lawgiving' (18 cases of *tsedeq*, 4 of *tsedaqah*, 6 of *tsaddiq*);[36] 'gracious, saving activity' in the sense that 'the nouns are virtually equivalent to "salvation"' (14 cases of *tsedeq*, 34 of *tsedaqah*, 5 of *tsaddiq*);[37] 'vindicating, giving victory or prosperity' (18 cases of *tsedeq*, 21 of *tsedaqah*, one of *tsaddiq*);[38] 'acting reliably, trustworthily, faithfully' (no cases of *tsedeq*, 5 of *tsedaqah*, 7 of *tsaddiq*);[39] 'right speaking' (2 cases of *tsedeq*, one of *tsedaqah*, none of *tsaddiq*);[40] 'God's forensic or relational righteousness' (no cases of *tsedeq* or *tsedaqah*, 3 of *tsaddiq*).[41]

With respect to the righteousness of things, Ziesler notes 14 cases of *tsedeq*. Ten times *tsedeq* refers to correct weights and measures, three times to peace-offerings and once to right paths.[42]

With special reference to Ziesler's analysis let us now make a few general observations concerning the Old Testament concept of righteousness. The main function of the adjective *tsaddiq* can be ascertained without difficulty. Out of a total of 208 occurrences of this term, 186 refer to man while only 22 refer to God. Thus it can be concluded that the adjective *tsaddiq* is used primarily to refer to man. With respect to the 186 references to man it should be noted that 108 are used in a general way to designate man's conduct insofar as it coincides with what is right in God's eyes and as such is opposed to what is wicked, and 51 are used specifically with reference to keeping the covenant.[43] Conduct which is right in God's eyes can hardly be opposed to keeping the covenant. Consequently, in 159 out of 186 cases the adjective *tsaddiq* appears to be used to designate proper religious conduct. Since this adjective is often used substantively to refer to 'the righteous', it appears that the latter are the ones who are properly religious. Since Ziesler's analysis shows that the meanings of the adjective *tsaddiq* overlap with the meanings of the nouns *tsedeq* and *tsedaqah*, the further generalization can be drawn that 'the righteous' are the properly religious because their conduct is governed by righteousness (*tsedeq/tsedaqah*). While it is evident that the foregoing description of the adjective *tsaddiq* does not exhaust the meaning of this term, it should be clear that this description isolates the primary meaning of *tsaddiq* in the Old Testament. In other words, with respect to the adjective *tsaddiq*, it is possible to speak in terms of a primary meaning and various secondary meanings.

The Old Testament usage of the nouns *tsedeq* and *tsedaqah* is more complex than that of the adjective *tsaddiq*. Let us first of all consider the relationship between the masculine noun *tsedeq* and the feminine noun *tsedaqah*. Some scholars have attempted to differentiate between these two terms with respect to meaning and/or function. Knight, for example, has proposed that 'The noun *tsedheq* is most frequently used of the righteousness of God; the feminine *tsedhaqah* is its effect in man. The former is the divine "right" which establishes salvation, the latter the human order which is an element of it.'[44] Ziesler's statistical analysis shows, however, that there is no such difference of meaning.[45]

It appears that the only distinction in usage between these two nouns is of a grammatical nature. As G. Quell has noted, *tsedeq*, because of its brevity in comparison to *tsedaqah*, is 'favoured as a gen. epexegeticus in the sense of *tsaddiq*'.[46]

Concerning the meaning of *tsedeq* and *tsedaqah*, one is forced to agree with Quell that in general 'there is no discernible shift of meaning as between the masc. and fem.'[47] This does not mean that there are no instances at all where one of these two terms does not have a distinctive meaning. Ziesler, for example, does note with reference to the category of God 'acting reliably, trustworthily, faithfully'[48] that there are 5 cases of *tsedaqah* but none of *tsedeq*. Such instances, however, appear to be minor exceptions when viewed against the total Old Testament usage. Ziesler's analysis clearly shows that the meanings of *tsedeq* and *tsedaqah* overlap to such an extent that these two nouns should essentially be seen as synonyms. Consequently, with reference to the Old Testament, one is forced to deal with *tsedeq/tsedaqah* as a single concept.

As Ziesler's analysis demonstrates, in the Old Testament a number of different meanings are attached to *tsedeq/tsedaqah*. It is unwarranted to differentiate between a primary meaning and various secondary ones. Instead, the distinction appears to be between a number of major and minor meanings. At this point let us focus on one of the minor and one of the major meanings which will be of particular importance for the present study.

Ziesler states that there is one case each of *tsedeq* (Is 58:8), *tsedaqah* (Prov 21:21) and *tsaddiq* (Ps 112:6) reflecting 'the common meaning of "almsgiving" or "benevolence" for *tsedaqah* among the Rabbis'.[49] While this is definitely true for Is 58:8 and Ps 112:6, this interpretation of *tsedaqah* in Prov 21:21 appears to be doubtful. There is, however, another passage, i.e. Dan 4:27(24), where this noun does refer to almsgiving. Ziesler tentatively includes this passage in the category of 'general or undefined ethical uprightness'.[50] G. von Rad, on the other hand, has argued convincingly that 'At the farthest edge of this canon there is heralded a decided narrowing and curtailment of the concept of *ts-d-q-h*, in so far as in Dan. IV.24(27) the Aramaic *ts-d-q-h* has the meaning of "good works", "almsgiving" . . .'[51]

Let us now consider one of the major meanings of *tsedeq/tsedaqah* in the Old Testament. Under the category of God's gracious, saving activity, Ziesler lists 14 cases of *tsedeq* and 34 of *tsedaqah* and notes that 'Here the nouns are virtually equivalent to "salvation".'[52] Von Rad shows that the concept of righteousness as the salvific gift of God reaches its climax in Deutero-Isaiah.[53] Indeed, it is obvious that in these cases righteousness (*tsedeq/tsedaqah*) is viewed as the gift of God rather than as a demand upon man.

That there are a significant number of passages in which righteousness (*tsedeq/tsedaqah*) designates God's gift for man is thus undeniable. The extent, however, to which this meaning should be seen as underlying the whole Old Testament concept of righteousness is debatable.

Schmid notes that the more recent scholars such as H. Cazelles, K. Koch, G. von Rad and F. Horst have stressed the salvific (*heilvollen*) character of *tsedeq/tsedaqah*, while previous scholars such as G. H. Dalman and F. Nötscher have stressed both the punitive (*strafende*) and salvific aspects of God's righteousness in the Old Testament.[54] Schmid himself arrives at the convincing conclusion that one should hold on to the salvific emphasis but at the same time view salvific and punitive righteousness as a unity.[55]

A debate closely allied to the question of the salvific meaning of *tsedeq/tsedaqah* concerns itself with the problem of whether righteousness should be viewed as a relationship or as a norm. Von Rad stresses that righteousness is strictly a relationship.[56] Quell views the terms *tsedeq* and *tsedaqah* among the 'normative terms for the concept of the law'.[57]

To von Rad righteousness not only governs man's relationship to God but also man's relationship to his fellows, the animals and his natural environment. Von Rad's main argument against the concept of norm is that an absolute norm cannot be identified in the Old Testament.[58]

Essentially, von Rad is forced into this position by his assertion that the righteousness which is bestowed upon Israel is always a saving gift, for no punitive righteousness can be adduced.[59] However, if it is argued that there is also a punitive aspect in the Old Testament concept of righteousness, it is necessary to think of *tsedeq/tsedaqah* in terms of a norm. Since Quell discusses these terms in the context of the concept of law in the Old Testament[60] it is logical that he focusses on the idea of norm.

Since it was concluded above that *tsedeq* and *tsedaqah* have both a salvific and punitive aspect, it is reasonable to infer that righteousness refers to both relationship and norm. A meaningful compromise is put forward by Ziesler when he suggests, 'In the end the difference is not great, for it is generally agreed that righteousness is behaviour proper to some relationship.'[61]

We shall now see the way in which these various possibilities are worked out in the later literature and what changes of meaning and emphasis are introduced.

2

TSEDEQ, *TSEDAQAH* AND *TSADDIQ* IN THE DEAD SEA SCROLLS

1 Introduction

This study of the words connected with the root *ts-d-q* in the Dead Sea Scrolls is not an end in itself but is undertaken for the purpose of providing a basis of comparison with the use of the concept of righteousness in the Gospel of Matthew. In the study of the Gospel of Matthew, stress will not only be placed on determining the meaning of terms such as *dikaiosynē* and *dikaios* but also on determining the overall significance of the use of the concept of righteousness in this gospel. In order to provide a valid basis of comparison, the twofold approach of determining specific meanings of various terms and their overall significance must also be applied to the study of the words connected with the root *ts-d-q* in the Dead Sea Scrolls.

In order to make a valid comparison, however, it is not sufficient merely to apply methodological principles consistently to various bodies of literature. It is of the utmost importance that the methodological principles be applied to bodies of literature which represent compatible literary categories. Specifically, the question must be asked whether the Gospel of Matthew can be compared to the Dead Sea Scrolls as a whole or whether distinctions must be made amongst the Dead Sea Scrolls. In other words, the question of the homogeneity of the Dead Sea Scrolls must be faced.

The New Testament discipline of *Redaktionsgeschichte* has shown that the Gospel of Matthew is composed of various traditional materials[1] which were brought together by a redactional process, the final stage being carried out by a specific individual or a group of persons. While discrete anterior traditions must therefore be taken into account, it is nevertheless evident that certain redactional motifs are inherent in the Gospel of Matthew, enabling us to treat it as a literary unity.

Soon after the discovery of the Dead Sea Scrolls, it was pointed out by scholars such as Reicke,[2] Burrows[3] and Teicher[4] that, like the New Testament, this literature is not homogeneous but reflects various stages of a historical development. Since that time many facts have emerged which support this conclusion.

It is now generally accepted that the Dead Sea Scrolls were written over a period of time and reflect a historical development. Although this general principle is accepted, there is wide divergence of opinion as to what constitutes the correct chronological sequence of the scrolls.[5]

Neither is there unanimity of opinion as to the time span between the appearance of the first and last of the scrolls. Most scholars agree that the scrolls found in the caves of Qumran were stored there no later than A.D. 70, the date of the destruction of the Temple of Jerusalem.[6] The *terminus ad quem* for the final redaction of the Dead Sea Scrolls is thus firmly established.

There is a great deal of controversy, however, as to the *terminus a quo*. As Dupont-Sommer[7] points out, even when archaeological data are taken into account, the historical background reflected in the Dead Sea Scrolls could conceivably refer to the pre-Maccabean period prior to 168 B.C., the Maccabean or Hasmonean epoch between 168 and 63 B.C. or the Roman period from 63 B.C. onwards. Consequently, we are dealing with a period of at least one hundred years during which the scrolls could have been composed. Vermes has suggested that the original composition of the Manual of Discipline (1QS) may date from the latter part of the second century B.C.[8] and that the War Scroll (1QM) was composed during the beginning of the first century A.D.[9]

Although the exact chronological sequence of the writings comprising the Dead Sea Scrolls may never be established with any degree of certainty, it is probable that a historical development is reflected in these writings. For example, Peter von der Osten-Sacken[10] has traced a development in the dualistic thought as portrayed by the scrolls. Rabinowitz[11] has demonstrated that the theme of persecution points to a development in time.

The problem of the dating of the scrolls is compounded by the fact that the individual writings themselves are not homogeneous but are composed of various strata. This is especially obvious in the Thanksgiving Hymns (1QH). Gert Jeremias has given a number of convincing arguments to support his conclusion that 1QH does not represent a literary unity.[12]

It has also been shown that the Manual of Discipline,[13] the War Scroll[14] and the Damascus Document (CD)[15] were compiled from various sources. Nevertheless, with the exception of the Thanksgiving Hymns, it appears that through a process of redaction the various sources have been integrated so that, even though differences are still visible, each writing does in fact show some degree of uniformity. There are, however, marked differences between the various writings. This is particularly evident when the Damascus Document is compared with the rest of the Dead Sea Scrolls.[16]

The Damascus Document has been known for a much longer period of time than the rest of the Dead Sea Scrolls. It was discovered in 1896 in the genizah of a synagogue in Old Cairo and published in 1910.[17] Sukenik was the first to suggest that the Damascus Document should be considered as one of the writings belonging to the Dead Sea Sect.[18] This suggestion seemed to be confirmed when fragments of this writing were indeed discovered in the caves of Qumran and today this view is generally accepted.

Yet the fact that the Damascus Document was transmitted independently of the rest of the Dead Sea Scrolls may be significant, for, as Burrows has noted, 'The relation between the Damascus Document in particular and the rest of the Qumran literature is not yet entirely clear. The combination of close resemblances at some points with marked differences at others indicates that either two distinct though related groups or two different stages in the history of the same movement are represented.'[19]

Attention has especially been drawn to the differences between the Damascus Document and the Manual of Discipline.[20] Butler has argued that the distinctive names such as 'volunteers', 'sons of light', 'sons of righteousness', 'sons of truth' and 'men of God's lot' used in 1QS indicate a longer period of separation from the mainstream of Judaism than is evident in CD and that CD is thus earlier than 1QS.[21] Most scholars, however, disagree with this conclusion and hold that CD is later than 1QS.[22]

It has also been suggested that 1QS and CD are two rule books which may not simply reflect different stages in the evolution of the Dead Sea Sect but also reflect the thought of different groups who had practices and beliefs of their own but remained within the larger community.[23]

Although it is granted that much more work needs to be done on the question of the homogeneity of the Dead Sea Scrolls before definitive conclusions can be reached, it is clear that any study of a specific aspect of the thought of the Dead Sea Sect must come to terms with this problem. The literary unity of the Dead Sea Scrolls should not be taken for granted.

Unfortunately, the whole problem of the homogeneity of the Dead Sea Scrolls has been ignored or at least deemed unimportant by a large number of scholars. Not only have obviously complex writings such as 1QH been treated as works by a single author[24] but even the Dead Sea Scrolls as a whole are regarded by many scholars as portraying a single, uniform point of view.

H. Ringgren, for example, chooses various topics within general subject areas such as God, Man and Eschatology, and, taking proof-texts from all available non-biblical texts found in Qumran, gives a 'systematic account of the doctrines and practices of the Qumran community'.[25] The result is essentially an eclectic account of beliefs which in all probability were never held by any particular group of persons at a specific time and place.

Some of the major studies of the words connected with the root *ts-d-q* in the Dead Sea Scrolls which have been undertaken for the purpose of providing comparative material for New Testament studies have also taken the homogeneity of the Dead Sea Scrolls for granted. Under the heading 'The Hebrew writings of the Intertestamental period', Ziesler[26] treats not only the Dead Sea Scrolls but also Sirach. His statistics and conclusions thus refer to this whole body of literature.

Consequently, when Ziesler compares the meaning of righteousness in Paul to that of the Dead Sea Scrolls and Sirach, he is comparing two very dissimilar bodies of literature. He is comparing the writings of one man, Paul, as they can best be determined,[27] to a very composite literature. He is comparing the view of a single man to that of one or more communities whose thought developed over a number of generations.

In contrast to Ziesler, who combines the Dead Sea Scrolls and Sirach, Kertelge[28] treats the Dead Sea Scrolls separately as background material for the study of God's righteousness in Paul. Like Ziesler, however, he fails to come to terms with possible variations of this concept amongst the various writings which constitute the Dead Sea Scrolls.

Although Kertelge[29] agrees with Becker that some variations in the meaning of the concept of God's righteousness exist in the Dead Sea Scrolls, he nevertheless goes on to stress the common rather than the divergent elements of this concept. Consequently, the comparison is between Paul's thought and that of a group of writings reflecting the thought of various individuals and/or groups of people through a period of time.

It is not the contention of the present study that no common motifs exist in the writings comprised by the Dead Sea Scrolls. It is, however, regarded as a proven fact that the Dead Sea Scrolls as a whole are not as homogeneous from a literary point of view as is the Gospel of Matthew. The Dead Sea Scrolls do not bear the imprint of a redaction by a single redactor as is the case with the Gospel of Matthew. Thus the procedure of taking proof-texts from the various scrolls may lead to a composite picture which in actual fact may never have been held by a specific member of the community.

It must be emphasized again that it is not argued that the method of taking proof-texts from various scrolls necessarily leads to a composite picture. It is only maintained that the possibility exists and that it is therefore imperative that no general conclusions as to the teaching of the Dead Sea Scrolls with respect to the concept of righteousness are made until it has definitely been established that no substantial differences exist between the various writings or strata within the writings.

The methodology of this study will therefore be to investigate the role of the concept of righteousness in each of the Dead Sea Scrolls. This does not mean that each writing is thought of as the product of a single author. It is, however, suggested that all the individual writings, except 1QH, are comparable to the Gospel of Matthew, inasmuch as each consists of various traditional materials which were brought together by a redactor and bear the imprint of his thought.[30]

Fiedler,[31] in his study of the concept of righteousness in the Gospel of Matthew, does in fact treat the writings of the Dead Sea Scrolls individually. But, as will be shown below, he stresses the Old Testament background of the passages in which the nouns *tsedeq* and *tsedaqah* are found to such an extent that he fails to grasp their contextual meaning in the Dead Sea Scrolls. Because of this emphasis he comes to the conclusion that the meaning of *tsedeq/tsedaqah* in the Dead Sea Scrolls concurs with the Old Testament meaning of *Heil*.

Although the defects of the various studies dealing with the concept of righteousness in the Dead Sea Scrolls as a background to the use of this concept in the New Testament are real, this does not mean that all the conclusions reached in these studies are invalid. Many observations are perceptive and some conclusions valid. The great drawback is that they are generally valid only within a very limited frame of reference. Consequently, a new, comprehensive study is needed which takes into account not only the meaning of the various words connected with the root *ts-d-q* but also their overall significance within the thought expressed by the individual writings.

2 The Damascus Document

The noun *tsedeq* occurs 12 times in CD. In 1:11 and 20:32 it is found in the title *moreh tsedeq*, and the use of *tsedeq* in this title is pivotal in the determination of the overall significance of the concept of righteousness in CD.

Strictly from a grammatical viewpoint the *nomen rectum tsedeq* in the construct-genitive expression *moreh tsedeq* could be translated substantively as 'teacher of righteousness' or adjectivally as 'righteous or right teacher'. In the former translation *tsedeq* is treated as an objective genitive while in the latter translation it is treated as an explicative genitive denoting an attribute[32] of a person. The decision as to which is the correct use in this case carries far-reaching consequences. If *moreh tsedeq* is translated as 'righteous or right teacher', then *tsedeq* is simply a term used to define the status of a certain office or person. If, on the other hand, it is translated as 'teacher of righteousness', that is, 'the one who teaches righteousness', then *tsedeq* could be an important term pointing to a central concept within

the thought of the author/redactor or even within the community to which
CD was directed.

There is no consensus as to the meaning of the title *moreh tsedeq*.
Weingreen, for example, claims that *tsedeq* is used adjectivally.

> It would seem, therefore, proper to conclude that, in the title we have
> under scrutiny, namely *m-w-r-h ts-d-q*, the noun *ts-d-q* has, first, the
> effect of an adjective and is to be understood as meaning 'true' in the
> sense of genuine. It expresses the idea of one publicly recognized in his
> title to office and in the exercise of his accredited functions. In this
> association the noun *ts-d-q* has no moral content at all; it is part of a
> conventional title and conveys the idea of legitimacy.[33]

As proof, Weingreen lists examples from the Old Testament,[34] the Rabbinic
literature[35] and contemporary usage[36] which he claims show that *tsedeq* is
always used adjectivally when it occurs in the genitive position in construct-
genitive expressions. Since there is evidence for continuity in such a usage,
he concludes that this principle must also hold true for the Dead Sea Scrolls.

It cannot be denied that Weingreen's conclusion is generally correct in
instances where the *nomen regens* in the construct-genitive expression is a
non-verbal noun. For example, the expression *mo'zne tsedeq* in Lev 19:36
could hardly refer to balances of righteousness. The translation 'righteous
or just balances', however, is meaningful.

In the case of verbal nouns such as *moreh*, on the other hand, it is possible that the *nomen rectum tsedeq* can be an objective genitive. In fact,
when one looks at the Damascus Document itself, there is evidence that in
the title *moreh tsedeq*, *tsedeq* is used as an objective genitive.[37] The passage
which most clearly provides such evidence is 6:11. Here the expression
yoreh ha-tsedeq occurs. The term *yoreh* could be the third person masculine
singular hiph'il imperfect of *y-r-h*. If this were the case then 6:11 would
have to be translated as 'he will teach righteousness'.

On the other hand, *yoreh* could also be the masculine, singular, qal
participle of *y-r-h*. Since the expression *yoreh ha-tsedeq* appears to be the
subject of *'amod*, this explanation is more plausible than the former.
Therefore 6:11 should be translated as 'he who teaches righteousness'.[38]
The noun *ha-tsedeq* is unmistakably the direct object of the participle
yoreh.[39]

There are no textual difficulties as far as the reading *yoreh ha-tsedeq* in
6:11 is concerned.[40] It should also be noted that similar expressions occur
in the Tannaitic literature and the OT. In Sifre Deuteronomy 144 on Deut
16:19 the following statement is found: *'ad sheyoreh tsedeq*.[41] Since the
relative pronoun *she* is used here it is certain that *tsedeq* is treated as the

direct object of *yoreh*. In Hos 10:12 we find the statement *'ad yabo'
weyoreh tsedeq lakem* ('until he comes and rains righteousness upon you').
Jeremias has noted that in this instance *tsedeq* must be objective.[42]

What is the relationship between the expressions *yoreh ha-tsedeq* (CD
6:11) and *moreh tsedeq* (1:11, 20:32)? Lohse translates both expressions
as 'Lehrer der Gerechtigkeit'[43] and on the basis of the respective contexts it
indeed appears certain that both expressions refer to the same person.[44]
The *moreh tsedeq* is the one who teaches *tsedeq*. Since *tsedeq* is objective in
the expression *yoreh ha-tsedeq* it is indeed probable that it is also objective
in the expression *moreh tsedeq*.[45] The Teacher of Righteousness is the one
who teaches righteousness.

Although CD 6:11 provides the best argument for the claim that *tsedeq*
in the title *moreh tsedeq* is an objective genitive, this passage by no means
exhausts the evidence. The phrase *kol yod'e tsedeq* in 1:1 also lends support to such a conclusion. As in the title *moreh tsedeq* we have here a
construct-genitive relationship. *Yod'e* is a construct participle and *tsedeq*
is in the genitive position. The translation 'all right/righteous knowers'
makes little sense. The context demands the translation 'all you who know
righteousness'. *Tsedeq* thus is an objective genitive. The emphasis is placed
on righteousness, not on the knowers. Since *tsedeq* is used substantively in
1:1 it would be strange indeed if it were not used in the same way in 1:11.
After all, from the context it appears natural that those 'who know righteousness' (1:1) in essence know that which has been communicated to them
by the Teacher of Righteousness (1:11).

In addition to 1:1, 11; 6:11 and 20:32, the noun *tsedeq* occurs in eight
further passages. In three of these, that is, 4:17 and 20:17 and 29, *tsedeq*
is definitely used substantively. In 20:17 and 29 it is a noun in the absolute
state. In 4:17 *tsedeq* occurs in the genitive position in the following construct-genitive expression: *lishloshet mine ha-tsedeq*. On the basis of the
three categories listed[46] it is obvious that 4:17 refers to 'three kinds of
righteousness' rather than to 'three right kinds'.

In the five remaining passages (1:16; 3:15; 20:11, 31, 33) *tsedeq* occurs
in the genitive position in various construct-genitive expressions. Although
the immediate context in each of the passages does not provide compelling
reasons for treating *tsedeq* substantively, neither are there compelling
reasons for treating it adjectivally.

On the basis of the evidence presented, we must therefore conclude that
the title *moreh tsedeq* should be translated as 'Teacher of Righteousness',
tsedeq being the object of the teaching of the Teacher.[47]

Although the evidence points to this conclusion, one should not over-
look the possibility that the whole question of the substantive and adjectival

use of *tsedeq* may have eluded the author/redactor of CD. The problem with which we have been dealing may in actual fact be a pseudo-problem arising solely out of difficulties inherent in the process of translating from Hebrew to English. The expression *moreh tsedeq* may have been used purposely because it was vague and could thus include both the idea of 'Teacher of Righteousness' and of 'Righteous Teacher'.[48] It should not be taken for granted that these two ideas are mutually exclusive.

On the basis of CD 6:11, however, it is clear that the *moreh tsedeq*, be he the 'Teacher of Righteousness' or the 'Righteous Teacher', teaches righteousness. Consequently, while keeping in mind the reservations just outlined, the best English translation of the title *moreh tsedeq* as used in CD still appears to be 'Teacher of Righteousness'.

Let us now turn to the question of the meaning and overall significance of the noun *tsedeq* in the Damascus Document. This writing begins with the following exhortation: 'Hear now, all you who know righteousness, and consider the works of God.'[49] The Damascus Document is addressed to those who know *tsedeq*. Righteousness is a term used to identify the community. The simple fact that this term is stressed at the beginning of the writing may be indicative of the importance attached to the concept of righteousness.

The nature of the righteousness which identifies the community is specified in the ensuing discussion. With respect to the Teacher of Righteousness, it is stated in 1:11f that he is to lead the people in the way of God's heart and to make known God's plans to the future generations. From the contrast between the 'waters of falsehood' (*meme kazab*) in 1:15 and the 'paths of righteousness' (*netibot tsedeq*) in 1:16, it is clear that *tsedeq* stands for all that is true as opposed to that which is false.

It can therefore be concluded that *tsedeq* refers to the content of the teaching of the Teacher of Righteousness. The teaching is to be true as opposed to the false teaching of others. Insofar as it reveals God's heretofore unknown plans for future generations, the teaching is to be esoteric.[50] In fact the teaching is to be in accordance with God's will. Those who know righteousness are those who are aware of the teaching which makes known the will of God.

The content of God's will is disclosed even more fully in 20:32f, the second passage in which the title *moreh tsedeq* occurs. Here it is stated that the Teacher of Righteousness teaches the precepts of righteousness (*huqqe ha-tsedeq*). From 20:11 it is clear that the *huqqe ha-tsedeq* refer to the law of the covenant made in the Land of Damascus[51] which is thought of as the New Covenant.[52] Consequently, L. Ginzberg's suggestion that *tsedeq* in the title *moreh tsedeq* refers to the proper understanding of Torah[53] is correct as long as Torah is defined not in terms of the covenant made at Sinai but in terms of the New Covenant made in the Land of Damascus. Accordingly, *tsedeq* refers not only to God's laws in general but also specifically to the totality of the rules and regulations of the community to which the Damascus Document is directed.[54]

The references to *tsedeq* in 20:29 and 31 must be seen in the context of 20:27-33. This passage starts with a general reference to the rules of the community and to the Teacher (*moreh*)[55] and ends with the specific reference to the Teacher of Righteousness and to the precepts of righteousness. As was demonstrated above, 20:32f shows that *tsedeq* refers to the norm for man's conduct, that is, to the totality of the rules and regulations of the community to which the Damascus Document is directed.

Since the beginning and end of 20:27-33 indicate a progression toward a very specific meaning for *tsedeq* it might be expected that this meaning would govern any other occurrences of this term in this relatively short passage. Consequently, it is surprising to note that Ziesler[56] categorizes the references to *tsedeq* in 20:29 and 31 as referring to God's as opposed to man's righteousness.

Technically Ziesler is right, for when 20:29 and 31 are seen out of context *tsedeq* does refer to God. In 20:29 it is stated that God's judgments are righteousness and truth towards man. Since 20:29-30 is parallel to 1QS 1:24-6 it has been suggested that this passage is based on a traditional formula of confession.[57] It is likely that in its original setting the stress in this confession was on God's righteousness.

In CD 20:31 the third person masculine singular pronominal suffix refers to God so that *mishpete tsidqo* does refer to God's ordinances of righteousness.[58]

However, when these two references to *tsedeq* are seen in the context of CD 20:27-33, a different picture emerges. This passage stresses that there is a norm which governs the conduct of man (e.g. 20:27, 28, 32, 33). It must be noted that in 20:29 and 31 it is not God's righteousness *per se* but the righteousness connected with his judgments and ordinances which is stressed. Is God's righteousness in this sense opposed to man's righteousness? Certainly not. God's righteousness in the form of his judgments and ordinances is seen as the norm governing man's conduct and thus man's righteousness. God's righteousness must therefore be viewed in terms of the specific laws governing man's conduct.

The reference to *tsedeq* in 3:15, 'His testimony of righteousness', also comes under the general category of the laws governing the conduct of man. That God's commandments are meant here is clear from the context which deals with the hidden things in which all Israel had strayed.

The reference to the teaching of righteousness in 6:11 is also to be understood primarily in terms of the law since it occurs in the context of the discussion of the law.[59]

There is yet another passage in which *tsedeq* is used with reference to the law insofar as it refers to man's juridical behaviour. In 20:17 it is noted that at a certain point in the future there will not be anyone who can reprove with righteousness (*betsedeq*). To reprove with righteousness means to reprove justly, that is, according to the commandments of the covenant.

The 11 references to *tsedeq* discussed thus far give rise to the conclusion that *tsedeq* is that which is taught by the Teacher of Righteousness, namely, that man's behaviour is to be in harmony with God's will. The latter is defined concretely by the commandments of the New Covenant made in the Land of Damascus. In other words, *tsedeq* is a technical term designating proper conduct according to a specific norm. With respect to the Old Testament debate whether righteousness should be viewed as norm or relationship, it must be concluded that in CD righteousness is viewed in terms of a norm.

The last passage under discussion in which the noun *tsedeq* occurs is 4:17. Here the three nets by which Belial ensnared Israel are described as 'three kinds of righteousness' (*lishloshet mine ha-tsedeq*) consisting of lust, riches and defilement of the Sanctuary. Ziesler notes that this passage is to be classified among those in which *tsedeq* refers to man's ethical behaviour in general rather than specifically juridical behaviour.[60] Although this explanation is correct, it fails to touch upon the real significance of the use of *tsedeq* in this passage; for in comparison to the other occurrences in the Damascus Document, 4:17 attributes an even broader meaning to *tsedeq*. Not only can it refer to behaviour which is proper in God's sight, but also to any type of normative conduct. According to Belial, lust, riches and defilement of the Sanctuary are representative of proper behaviour. Hence they can be designated as *tsedeq*.

Thus 4:17 represents not so much a deviation in meaning as an expansion of meaning. It can thus be concluded that in the Damascus Document the term *tsedeq* embraces the whole concept of the behaviour of man. Any type of normative behaviour can be designated as *tsedeq*.

Just as the noun *tsedeq* is a technical term for the proper conduct of man, so the adjective *tsaddiq* is used in the Damascus Document to designate those whose conduct is in accordance with *tsedeq*. The adjective *tsaddiq* occurs 5 times in CD.[61] In 4 cases *tsaddiq* is placed in opposition to *rashaʿ*. From 20:20 it is clear that the contrast is between two diametrically opposed categories of people. The righteous one (*tsaddiq*) is the one who serves God while the wicked one (*rashaʿ*) is the one who does not. In

4:7 the *tsaddiq* is also contrasted with the *rasha'*, and the criterion here appears to be that the righteous one follows Torah while the wicked one does not. In 1:19 both the *tsaddiq* and *rasha'* are mentioned and then in 1:20 it is implied that the righteous one walks in perfection.

In 11:21 the terms *tsaddiqim*[62] and *resha'im* occur in a quotation of Prov 15:8. It is of course impossible to be absolutely certain which text of Prov 15:8 the author of CD 11:21 was following, yet it is possible that the text of Prov 15:8 read *yesharim*[63] instead of *tsaddiqim*. Schechter suggests that the text of CD 11:21 is corrupt and points to a confusion with Prov 15:29.[64] However, another explanation is possible. It could be that the adjective *tsaddiq* was substituted for *yashar* because the contrast between *rasha'* and *tsaddiq* was firmly entrenched in the thought of the author/ redactor of this passage.

It can be stated with certainty that in the Damascus Document *tsaddiq* is the primary designation for those who are properly religious. Other terms such as seers of truth,[65] the upright[66] and men of perfect holiness[67] also occur. Yet in passages dealing with the fundamental distinction between those who are and those who are not properly religious the terms used are *tsaddiq* and *rasha'*.

Having established that *tsedeq* and *tsaddiq* are important terms in the Damascus Document, let us now inquire as to the use and meaning of the noun *tsedaqah*. This noun occurs only twice in CD. In 8:14/19:27[68] Deut 9:5 is quoted. The expression *betsidqateka*, however, is not the part of the quotation which in fact is relevant to the context.

The occurrence of the term *tsedaqah* in CD 20:20, on the other hand, is significant. As Ziesler points out, *tsedaqah* here refers to God's saving, gracious activity.[69] As is clear from the foregoing discussion, this meaning does not overlap with the meaning of *tsedeq*. It is thus difficult to conceive how Fiedler could reach the conclusion that in the Damascus Document *tsedeq/tsedaqah* has the Old Testament meaning of *Heil*.[70] With respect to the Damascus Document it is clear that the nouns *tsedeq* and *tsedaqah* do not refer to a single concept. Each noun is used with its own distinct meaning. The noun *tsedaqah* refers to God's saving, gracious activity and in comparison to *tsedeq* plays a relatively minor role in the Damascus Document. *Tsedeq*, on the other hand, is both the primary designation for man's proper conduct according to a specific norm and for the norm itself.

3 The Manual of Discipline

In the Manual of Discipline the adjective *tsaddiq*[71] and the title *moreh tsedeq*[72] do not occur. The noun *tsedeq*, however, does occur 17 times[73] in 1QS in expressions other than the title *moreh tsedeq*.

In 5 instances[74] *tsedeq* occurs as a noun in the absolute state. In 11 instances[75] it occurs in the genitive position of various construct-genitive expressions and in one case[76] it is preceded by a lacuna so that its grammatical usage remains undetermined.

In some of the construct-genitive expressions it is evident that *tsedeq* is used substantively. For example, in 4:9 the translation of *ba'abodat tsedeq* as 'in the service of righteousness'[77] or 'in serving righteousness'[78] fits the context much better than the grammatically possible translation 'in the right service'. Also in 9:5 the meaning expressed by the translation 'an agreeable odour of righteousness'[79] best fits the context.

Another factor supporting the conclusion that *tsedeq* can be used substantively while in the genitive position is the analogy to the use of the terms 'truth' and 'perversity'. In 3:19 the expressions *toledot ha-'emet* and *toledot ha-'awel* must be translated as 'the origin of truth' and 'the origin of perversity'[80] respectively, for a translation such as 'the true origin' would not fit the context. Accordingly, *ruhot ha-'emet weha-'awel* which occurs in the same context must mean 'the spirits of truth and perversity'. *'Emet* and *'awel* are thus treated as nouns when they occur in the genitive position. Therefore the translations 'sons of truth' (4:5, 6) and 'sons of perversity' (3:21) must also be correct, and by analogy the expression *bene tsedeq* in 3:20, 22 should mean 'sons of righteousness'.

These arguments in conjunction with the fact that in 5 instances *tsedeq* does occur as a noun in the absolute state do not necessarily prove that *tsedeq* is always used substantively.[81] These factors, however, do indicate that in general *tsedeq* has the meaning *righteousness* rather than *right*. Consequently, all references to *tsedeq* should be considered in determining the meaning of the concept of righteousness in the Manual of Discipline.

Ziesler divides the 15 references[82] to *tsedeq* according to the following categories: man's general ethical behaviour,[83] the behaviour of the covenant people,[84] man's juridical behaviour,[85] God's judgment,[86] God's ordinances[87] and God's righteousness seen primarily as his saving, gracious activity.[88]

There are a number of problems with this classification. The distinction between the general ethical and the juridical meaning of *tsedeq* with respec᛫ to man's behaviour seems to be based primarily on the fact that the majorit᛫ of passages listed as belonging to the former category are very vague in indi᛫ cating the meaning of *tsedeq*. It must also be pointed out that Ziesler's distinction between man in general and the covenant people in particular is misleading. Although the covenant people are not specifically mentioned᛫ in some passages, it is by no means the case that such passages do not appl᛫ to them. Consequently, the only valid conclusion which can be drawn on the basis of the ten passages where *tsedeq* refers to man (plus 1:26 and

9:14, the passages which Ziesler does not treat but which should be included) is that in these passages *tsedeq* refers to man's general conduct, both ethical and juridical.

Ziesler's presentation of God's righteousness is also somewhat misleading. In actual fact, of the five passages listed by Ziesler only 1QS 10:11 and possibly 11:15 refer specifically to God's righteousness.[89] The three other passages, namely 1:13, 3:1 and 4:4, refer to God's righteousness in the form of his ordinances and judgment primarily with the intent of showing that this is to be a norm for man's conduct. In these passages *tsedeq* refers to man's behaviour as revealed by God.

In 10:11 *tsedeq* definitely refers to God's saving, gracious activity.[90] In 10:26, *tsedeq* could also have this meaning. The decision as to whether or not it does depends largely on how the lacuna before it is filled.

With respect to 11:15, Ziesler notes that the meaning of *tsedeq* could be both legal and gracious.[91] However, since *tsidqo* is parallel to *tip'arto* ('his majesty') it is probable that the meaning tends more to the legal than the gracious side.

Before discussing the overall significance of the use of *tsedeq* in 1QS, it is necessary to inquire into the meaning of the noun *tsedaqah*. This noun occurs 12 times in 1QS. Three times it refers to man's righteousness and 9 times to God's righteousness.[92]

The passages in which *tsedaqah* is used with respect to man are 1:5, 5:4 and 8:2. It must be noted that in these passages *tsedaqah* occurs as part of a series of terms which refer to man's conduct. 1QS 5:4 and 8:2 seem to be loose quotations of Mic 6:8; that is, the list of virtues given in Mic 6:8 is expanded to include *tsedaqah*. It is unlikely that *tsedaqah* refers to man's gracious activity analogous to God's gracious activity (e.g. 1QS 11:12) or to man's strict justice analogous to God's strict justice (e.g. 1QS 10:25) since terms with such meanings already occur in the lists, namely *hesed* and *mishpat* respectively.

As will be shown in the discussion of the Tannaitic literature, the most common meaning of *tsedaqah* during the Tannaitic period was *almsgiving*. For want of a better explanation, let us suggest that in 1QS 5:4 and 8:2 *tsedaqah* refers to almsgiving.[93] This meaning may also apply to 1:5, although in this list only *'emet* and *mishpat* occur in addition to *tsedaqah*.

The 9 occurrences of *tsedaqah* referring to God are classified as follows by Ziesler.[94] 1QS 1:21; 10:23, 25; 11:3, 12, 14 (twice) refer to God's righteousness in the sense of his saving, gracious activity, with 10:25 and 11:14 also having legal overtones. 1QS 11:5, 6 are listed with examples from 1QH under the general category of God's righteousness in the sense of his acting reliably, faithfully, within his own covenant. Ziesler notes, however, that in the case of the 1QS passages there is a strong note of graciousness. The latter two passages should therefore be included in the saving, gracious activity category. 1QS 10:25, on the other hand, should not be included in this category since the legal aspect seems to dominate. It thus appears that in all passages except 10:25, *tsedaqah* refers primarily to God's saving, gracious activity.

In 10:25 *tsedaqah* refers to God's strict justice, for this passage states, 'with prudent knowledge I will fence [it] in with a firm boundary,[95] to keep the faith and the law strictly according to the righteousness of God'. The meaning of *tsedaqah* in this passage is identical with the meaning of *tsedeq* in 1:13, 3:1 and 4:4. In these passages both terms refer to the strict justice of God which serves as a norm for man's conduct.

It is thus clear that there is some overlap in the meanings of *tsedeq* and *tsedaqah*. Both terms are used to refer to God's saving, gracious activity and to God's strict justice which is to be a norm for man's conduct. It should be noted that 10:11, where *tsedeq* definitely refers to God's saving, gracious activity, and 10:26 and 11:15, where *tsedeq* may also have such a meaning, all occur in that part of 1QS which is generally known as the Hymn (10:9–11:22).[96] Although there is no consensus as to the number of literary sources from which 1QS has been compiled, it is generally acknowledged that the Hymn represents one such source.[97] The overlap in meaning between *tsedeq* and *tsedaqah* in 1QS is therefore primarily due to the fact that 1QS incorporates various sources. Since 10:9–11:22 is in the form of a hymn, reminiscent of the genre of the Psalms, it is probable that the overlap in meaning reflects the usage of the Old Testament where *tsedeq/tsedaqah* can refer to the gift of God.

The reason for the occasional overlap in meaning between *tsedeq* and *tsedaqah* with reference to God's saving, gracious activity can therefore be accounted for. Consequently, it is unwarranted to generalize and conclude that the terms *tsedeq* and *tsedaqah* refer to a single concept. Thus Fiedler's conclusion that in 1QS the basic meaning of *tsedeq/tsedaqah* is *Heil*[98] is misleading. Although there is some overlap, it is nevertheless evident that *tsedeq* primarily refers to God's and man's righteousness insofar as God's law is a norm for man's conduct and *tsedaqah* is primarily used to refer to God's saving, gracious activity.

While Fiedler's conclusion is thus unwarranted, the fact that there is any overlap in meaning at all between *tsedeq* and *tsedaqah* does indicate that the final redactor of 1QS was not perturbed by the lack of preciseness in the use of these terms. Consequently, the question must be posed whether *tsedeq* plays as significant a role in 1QS as in CD where it was used as an important technical term.

As the ensuing discussion will show, *tsedeq* in fact does not play as decisive a role in 1QS as in CD. This conclusion, however, is not based so much on the fact of the overlapping meanings of *tsedeq* and *tsedaqah* as on the fact that *tsedeq* plays a relatively minor role in 1QS when compared to the term *'emet* (truth).

It has been noted by a number of scholars that the terms *tsedeq* and *'emet* are often used synonymously in the Dead Sea Scrolls.[99] While this is undoubtedly true, it should not be concluded that these two terms are treated with equal importance in the various writings. In both 1QS[100] and CD[101] a number of passages show that *tsedeq* is synonymous with *'emet*. Nevertheless, it is clear that in CD *tsedeq* is the primary term used to define man's proper conduct while in 1QS this role is played by *'emet*.

A simple word count points to this conclusion. In 1QS *tsedeq* occurs 17 times while *'emet* occurs 43 times. In CD, on the other hand, *tsedeq* occurs 12 times while *'emet* occurs only 4 times.

The conclusion that *tsedeq* and *'emet* are the primary terms used to define man's conduct in CD and 1QS respectively is corroborated by the fact that, in the passages in which both *'emet* and *tsedeq* occur, in CD *tsedeq* plays the more important role while in 1QS *'emet* does. In CD *'emet* occurs only once independently of *tsedeq*; that is, in 2:13 the 'seers of truth'[102] (*hoze 'emet*) are mentioned. In the other passages *'emet* and *tsedeq* are always mentioned together, *tsedeq* always being mentioned first.[103] The order is especially significant in 20:29f, for in the parallel passage in 1QS 1:26, *'emet* is mentioned first.

In 1QS 1:13 the noun *tsedeq* occurs only after it has been stated in 1:11f that the volunteers are to cling to God's *truth* and purify their understanding in the *truth* of the precepts of God. In 2:24 *tsedeq* occurs in a list of expressions which begins with 'the community of truth'. It appears that *'emet* is the basic term in this passage.

In 1QS 9:5 'odour of righteousness' is parallel to 'perfection of way' with both expressions being subordinate to the idea that everything is to be 'in accordance with eternal truth' (9:3). Even the reference to God's righteousness in 11:15 is not without parallel, for in 11:4 there is a reference to God's truth.

In the section dealing with the two spirits (3:13–4:26) there are a total of 6 references to *tsedeq*.[104] Here too, however, it is *'emet* rather than *tsedeq* which is of prime significance. The main theme of this section is the interaction of the spirits of truth and perversity. The term *'emet* occurs 15 times in this section. *Tsedeq* is simply one of the synonyms for *'emet*. This is particularly evident in 4:23ff:

Till now the Spirits of truth and perversity battle in the hearts of every man; (24) (they) walk in Wisdom and Folly. And according to each man's share of Truth and Righteousness, so does he hate Perversity. And according to his portion in the lot of Perversity, and (according to) the wickedness (which is) in him, so does (25) he abominate Truth.[105]

In v. 23 of the foregoing passage 'truth' ('emet) and 'perversity' ('awel) are placed in opposition. Then in the first part of v. 24 'truth' ('emet) and 'righteousness' (tsedeq) are contrasted with 'perversity' ('awlah). Finally at the end of v. 24 we return to the original contrast as stated in v. 23. In this passage tsedeq is a synonym for 'emet or simply a part of the concept of truth.

Leaney's analysis of 3:13–4:26 lends support to the conclusion that 'emet rather than tsedeq is of primary significance in this section. He suggests that in this section of 1QS 'the thought certainly oscillates between two sets of terms, truth/perversity, light/darkness'.[106] The fact that 'emet rather than tsedeq is of prime importance in this section attains added significance, for as Leaney has pointed out 'This passage is given a heading (3.13ff.) which shows its fundamental importance to the men of the sect.'[107]

With respect to the concept of truth, Leaney goes on to explain that in 1QS '"To know the truth" is a state of mind parallel with the action, "to keep the Law"; and "to practise the truth" . . . means "to keep the Law".'[108] As was shown above, in CD such a meaning is attached to tsedeq.

The expressions used in 1QS to designate those who are properly religious also indicate that 'emet rather than tsedeq is the term designating the proper conduct of man. In the Damascus Document there was no doubt that the term tsaddiq was the principal designation for the one who was properly religious. In 1QS this term does not occur. The expression 'sons of righteousness' (bene tsedeq), on the other hand, does occur 3 times in 1QS.[109] It is, however, by no means the principal designation for those who are properly religious. Other terms such as 'sons of truth'[110] and 'sons of light'[111] seem to be much more important. It is these expressions which, with their respective counterparts, 'sons of perversity'[112] and 'sons of darkness',[113] relate most closely to the terms truth/perversity ('emet/'awel) and light/darkness ('or/hoshek) around which the thought of 1QS revolves.

It should be noted at this point that 'emet is at times a synonym for tsedeq in the Old Testament. For example, this appears to be the case in Ps 15:2, 45:4 and 119:142. In 1QS, however, it is not simply the case that 'emet is a synonym for tsedeq, but the latter is subordinated to the former.

Let us now see how the use of the words connected with the root ts-d-q in the rest of the Dead Sea Scrolls compares to that of CD and 1QS. In oth-

words, do the remaining writings reflect the usage of CD where *tsedeq* is the principal designation defining proper conduct and *tsaddiq* is the primary term used to designate those who are properly religious insofar as they practise *tsedeq*, or do they reflect the usage of 1QS where the term *'emet* rather than *tsedeq* designates proper conduct?

As was noted previously, the purpose of this study is not only to investigate the meaning of the words connected with the root *ts-d-q* but also their overall significance in the thought expressed by the various writings. Since many of the writings are either very short and/or preserved in a very fragmentary condition, they do not provide suitable research material for such a study. However, in order to gain a better understanding of how extensive the use of the words connected with the root *ts-d-q* is in the Dead Sea Scrolls, we shall nevertheless briefly deal with this material before turning to those writings which are more significant with respect to the purpose of this study.

4 Miscellaneous writings

In the Micah Commentary (1QpMic) there is a reference to the Teacher of Righteousness.[114] The great number of lacunae, however, make it impossible to reconstruct the context in which this title is found.[115]

In Florilegium (4QF1) 2:4 the expression *wetsaddiqim* occurs.[116] Since the expression is surrounded by lacunae, it is not possible to determine how this term is used.

In Patriarchal Blessings (4QPatr), line 3, the title *meshiah ha-tsedeq*[117] is found. It is clear from line 5 that the *meshiah ha-tsedeq* 'has kept [. . .] the Law with the members of the Community'.[118] Consequently, *tsedeq* is related to the concept of the Law in this passage. Since this writing consists of only six lines, it is impossible to arrive at a conclusion as to the overall significance of the concept of righteousness in the thought of the author of this writing.

In Testimonia (4QTest), the Commentary on Nahum (4QpNah) and the Rule Annexe (1QSa) neither of the nouns *tsedeq* nor *'emet* is found. In the Book of Blessings (1QSb), on the other hand, the nouns *tsedeq*[119] and *'emet*[120] each occur 3 times. In 1QSb 3:24 *tsedeq* and *'emet* are used synonymously. It is difficult to determine which term has the greater significance in this writing. It should be noted that although only parts of five columns remain, this writing probably consisted of more than five columns.[121] Caution should thus be exercised in arriving at any definite conclusions about this writing until a greater part of the text has come to light.[122]

5 The Thanksgiving Hymns

In 1QH there are 14 occurrences of the noun *tsedeq*. In 5 instances *tsedeq* is specifically used with reference to man, referring to man's ethical behaviour in 2:13, 5:22, 6:19 and 16:5 and to man's legal activity in 6:4. In eight passages *tsedeq* refers to God. In 1:23, 26, 30; 9:33 and possibly in 10:36 it refers to God's judgment and punishment of man. In 4:40 and 13:19 it refers to God's deeds in general while in 11:18 it specifically refers to God's saving, gracious activity.[123]

It was noted with respect to 1QS that the attempt to draw a clear-cut distinction between God's as opposed to man's righteousness was impossible since the two concepts were closely related. In the case of 1QH, on the other hand, such a distinction is possible. This does not mean that there is no relationship at all between the two concepts. For example, in 1QH 1:26f *tsedeq* is used in a passage which contrasts God's and man's behaviour, and there certainly is a point of contact between the way man (6:4) and God (1:23, 30) reprove with righteousness. But the view that God's righteousness is the norm for man's righteousness is not as intrinsic to the thought of 1QH as it is in CD.

The reason for the lack of uniformity in the use of *tsedeq* in 1QH may very well stem from the fact that it is a collection of hymns which do not reflect a uniform background. Because of the problem of the lack of homogeneity it is difficult if not impossible to draw a general conclusion as to the relative importance of the terms *tsedeq* and *'emet* in 1QH. The facts that there are 53 occurrences of *'emet* as opposed to 14 occurrences of *tsedeq* and that these two nouns are treated as synonyms in a number of cases[124] seem to indicate that *'emet* is a more important term in 1QH than *tsedeq*. This conclusion is in actual fact misleading, for there are significant variations in the use of these terms among the hymns.

1QH 7:26-33 represents a hymn which except for some minor lacunae has been preserved in its entirety.[125] In this hymn the terms *tsedeq*, *tsedaqah* and *tsaddiq* do not occur. There are, however, two references to God's truth (7:26, 28) and one reference to the sons of God's truth (7:29f). In this hymn *'emet* is the term which above all stands for that which is right.

1QH 1:3-39 represents the major part of a hymn whose beginning and end are not extant.[126] The noun *'emet* occurs twice (1:27, 30) while the noun *tsedeq* is found 3 times (1:23, 26, 30). The adjective *tsaddiq* is found in 1:36, designating those who are properly religious. It appears that in this hymn *tsedeq* rather than *'emet* is the primary term designating that which is right.

Holm-Nielsen has noted that the two hymns mentioned above make very little use of Scripture.[127] Consequently, the variation in the use of the terms *tsedeq* and *'emet* may have a basis other than the imitation of scriptural modes of expression.

Like *tsedeq*, the noun *tsedaqah* also has a number of meanings in 1QH. In 4:37; 7:19; 11:31; 16:9; 17:17, 20(twice) and perhaps also in 11:7 and 14:16 *tsedaqah* refers to God's saving, gracious activity. In 5 instances, however, the meaning of *tsedaqah* diverges greatly from that of mercy. In 1:26f 'works of righteousness' are contrasted with 'service of iniquity'. In both 4:30 and 31 *tsedaqah* refers to man's conduct, in the sense that it should be perfect. The expression 'the paths of righteousness' in 7:14 also refers to man's ethical conduct.

In 7:17 *tsedaqah* means the very opposite of mercy. Although there are some lacunae in 7:17f, the general meaning of the passage is clear. It is stated that one is not delivered by righteous deeds (*tsedaqot*) but by God's grace (*hesed*). Man's righteous deeds are thus clearly distinguished from grace.[128]

It should be noted that in all the five passages just discussed in which the meaning of *tsedaqah* deviated from that of mercy, the term *tsedaqah* was used with reference to man rather than God. As a matter of fact, this distinction holds true for the Dead Sea Scrolls as a whole; that is, *tsedaqah* means mercy only when referring to God.

The adjective *tsaddiq* occurs 8 times in 1QH. The occurrence in 16:1 is insignificant, since it is surrounded by lacunae. In 1:36, 4:38, 7:12, 15:15 and 16:10 *tsaddiq* is used to refer to man. In 4:38 and 7:12 the righteous one (*tsaddiq*) is contrasted to the wicked one (*rasha'*). In 1:36 the *tsaddiqim* are defined as the perfect of way and in 15:15 the one who walks according to the covenant is said to be righteous.

On the basis of the passages just discussed, it appears that the use of the adjective *tsaddiq* in 1QH is parallel to that of CD. There is, however, one additional use of *tsaddiq* in 1QH which is not found in CD; namely, in 1QH 12:19 and 14:15 God is described as being righteous (*tsaddiq*). It should also be noted that, while in CD the term *tsaddiq* is the principal designation for those who are properly religious, this does not seem to be the case in 1QH. For example, the expression 'seers of truth' occurs only once in CD (2:13), while in 1QH the expression 'sons of truth' occurs 5 times[129] and 'men of truth' twice.[130] Because of the problem of the lack of homogeneity of 1QH, no general conclusions can be drawn as to the primary designation for those who are properly religious.

In conclusion it can only be stated that with respect to the use of *tsedeq*, *tsedaqah*, *'emet* and *tsaddiq* in 1QH, there are some factors which suggest an affinity with 1QS, while other factors point to an affinity with CD. The lack of uniformity in usage is indicative of the fact that rather than representing a literary unity, the hymns in 1QH represent the thought of various authors during various stages of the development of the Dead Sea Sect. Although a more thorough study of the relationship between sources and usage could hypothetically be made, this has not been attempted in this study, for the final result of such an investigation would of necessity be inconclusive since the majority of the hymns have not been preserved in their entirety.[131]

6 The War Scroll

In 1QM there are 7 occurrences of the noun *tsedeq*. In 5 cases[132] the meaning appears to correspond to the primary meaning of *tsedeq* in 1QS; that is, *tsedeq* refers to man's conduct insofar as this conduct is in agreement with God's righteousness. God's righteousness in this case refers to his will as made known specifically through his ordinances.

In the two remaining passages *tsedeq* refers solely to God's activity. In 1QM 18:8 *'el ha-[tse]deq* refers to God's saving, gracious activity.[133] In 4:6 the expression *'el tsedeq* occurs as one of the titles which are written on the banners of the four levite families.[134] Since *mishpat 'el* is one of the other titles, Ziesler[135] is probably right in assuming that *tsedeq* here too refers to God's saving, gracious activity.

The two meanings of *tsedeq* found in 1QS thus also occur in 1QM. Similarly to 1QS it is the case in 1QM that *tsedeq* is not the primary designation for that which is right. There are 12 occurrences[136] of *'emet* and it appears that this term is more significant than *tsedeq*.

The noun *tsedaqah* does not occur in 1QM. Nor is the adjective *tsaddiq* found. Although there may be a reference to 'the sons of righteousness' in 13:10[137] it is obvious that the primary expression for those who are properly religious is 'sons of light'[138] and for those who are not, 'sons of darkness'.[139] The expression 'sons of truth' is also found in 1QM.[140]

On the basis of the foregoing data it is possible to conclude that the use of the words connected with the root *ts-d-q* in 1QM shows a greater affinity to 1QS than to CD.

7 The Habakkuk Commentary

In 1QpHab the nouns *tsedeq* and *tsedaqah* occur 6 times[141] and once[142] respectively with their use being restricted to the title 'Teacher of Righteousness'. The use of the adjective *tsaddiq* is restricted to quotations from the text of Habakkuk.[143]

It appears that the variation in the use of *tsedeq* and *tsedaqah* in the title 'Teacher of Righteousness' does not reflect an intentional attempt to distinguish between two distinct titles. According to 2:2 the *moreh*

ha-tsedaqah is 'the one who teaches things which he has directly received
from the mouth of God' and as such is contrasted to 'the Man of Lies'
(*'ish ha-kazab*). Similarly in 5:10f the *moreh ha-tsedeq* is contrasted to
'the Man of Lies' and in 7:4f it is stated that God has made known all the
mysteries to the *moreh ha-tsedeq*. Consequently, the functions of the
moreh ha-tsedaqah and the *moreh ha-tsedeq* seem to be identical.[144] The
reading *moreh ha-tsedaqah* in 2:2 may therefore either rest on a simple
copying error[145] or it may be indicative of the fact that the title 'Teacher
of Righteousness' was not such a well-established technical term in the
thought of the author/redactor of 1QpHab as might be expected.

The latter possibility is supported by the fact that the noun *tsedeq* does
not play a prominent role in 1QpHab. As mentioned above, it does not
occur outside of the title 'Teacher of Righteousness'. Consequently, it is
by no means a proven fact that *tsedeq* is the primary term designating
what is right. Such a role could very well be attributed to *'emet*. In 8:9 it
is noted that when the Wicked Priest first came, he was called by the name
of truth. In this context *'emet* is a term designating everything that is right.
The term *'emet* also occurs in 7:10–12 where it is stated that the men of
truth and doers of Torah do not slacken in the service of truth.

In the passage above, those who are properly religious are called 'men of
truth' and 'doers of Torah'. In 8:1 the doers of Torah are mentioned again
and it is made clear that they are the followers of the Teacher of Righteousness. It should be noted that the expression 'doers of Torah' in 8:1 is substituted for the term *tsaddiq* of Hab 2:4 which in all probability filled the
lacuna in 1QpHab 7:17.[146] It thus appears that the primary term for those
who are properly religious is not *tsaddiq*.

Thus it can be concluded that although 1QpHab, like CD, makes use of
the title 'Teacher of Righteousness', the overall importance attached to the
terms *tsedeq* and *tsaddiq* in 1QpHab is more in line with that of 1QS than
CD.

8 The Commentary on Ps 37

In 4QpPs37 the nouns *tsedeq* and *tsedaqah* do not occur but the adjective
tsaddiq occurs twice[147] in the actual commentary and 5 times[148] in biblical
quotations.

Since it is surrounded by lacunae, the expression *b-ts-d-y-[q-y-m*[149] in
2:26 does not elucidate the usage of the adjective *tsaddiq*. In 4:8 the
expression *ha-tsadd[iq*[150] occurs in the course of the interpretation of Ps
37:32 where it is stated that 'the wicked watches the righteous' (*rasha'
latsaddiq*). In the interpretation *rasha'* is said to refer to the Wicked Priest
and *tsaddiq* to the righteous one (*ha-tsadd[iq*) whom the Wicked Priest is
attempting to kill.

Let us now see how some other occurrences of the term *tsaddiq* which are quoted from Ps 37 are interpreted. Twice *tsaddiq* is said to refer to 'the doers of Torah'[151] and once to 'the congregation of the poor'.[152]

There are also some lacunae which can be filled with the proper quotations from Ps 37 with a high degree of certainty. On the basis of these passages *tsaddiq* is interpreted to refer to 'the men of God's good pleasure',[153] to 'the teacher',[154] indirectly to 'the righteous' themselves[155] and to 'someone who spoke the truth'.[156]

On the basis of these passages it can be concluded that the commentator did understand the term *tsaddiq* to apply to those who are properly religious. After all, he uses it to refer to his own group. On the other hand, the term *tsaddiq* is by no means used in 4QpPs37 as the most prominent designation for those who are properly religious. Instead of making the fullest use of this term, the commentator on many occasions replaces the term *tsaddiq* of the biblical quotations with other terms in the commentary.

Let us now turn to the question of the significance of the noun *tsedeq* in 4QpPs37. As was pointed out above, the nouns *tsedaqah* and *tsedeq* are not found in this writing. However, the term *moreh* followed by a lacuna occurs 3 times and it has been suggested that in each case the lacuna should be filled with the noun *tsedeq*. For example, Lohse[157] gives the following readings: 3:15, *moreh ha-*[*tsedeq*;[158] 3:19, *more*[*h ha-tsedeq*;[159] 4:27, *moreh* [*ha-tsedeq*.[160]

Allegro has added 4:8 as another passage referring to the Teacher of Righteousness. He restores the text as follows: *p-sh-r-w '-l* [*h-k-w-h-*]*n h-r-sh-' '-sh-r sh-*[*1-h '-1 m-w-r-h h-ts-d-q?*] *1-h-m-y-t-w.*[161]

A number of scholars have followed Allegro's suggestion.[162] Carmignac specifically lists this passage among those which provide the best evidence for the proper description of the Teacher of Righteousness.[163] It now appears that Allegro's restoration of the text may have been faulty, for another restoration in which the term *moreh* cannot occur seems more probable. According to Lohse the text should read: *pishro 'al* [*ha-ko*]*hen ha-rasha' 'asher ts*[*ope*]*h ha-tsadd*[*iq umebaqqesh*] *lahamito.*[164]

This passage could thus refer to the righteous one rather than to the Teacher of Righteousness. Since it appears that scholars were probably mistaken in the case of 4:8, care should be taken in the restoration of the text in 3:15, 19 and 4:27 where the term *moreh* occurs. For example, with respect to 3:15 it should be made clear that *tsedeq* is a restoration of the text. It cannot be assumed as Gert Jeremias[165] has done that *moreh ha-*[*tsedeq* is the only possible reading, especially since in CD 20:1 the expression *moreh ha-yahid* occurs. It should also be noted that *'emet* rather than *tsedeq* could be the primary designation for that which is right. The noun *tsedeq* is only postulated as occurring in 4QpPs37, while the noun *'emet* in fact is found in this writing. In 3:15ff it is stated that God leads the teacher (*moreh*) in his truth (*la'amito*)[166] and in 4:3f the interpretation of Ps 37:30, a passage in which the adjective *tsaddiq* occurs, makes reference to someone who spoke the truth (*ha-'emet*).[167]

Since the text of 4QpPs37 has not come down to us in a good state of preservation, all the facts concerning the use of the words connected with the root *ts-d-q* may never be known. This much is certain, however; it is not a foregone conclusion that righteousness is viewed as an important concept in this writing. As a matter of fact, it appears that in the Damascus Document the concept of righteousness plays a far more significant role than in 4QpPs37.

9 The concept of righteousness in the Dead Sea Scrolls

On the basis of the foregoing study it is evident that the Dead Sea Scrolls do not display uniformity in the usage of the terms *tsedeq*, *tsedaqah* and *tsaddiq*. The divergence in usage is particularly evident when comparing the Damascus Document and the Manual of Discipline. Although the content and purpose are markedly similar in these two writings, insofar as they are both rule books, it is only in the Damascus Document that the term *tsedeq* plays a vital role in the formulation of the message expressed by this writing. In the Manual of Discipline *tsedeq* is subordinated to *'emet*. Consequently, in comparison to the Damascus Document, the concept of righteousness is relatively insignificant in the Manual of Discipline. As a matter of fact, it appears that of all the writings constituting the Dead Sea Scrolls it is only in the Damascus Document that *tsedeq* is used as a major conceptual term.

What is the concept of righteousness in the Damascus Document? In CD the term righteousness, *tsedeq*, is raised to the position of a technical term, or possibly in the eyes of the ordinary members of the community to the level of a popular slogan, symbolizing everything that is right in the sight of God.

The members of the community know righteousness only through the teaching of the Teacher of Righteousness, for the content of his teaching is *righteousness*. The Teacher of Righteousness makes known and interprets God's righteousness (*tsedeq*) which is primarily understood in terms of God's ordinances which were revealed to the community in the Land of Damascus and are referred to as the New Covenant. God's righteousness understood in this way is to be the norm for man's righteousness. Man's righteousness is understood in terms of the ideal of perfect adherence to God's ordinances. From man's point of view, righteousness thus refers to perfect conduct in the sight of God, especially when viewed with reference to the sectarian use of the expression 'precepts of righteousness' (*ḥuqqe ha-tsedeq*).

The man who strives to live according to this ideal is righteous (*tsaddiq*) and as such is sharply contrasted to the person who is wicked (*rasha'*) and does not live according to *tsedeq*.

Although the ideal expressed in the Damascus Document is perfection of way, it is clear that this goal is not actualized in everyday life. This is evident from the fact that the possibility of deviating from the path of perfection has been taken into account and specific punishments for specific transgressions are outlined.[168]

It should be noted that although God's saving, gracious activity (*tsedaqah*) is mentioned in the Damascus Document[169] this activity is not seen as governing man's conduct. In other words, God is not seen as imputing *tsedaqah* in order that man can lead a properly religious life and thus have *tsedeq*. *Tsedaqah* refers to the gift of salvation. *Tsedeq* refers to the demand of God upon man to lead a properly religious life. By doing *tsedeq* man does not earn salvation but shows that he is not rejecting God's gift of salvation insofar as he is willing to live according to God's demands. When man deviates from the norm for proper conduct, he is punished. The concept of righteousness (*tsedeq*) stresses the ideal of perfection of way.[170] Man's *tsedeq* is not dependent on God's *tsedaqah*.

Consequently, it is evident that the principle stated by Fiedler[171] that man can do *tsedeq* only after God has shown his *tsedaqah* to him is in actual fact not found in the Damascus Document. Even in the Hymn[172] at the end of the Manual of Discipline and in the Thanksgiving Hymns[173] where it is stressed that God's *tsedaqah* is beneficial for man, the benefit is seen primarily in terms of man's salvation rather than man's ability to lead a properly religious life (*tsedeq*).[174] If at times in the Thanksgiving Hymns God's *tsedaqah* appears to govern all of man's actions, the explanation for this phenomenon lies in the attitude presupposed in this type of writing. The Hymns are characterized by an attitude of prayer. As man comes humbly before his creator his thoughts naturally turn to God's grace. Man is so overawed by God's greatness that he feels unable to do anything without his help. This attitude, however, should not be seen as governing the thought expressed in the non-hymnic writings. In the halakic discussions of these writings man is concerned with his religious duties. He thinks in terms of what he can and indeed must do in order to live according to *tsedeq*, the demand of God upon man.

Another factor which must be taken into account when comparing the thought expressed in the hymnic as opposed to the non-hymnic writings

is the influence of the Old Testament. It is generally acknowledged that
the hymnic writings are influenced by the Old Testament to a much greater
extent than the rest of the Dead Sea Scrolls.[175] Because of the use of Old
Testament modes of thought some of the terminology incorporated into
the hymnic writings is not fully representative of sectarian usage.[176] In this
way ideas which were not necessarily in complete harmony with sectarian
teaching could find their way into the hymnic writings. This does not mean
that all ideas expressed in these writings are suspect. It does indicate, however, that one should not attach overwhelming importance to these ideas
so that they are seen as governing the thought expressed in the non-hymnic
writings.

For example, as was pointed out above, in the Damascus Document
there is room for both God's *tsedaqah* and man's *tsedeq*. Even though man's
tsedeq is not dependent on God's *tsedaqah*, God's grace with respect to
man's salvation is in no way denied. However, within the thought of CD
much greater stress is placed on man's responsibility to lead a properly
religious life according to the demand of God upon man than on God's
saving, gracious activity. If man commits a transgression he is punished. If
he actually despises the commandments of God he is expelled from the
community.[177] In the concept of righteousness expressed in the Damascus
Document, not *tsedaqah* but *tsedeq* is stressed, for *tsedeq* represents all
that is right in the sight of God and as such is to be the goal of man's personal effort.

The term *tsedeq* does not play such a decisive role in the remainder of
the Dead Sea Scrolls. G. Jeremias's generalization that the term *tsedeq* is
used as a religious password (*religiöses Kennwort*) or a slogan (*Schlagwort*)
in the Dead Sea Scrolls in general is therefore not entirely correct.[178]
Especially the implication that such a use leads to a deterioration (*Ver-
flachung*)[179] of the meaning of *tsedeq* does not hold true for the Damascus
Document. In CD the use of *tsedeq* as a slogan is to be viewed in a positive
rather than a negative sense. For the rest of the Dead Sea Scrolls, on the
other hand, Jeremias's observations may apply. Especially in 1QS and 1QM
where the term truth (*'emet*) is stressed as the term designating that which
is right in the sight of God, and *tsedeq* is used as a synonym for *'emet*, there
may be a deterioration of the meaning of *tsedeq*.

It was noted above[180] that in the Old Testament it is necessary to speak
of a concept of *tsedeq/tsedaqah* since these two terms are used interchangeably. In the Dead Sea Scrolls, on the other hand, there is a definite trend
to assign distinct meanings to these two terms.

In CD and 1QS apart from the Hymn (10:9–11:22), it is clear that
tsedaqah refers to God's saving, gracious activity and that *tsedeq* designates

the norm for man's conduct. With respect to the latter a difference exists between CD and 1QS, for in the former the norm is specified as being the laws of the New Covenant[181] which was made in the Land of Damascus while in the latter the norm appears to be the laws of the covenant made at Sinai but as interpreted by the sectarians.[182]

In the rest of the Dead Sea Scrolls, that is, other than CD and 1QS except for the Hymn, there is some overlap in meaning between *tsedeq* and *tsedaqah*. In 1QS 10:11; 1QH 11:18; 1QM 18:8 and possibly 1QS 10:26, 11:15; 1QM 4:6 *tsedeq* refers to God's saving, gracious activity. In 1QS 10:25; 1QH 1:26; 4:30, 31; 7:14, 17; 1QpHab 2:2 *tsedaqah* takes on the usual meaning of *tsedeq*, insofar as *tsedeq* refers to man's conduct.

It should be noted that the majority of the passages just listed are from the Hymn in 1QS and from 1QH. As was noted previously, it is in the hymnic materials of the Dead Sea Scrolls that the Old Testament usage of the terms *tsedeq* and *tsedaqah* is seen most strongly. This should not be surprising, for traditional modes of thought and expression would naturally continue to survive most easily in hymns which constituted part of the worship of the community.

The instances of overlap, therefore, are not so extensive as to obliterate the trend to differentiate between the terms *tsedeq* and *tsedaqah*. It can be concluded that whereas in the Old Testament it is necessary to think in terms of a concept of *tsedeq/tsedaqah*, in the Dead Sea Scrolls distinctive meanings are attached to these two terms.

Furthermore, in contrast to the Old Testament where it was difficult to ascertain whether in fact *tsedeq/tsedaqah* referred to a norm or relationship, in the Dead Sea Scrolls *tsedeq* is considered a norm. This is evident not only in the Damascus Document but also in the other Dead Sea Scrolls in which the term *tsedeq* occurs.[183]

3

TSEDEQ, TSEDAQAH AND TSADDIQ IN THE TANNAITIC LITERATURE

1 Introduction

In the discussion concerning the method of the present study the general rationale behind the treatment of the Tannaitic literature was outlined.[1] Before turning to the analysis of the terms *tsedeq*, *tsedaqah* and *tsaddiq* it is, however, necessary to deal specifically with the nature of this literature.

The Tannaitic period is generally defined as spanning A.D. 10 to A.D. 220, that is, beginning with the disciples of Shammai and Hillel and ending with the contemporaries of R. Judah ha-Nasi.[2] The Rabbis[3] who lived during this period are known as the Tannaim and their sayings and discussions form the Tannaitic literature.

The Tannaitic literature has been preserved in two distinct forms. In the mishnaic form the materials are arranged according to topical criteria, while in the midrashic form the materials follow the sequence of the biblical book which is commented upon. Both types of writings are primarily halakic rather than haggadic in content.

The Tannaitic literature of the mishnaic form consists of the Mishnah, Tosefta and various traditions in the Palestinian and Babylonian Talmuds which are attributed to Tannaim. The latter sayings are generally referred to as *baraitot*.[4] The Tannaitic literature of the midrashic form consists of the halakic midrashim such as the Mekilta on Exodus, Sifra on Leviticus, Sifre on Numbers and Deuteronomy, Sifre Zuta on Numbers, Mekilta of R. Simeon b. Yohai on Exodus, Midrash Tannaim on Deuteronomy and *baraitot* in later midrashim such as Midrash Rabbah.

Although all the materials just mentioned can technically be termed Tannaitic, not all are on the same level of reliability. In this study we shall concentrate only on those writings which appear to be most authentic. Consequently, the following materials will be excluded. We will not deal with traditions found only as *baraitot* in the Palestinian and Babylonian Talmuds and the later midrashim such as Midrash Rabbah. Since these writings were compiled two or more centuries after the close of the Tannaitic period, it is indeed likely that some *baraitot* underwent redactional changes.

Neither will we deal with the Tannaitic midrashim known as the Mekilta of R. Simeon b. Yohai on Exodus, Sifre Zuta on Numbers and Midrash Tannaim on Deuteronomy. While these midrashim may at one time have existed as distinct entities, today they are known to us only through later sources and have been reconstructed from them. The reliability of such reconstructed writings is suspect.

It is not implied that the Tannaitic traditions found in the writings which are excluded from this study are totally unreliable and thus worthless. On the contrary, some of these sayings may indeed cast additional light on the concept of righteousness as understood by the Tannaim. It is, however, beyond the scope of the present study to implement a critical analysis of these writings in order to determine which of the sayings are in fact Tannaitic and which show later redactional influences. As a first step it has been deemed advisable to deal only with the most authentic literary sources of the Tannaitic period.

We will therefore deal exclusively with the Mishnah, Tosefta, and the halakic midrashim known as the Mekilta on Exodus, Sifra on Leviticus and Sifre on Numbers and Deuteronomy. These writings correspond to the first two of five categories of Tannaitic traditions considered most reliable by Neusner. It should be noted that Neusner places the Mishnah-Tosefta ahead of the Tannaitic midrashim in his scale of reliability. Both types of materials in turn are deemed more reliable than the *baraitot* in the Talmuds and the later midrashim.[5]

The compilation of the Mishnah by R. Judah ha-Nasi took place *c*. A.D. 200.[6] Undoubtedly this work was enlarged by later additions[7] but basically the Mishnah deals with traditions up to *c*. A.D. 200.

As J. Bowker has noted, the relationship between the Mishnah and Tosefta 'remains one of the most vexing problems of rabbinic scholarship'.[8] For the purpose of this study we will follow the traditional view that the Tosefta was compiled at roughly the same time as the Mishnah[9] and follow Neusner's[10] conclusions as to its reliability.

With respect to the dating of the Tannaitic midrashim it must be pointed out that B. Z. Wacholder has argued that the Mekilta on Exodus was composed by a writer in the eighth century, that is, after the completion of the Babylonian Talmud.[11] It appears that Wacholder holds a similar view as to the date of Sifra on Leviticus and Sifre on Numbers and Deuteronomy.[12]

M. Smith has strongly attacked Wacholder's dating of the halakic midrashim as 'peculiar opinions'.[13] Indeed, Wacholder's view runs counter to the overwhelming scholarly consensus that the Mekilta on Exodus, Sifra on Leviticus and Sifre on Numbers and Deuteronomy are Tannaitic.[14] The compilation of these midrashim, however, seems to have taken place after that of the Mishnah. E. Z. Melamed has suggested that the final redaction of the halakic midrashim took place two generations after that of the Mishnah.[15]

It was noted that the Tannaitic period stretches from A.D. 10 to 220. The bulk of the Tannaitic literature, however, deals with the Rabbinic discussions from the fall of Jerusalem (A.D. 70) to 220.[16] Since the final redaction of the Gospel of Matthew took place after the fall of Jerusalem, perhaps as late as A.D. 80-100,[17] there is definitely an overlap in time between the thought expressed in the writings under discussion and the redactional activity of Matthew.[18]

While it is easy to discern that the Tannaitic literature is relevant as a background to the time of the final redaction of the Gospel of Matthew, it is not absolutely clear to what extent this literature is relevant to the time of the activity of Jesus. For example, of what value is the Tannaitic literature as a background to the debates between Jesus and the Pharisees as depicted in the Gospel of Matthew?

It cannot be taken for granted that the Rabbis continued the Pharisaic traditions. On the other hand, it would indeed be surprising if there were no continuity of thought. Indeed, S. Zeitlin has argued that Pharisaic views can be established from Rabbinic materials.[19] Thus while the Tannaitic literature is most relevant to the time of the final redaction of the Gospel of Matthew, it is not totally unrelated to the time of Jesus. Consequently, a study of the righteousness terminology in the Tannaitic literature is appropriate.

The present study will deal in detail only with the terms *tsedeq*, *tsedaqah* and *tsaddiq*, and of these three terms only *tsedeq* and *tsedaqah* will be treated exhaustively.[20] Other related terms will not be investigated. For example, the meaning of the term 'merit' (*zekut*) is in certain cases related to the meaning of *tsedeq*.[21] While an investigation of this term could be of benefit, preliminary research has shown that an understanding of the concept of merit (*zekut*) is not crucial for an understanding of the concept of righteousness (*tsedeq*).[22] Since every study is bound by certain limitations of time and space, and the value of the study of related terms was not found to be critical, it was decided to concentrate on the three terms mentioned above. Consequently, this study has restricted itself both to the most authentic writings comprised by the Tannaitic literature and to the primary terms dealing with the concept of righteousness.

The treatment of the adjective *tsaddiq* will not be as detailed and exhaustive as that of the nouns *tsedeq* and *tsedaqah* since an investigation of the nouns is more crucial for the main purpose of this study. In previous studies the nouns have received less attention than the adjective. For example, a detailed analysis of the adjective has been made by R. Mach[23] whereas many of the Tannaitic passages dealing with the nouns have not been analysed so as to provide background information for the study of the New Testament.

In the study of the Dead Sea Scrolls each writing was discussed separately. This was done in order to point out significant variations among these writings in the use of the righteousness terminology.

When this study was prepared as a doctoral dissertation,[24] the method of presentation of the Tannaitic literature followed that of the Dead Sea Scrolls; that is, each writing was discussed separately. It was discovered, however, that unlike the Dead Sea Scrolls, the various writings constituting the Tannaitic literature do not display significant variations in terms of meaning and function in the use of the righteousness terminology. Consequently, rather than helping to clarify the discussion, this method of presentation tended to impede it insofar as it led to a needlessly fragmented picture of the concept of righteousness. In the present form of this study it was decided to correct this fault. Instead of discussing each writing in turn, the Tannaitic literature will be considered as a whole, each of the terms *tsedeq*, *tsedaqah* and *tsaddiq* being treated thematically.

2 The adjective *tsaddiq*

As was noted above, the investigation of the term *tsaddiq* is not intended to be exhaustive. Rather, a general overview of the extent of meaning will be presented, with a more detailed analysis of specific themes which will serve as significant background material for the elucidation of the concept of righteousness in the Gospel of Matthew.

On the basis of the number of occurrences it is obvious that in the Tannaitic literature the term *tsaddiq* is used primarily with respect to man. There are, however, a number of significant passages in which this term is also used to describe God.

In Mek. Pisḥa 16[25] the term *tsaddiq* refers directly to God. 'Rabbi[26] says: "The memory of the righteous shall be for a blessing" (Prov 10.7), means, whenever one mentions the Righteous One, the Righteous One who lives eternally – as it is said: "The Lord is righteous in all His ways (Ps 145.17), – give Him praise by saying Amen."'[27] From this passage it is not clear what in fact is meant by calling God 'righteous'. On the basis of other passages, however, it becomes clear that God is called righteous with reference to his role as judge. For example, in Sifre Deut 307 on 32:4 (p. 346) the term *tsaddiq* found in Deut 32:4 is interpreted as signifying that God is a righteous judge and that he is so acknowledged by man. Also both in Zeph 3:5 which is quoted in Mek. Beshallaḥ 6[28] and in Ex 9:27 which is quoted in Shirata 9,[29] God is referred to as being righteous. In Mek. Beshallaḥ 6 the fact that God is righteous means that 'He will bring to light Israel's judgment every morning.'[30] In Mek. Shirata 9, on the other hand, the fact that God is righteous is interpreted to mean that he tempers judgment with mercy.

> By virtue of what was burial granted to them? By virtue of (Pharaoh's) having said, 'The Lord is righteous' etc. (Exod 9:27). Said the Holy One, blessed be He, to them: 'You acknowledged the justice of the sentence upon you, in turn I shall not shortchange you, and I will grant you burial.' As it is said, 'Thou stretchedst out Thy right hand – the earth swallowed them.'[31]

Before turning from God to man let us look at the relationship between the use of the adjective *tsaddiq* with respect to God and man. Is the same term used with different meanings so that there are some qualities which are reserved for God? Or can man be righteous in the same manner that God is righteous?

There are two passages in Sifre Deuteronomy which provide very explicit answers to the questions just posed. In Sifre Deut 307 on 32:4 (p. 344) the statement from Deut 32:4, 'just (*tsaddiq*) and right (*yashar*) is he', is quoted as proof that God did not create man to be wicked but to be righteous as he himself is.[32]

In Sifre Deut 49 on 11:22 (p. 114) Joel 2:32[33] is quoted: 'All who call upon the name of the Lord shall be delivered.'[34] The question is then posed: 'How is it possible for man to be called by the name of God (*maqom*)?' Various illustrations are then given to answer this question. One of them is: '(Just as) God (*ha-maqom*) is called righteous (*tsaddiq*), as it is said: "For the Lord is righteous (*tsaddiq*), he loves righteous deeds (*tsedaqot*)" (Ps 11:7), so you are righteous (*tsaddiq*).'[35]

On the basis of these passages it is clear that there is no essential difference between the assertions that God is *tsaddiq* and that man can be *tsaddiq*. It should be noted at the outset that these passages in no way imply that God imputes righteousness to man. These passages simply indicate that just as God is righteous so man can and ought to be righteous.

If man can be righteous just as God is righteous, one might expect a righteous man to be very important. This is indeed the case. In Mek. Shirata 1[36] it is stated that one righteous person is as important as the whole world.

In Sifre Deut 38 on 11:10 (p. 76) and in 47 on 11:21 (p. 107) it is stated that the world was created for the sake of the righteous. In Sifre Deut 47 on 11:21 (p. 106) it is noted that the righteous are high and exalted above all who come into the world and that they rule and have power from one

end of the world to the other. According to Sifre Num 136 on Deut 3:27
(p. 182) the righteous, just like Moses, will be able to see from one end of
the world to the other. Indeed, it is the righteous who sustain[37] and benefit[38]
the world. Every place where they walk, a blessing follows their feet.[39]
Great benefits can be obtained by honouring the righteous. For example, it
is said that the Canaanites had peace because they honoured the righteous
one, Abraham.[40]

What are the qualities which make the righteous so special? From the
quotation of Is 26:2 in Mek. Beshallaḥ 7[41] and Hab 2:4 in Mek. Beshallaḥ
7[42] it appears that the individual *tsaddiq* is a man of faith. On the basis of
the example of Moses it is generalized that the righteous are very selfless.[43]
R. Akiba states that there is no enmity, hatred or jealousy among the
righteous.[44] Indeed, even the mere presence of the righteous is readily
noticeable, for according to Sifre Deut 47 on 11:21 (p. 104) their faces are
like the sun (*yom*).[45]

If the righteous can imitate God, are very important and exhibit such
remarkable qualities, can they be perfect? In order to answer this question
let us first of all list some of the individuals who are specifically designated
in the Tannaitic literature as being *tsaddiq*.

Both the singular and plural forms of the adjective are used to refer to
righteous individuals.[46] Some of the men who are said to be *tsaddiq* are
Abraham,[47] Benjamin,[48] Joseph,[49] Methuselah,[50] Moses[51] and Simeon.[52]
The singular adjective is also used to refer to specific women. For example,
in Sifre Deut 1 on 1:1 (p. 5) Miriam the righteous[53] is referred to.

Similarly the plural adjective is employed to refer to men and also to
men and women. For example, in Sifre Deut 33 on 6:6 (pp. 59f) R. Josia
refers to the *tsaddiqim* and then specifically mentions Abraham, Boaz and
Elisha. In Sifre Num 133 on 27:1 (p. 176) the term *tsaddiqim* refers to
Isaac and Rebekah.

The persons listed thus far lived prior to the Tannaitic period and it
must be granted that in the Tannaitic literature it is primarily such people
who are designated as being *tsaddiq*. This does not mean, however, that this
term could not be used to refer to specific persons living in the Tannaitic
period. At least two passages can be cited where specific Tannaim are designated as being *tsaddiq*, even if only in an indirect way. In Mek. Nezikin 18[54]
Is 57:1, 'the righteous (*ha-tsaddiq*) perisheth', is quoted by R. Akiba with
respect to the death of R. Simeon and R. Ishmael, and in Sifra Emor parash;
1:14 on Lev 21:3 the term *tsaddiq* is applied to Joseph b. Paksas.

Let us now return to the question concerning the perfection of the
righteous. Was the *tsaddiq* par excellence, Moses, perfect?

That the Tannaim indeed thought of Moses as the greatest among the
righteous is demonstrated by the following passage found in Mek. Shirata 9.[55]

On one occasion Rabbi sat holding a discourse to the effect that in
Egypt one (Hebrew) woman gave birth to sixty myriads. One of the
disciples in his company spoke up and said to him: 'Master, what is of
greater import, the world or a righteous man?' 'The righteous man',
Rabbi replied. 'How so?' Said Rabbi to him: 'Take the case of Jochebed,
who gave birth to Moses, (and) he was the equal of them all.'[56]

The preeminence of Moses among the righteous is also reflected in
passages where Moses is mentioned first and then the rest of the righteous.
For example, in Sifre Num 106 on 12:15 (p. 105) it is stated that God loves
the righteous so much that he will not only take Moses but all the righteous
to himself.

Yet despite this high praise it is clear on the basis of Mek. Amalek 3[57]
that Moses was by no means perfect.

R. Joshua b. Karḥa says: Great is circumcision, for no merit of Moses
could suspend the punishment for its neglect even for one hour . . .
Rabbi says: Great is circumcision, for all the merits of Moses availed
him not in the time of his trouble about it. He was going to bring out
Israel from Egypt and yet because for one hour he was negligent about
the performance of circumcision, the angel sought to kill him.[58]

That the righteous were not perfect can be demonstrated in yet other
ways. R. Eleazer of Modiim states in Sifre Num 137 on 27:14 (p. 184) that
when God announces the death of the righteous he at the same time reports
their sin.[59] The reporting of the sin is not viewed in an unfavourable way
but rather as a gracious act. It is in this way that God lets it be known that
a particular *tsaddiq* committed only a single sin. All speculation with respect
to the hidden sins of the righteous is thus precluded. Yet the fact remains
that this passage shows that the righteous die as the result of transgressions
and thus are not thought of as being perfect.

The fact that there are distinctions among the righteous also presupposes
that there must be levels of imperfection amongst them. This is evident from
Sifre Deut 10 on 1:10 (p. 18) which states: 'Seven classes of righteous
men (there will be) in the Garden of Eden, one higher than the other.'[60]
Then one or more biblical quotations are given to illustrate each class. The
lower class is described by Ps 140:13,[61] 'Surely the righteous shall give
thanks to thy name; the upright shall dwell in thy presence.' The highest
class is described by Ps 24:3, 'And who shall stand in his holy place?'[62]

For our final example of the lack of perfection of the *tsaddiqim* we will
consider Sifra Shemini Millu'im 22-7 on Lev 10:1-5. In this passage the
death of Nadab and Abihu, the sons of Aaron, is discussed. The discussion
ends as follows: 'If for those who offended him by bringing before him

that which was not in accord with his will, God (*ha-maqom*) acted thus, how much more (will he do good) for the rest of the righteous (*ha-tsaddiqim*).'[63] It is clearly implied that although Nadab and Abihu sinned to the extent that God felt it necessary to put an immediate end to their lives, they nevertheless were considered among the righteous.[64]

If the righteous are not perfect, is there perhaps a still higher category of individuals who are? At first the expression *tsaddiq gamur*[65] (perfectly righteous)[66] seems to indicate that there is. Upon closer investigation, however, it is obvious that even the perfectly righteous are not considered to be perfect with respect to transgressions. This fact emerges on the basis of Sifre Deut 307 on 32:4 (p. 345).

> 'A God of faithfulness' (Deut 32:4). Just as he pays the perfectly righteous (*tsaddiq gamur*) the reward of a commandment (*mitsvah*) which he fulfilled in this world (after he is) in the world to come, so he pays the perfectly wicked (*rasha' gamur*) the reward of a minor commandment which he fulfilled in this world (while he is) in this world. And just as he punishes the perfectly wicked (*rasha' gamur*) in the world to come for a transgression which he committed in this world, so he punishes the perfectly righteous (*tsaddiq gamur*) in this world for a minor transgression which he committed in this world.[67]

This passage states that neither the perfectly righteous nor the perfectly wicked are in actual fact perfect in their righteousness and perfect in their wickedness. It is taken for granted that the perfectly righteous one can commit a minor transgression and that the perfectly wicked one can fulfil a minor commandment. It should be noted that only minor commandments and minor transgressions are referred to. It seems to be taken for granted that the perfectly wicked cannot fulfil major commandments nor the perfectly righteous commit major transgressions.[68]

There may be another reference to the perfectly righteous in Sifre Deut 40 on 11:12 (p. 81). The reading, however, is uncertain.[69] The point raised in this passage is that if the people of Israel are perfectly righteous at the beginning of the year and God therefore decides to provide plenty of rain for them, he cannot change this decision even though the people change for the worse. God is, however, able to send the rain at an inopportune time.

It is obvious that people who are perfectly righteous at one time do not necessarily remain that way. Consequently, in this passage, as in the previous one, the term *gamur* does not imply a hundred per cent type of perfection.

In the foregoing discussion the perfectly righteous were placed in opposition to the perfectly wicked. Indeed, the contrast between the righteous and the wicked (*tsaddiqim* and *resha'im*) plays a major role in the use of the adjective *tsaddiq* in the Tannaitic literature. For example, in the Mishnah there are 18 occurrences of the adjective *tsaddiq* outside of biblical quotations and in 11 cases[70] the contrast is between the righteous and the wicked.

The terms *tsaddiqim* and *resha'im* are used to depict two entirely different types of people. The contrast is like day and night. The wicked destroy the world while the righteous sustain it.[71] The prayers of the righteous are heard in the morning while God will punish the wicked in Gehinnom in the morning.[72] The righteous control their *yetser* while the wicked do not.[73]

A point of contrast between the *tsaddiqim* and *resha'im* which must be treated in greater detail than the preceding ones is that of the type of existence in this world and the world to come. With respect to life in this world it is often stressed that the righteous suffer while the wicked prosper.[74] E. P. Sanders[75] has argued convincingly that this view reflects primarily R. Akiba and his school during the time of the Hadrianic persecution. Before and after this period there were also different views.

According to T. Sanhedrin 11:8, R. Simeon b. Judah says in the name of R. Simeon that 'Beauty and power and wisdom and wealth and old age and glory and honour and sons, are good for the righteous and good for the whole world.'[76] R. Simeon b. Menasya then goes on to say that 'These seven qualities which the wise have counted among the virtues of the righteous were all exemplified in Rabbi and his sons.'[77] It thus appears that at the end of the Tannaitic period some of the righteous led a very comfortable existence.

With respect to life in the world to come it is clear that the wicked will suffer while the righteous will prosper.[78] The righteous have the assurance that God will take not only Moses but all of them to himself.[79] They can even look forward to a more pleasant death than the wicked.[80]

There are a number of passages which specify the reward of the righteous in the world to come. Every righteous one[81] will inherit 310 worlds[82] and together they will receive all the silver, gold and diamonds at the bottom of the sea.[83]

Although all the righteous will be in the Garden of Eden[84] there will not be total equality among them. As we saw above, it is suggested that 'Seven classes of righteous men (there will be) in the Garden of Eden, one higher than the other.'[85] According to R. Simeon b. Yohai the distinctions between the righteous will be according to the brilliance of their faces. 'To seven joys the faces of the righteous (will be) similar in the future: to the sun, moon, sky, stars, lightning, lilies and candlesticks of the Temple.'[86]

The foregoing discussion has shown that it is a matter of utmost concern whether one belongs to the *tsaddiqim* or the *resha'im*. Let us therefore consider the criteria for belonging to the *tsaddiqim*.

On the basis of Mek. Pisḥa 16[87] it could possibly be inferred that God predestines who is to be counted among the righteous and the wicked.

> We find that the names of the righteous and their deeds are revealed before God even before they are born, as it is said: 'Before I formed thee in the belly I knew thee', etc. (Jer 1:5). We thus learn that the names of the righteous and their deeds are revealed before God. How about those of the wicked? Scripture says: 'The wicked are estranged from the womb', etc. (Ps 58.4).[88]

Although an interpretation in terms of predestination may be possible, it is not probable. What is most likely involved is foreknowledge on the part of God, for there are other more explicit passages which show that being righteous or wicked is not predetermined. For example, in T. Sanhedrin 8:4 it is argued that only a single man was created in the beginning so that the righteous could not say that they were children of a righteous man and the wicked that they were the children of a wicked man.

Also the fact that God is portrayed as caring both about the wicked and the righteous rules out a strict predeterminism. For example, in Mek. Amalek 3[89] R. Zadok is quoted as saying: 'It is the Holy One, blessed be He, who gives to every one his wants and to everybody according to his needs. And not to good people (*kesherim*) (and righteous people)[90] alone, but also to wicked people (*resha'im*) and even to people who are worshipping idols.'[91]

Is nationality a criterion for being righteous? In other words, can only Jews be *tsaddiq*? On this point there is divergence of opinion among the Tannaim. On the one hand, strong opinions are expressed that Gentiles can be righteous. R. Jeremiah[92] is quoted as saying that under certain conditions a Gentile can be equal to the High Priest.[93] This opinion is echoed in T. Sanhedrin 13:2 according to which R. Joshua states that there are righteous Gentiles who have a share in the world to come. More specifically, a group of Philistines is designated as being righteous in Sifre Num 88 on 11:6-7 (p. 88). The ones who said, 'Woe to us! Who can deliver us from the power of these mighty gods?' (1 Sam 4:8a) are portrayed as the *tsaddiqim*, while the ones who said, 'These are the gods who smote the Egyptians with every sort of plague in the wilderness' (1 Sam 4:8b) are portrayed as the *resha'im*.

On the other hand, there is the opposing view that only Jews can be righteous. For example, in T. Sanhedrin 13:2 R. Eliezer states that no Gentiles have a share in the world to come.

It should be noted, however, that it is never taken for granted that Jews *per se* are righteous. Indeed, in Sifre Num 119 on 18:20 (p. 144) some priests are called wicked. 'Greater is the covenant that was made with Aarc than the covenant that was made with David. Aaron transmitted (the privilege of the priesthood) to the righteous (*tsaddiqim*) and the wicked (*resha'im*) while David transmitted (the privilege of kingship) to the righteous and not the wicked.'[94]

It thus appears that predeterminism and nationality are not generally accepted criteria for judging who is or is not righteous. One's relationship to the law, on the other hand, is a crucial criterion. According to Sifra Qedoshim pereq 11:6 on Lev 20:16 the righteous are defined as those who practise Torah and do the will of their father who is in heaven. The same criterion is presented in Sifra Aḥare pereq 13:13 on Lev 18:5. In this passage the adjective *tsaddiq* occurs in quotations from Is 26:2, Ps 118:20 and 33:1, and in the discussion of who is righteous R. Jeremiah[95] stipulates that a Gentile can be as righteous as a High Priest if he practises the law. Also Rabbi supports the criterion of observing the law when he notes that the righteous fear the commandments.[96]

The final authority as to who is righteous, however, is not man but God. This is clearly shown in Mek. Kaspa 3.[97] In this passage Ex 23:7, 'And the innocent (*naqi*) and righteous (*tsaddiq*) slay thou not', is quoted five times. At first the stress is on the meaning of *naqi* but toward the end of the discussion the following argument is advanced:

Suppose one comes out from the court acquitted (*zakka'i*) and after a while they find evidence of his guilt. I might understand that they should bring him back for a new trial. But it says: 'And the righteous (*tsaddiq*) slay thou not.' You might think that just as he came out acquitted (*zakka'i*)[98] from your court, he also came out acquitted from My court. It says however: 'For I will not justify the wicked (*'atsdiq rasha'*).'[99]

In this passage a distinction is made between the one whom man declares to be righteous and the one whom God declares to be so. As far as man is concerned a person is considered to be innocent, i.e. *zakka'i* and *tsaddiq*,[100] if he is acquitted by the court even though he is later found to be guilty. God, however, does not consider such a person to be *tsaddiq* but declares him to be *rasha'*.[101]

Although Mach and Ziesler agree that such a use is rare, they draw attention to this passage as showing that *tsaddiq* can be used in a purely forensic sense; that is, man is declared innocent though he is not.[102] It should be noted, however, that this passage only posits such a possibility with respect to a human court, not with respect to God. In addition, this purely forensic use has no bearing on soteriology but simply refers to a case tried in a human court. As far as God is concerned, he only declares those righteous who are in fact righteous; that is, those who live in accordance with Torah.

Thus far it has been established that although God is the final authority as to who is righteous and who is wicked, it is nevertheless clear that the righteous are those who practise Torah. On the basis of evidence such as this, in conjunction with the fact that only the righteous inherit the world to come, many scholars have made the practice of Torah, in the sense of doing good works, into a soteriological principle. It is argued that a righteous man is one whose righteous deeds outweigh his evil deeds.[103] In the literature under discussion the following passages have been used to support this view. In T. Kiddushin 1:15f, R. Simeon (b. Yohai, according to B. Kiddushin 40b) compares the righteous man to the wicked man.[104]

> If a man has been righteous (*tsaddiq*) all his days and rebels at the end, he destroys it all, for it is said, 'The righteousness of the righteous man (*tsidqat ha-tsaddiq*) will not save him in the day when he transgresses' (Ezek 33:12). If a man has been wicked (*rasha'*) all his days and repents at the end, God receives him, for it is said, 'And as for the wickedness of the wicked (*werish'at ha-rasha'*), he shall not fall by it when he turns from his wickedness' (Ezek 33:12).

Mach uses the passage above as proof for the view that every individual is judged according to the majority of his deeds.[105] In actual fact this passage teaches nothing of the kind. Rather than referring to the weighing of good and bad deeds, this passage implies that by rebelling at the end of his life, a righteous man can undo the effect of all the good deeds which he had performed previously. Also, if this passage is seen in its context – that is if 1:16 is taken into account – it is clear that a man's future is not only decided by his deeds, but by acts of repentance. Even if a man has been wicked, God will still receive him as long as he repents.

Another passage which has been used to support the idea of weighing is T. Sanhedrin 13:3. Here the expression *resha'im gemurim* is found. According to the School of Shammai there are three classes of people, that is, those who will enter into everlasting life, those who will suffer shame and everlasting contempt and those who will go down to Gehenna but in the end receive healing. It is explicitly stated that the perfectly wicked make up the second class.

Although no specific name is attributed to the first class, Mach is probably right in stating that they are the perfectly righteous.[106] On the other hand, Mach's assertion that the third class are those whose good and bad deeds are evenly balanced and that the whole passage provides proof for the general principle that every individual is judged according to the majority of his deeds is not convincing. At best it can be said that this passage rather than pointing to a generally accepted principle, points to a view held by the School of Shammai. As is clear from the ensuing discussion in T. Sanhedrin 13:3, the School of Hillel did not hold to this threefold distinction but argued that God leans in the direction of mercy. Since T. Kiddushin 1:15f also sees repentance as a criterion for the decision as to man's final judgment, it is unwarranted to take the idea of weighing of good and bad deeds as the sole basis for the final judgment of the righteous and the wicked.[107]

It is evident not only from the foregoing passages but also from others that repentance plays a crucial role in the soteriological system of the Tannaim. For example, in Sifra Hobah parasha 12:9 on Lev 5:17, R. Jose mentions the reward which will be given in the future to the righteous who repent and fast on the Day of Atonement. It is clear that repentance rather than deeds is stressed when soteriology is involved.

It is not the intention of the present study to give a detailed analysis of the soteriological system of the Tannaim.[108] On the other hand, the role of repentance does have to be noted so as not to give the impression that being righteous (*tsaddiq*), that is, practising the law, in and of itself, aside from grace and repentance is the sole criterion for salvation. As E. P. Sanders has demonstrated, 'Being righteous in the sense of obeying the law to the best of one's ability and repenting and atoning for transgression *preserves* one's place in the covenant (it is the opposite of rebelling), but it does not *earn* it.'[109] In other words, being righteous is a necessary but not sufficient ground for salvation. Being righteous simply demonstrates that one intends to remain within the covenant by following the laws of the covenant given to Moses on Mount Sinai. Transgression of the law, however, has to be atoned for and repentance is crucial in the process of atonement.

That repentance is indeed the crucial criterion in the soteriological system of the Tannaim is demonstrated yet more clearly in passages dealing specifically with the concept of salvation rather than in those where repentance is mentioned in conjunction with the *tsaddiqim*.

There are a number of passages which classify types of transgression with corresponding means of atonement.[110] Various offerings and sacrifices, the Day of Atonement as such, suffering and death are mentioned. Repentance, while at times appearing to be one of many means of atonement, at other times is described as the general attitude which has to accompany the other means of atonement.[111] Consequently repentance plays a crucial role in the soteriological system of the Tannaim.

The following distinction must therefore be kept in mind at all times when referring to the Tannaitic concept of the righteous. While only the righteous will inherit the world to come (after all, they are the ones who demonstrate that they want to remain in the covenant), being righteous (*tsaddiq*), that is, obeying the law and thus doing good deeds, is a necessary but not sufficient ground for salvation. As was shown above, even those who were considered to be 'perfectly righteous' were not regarded as having committed no transgressions at all. But, in order to inherit the world to come, transgressions have to be atoned for and atonement involves repentance.

The conclusion emerging from the investigation of the adjective *tsaddiq* is that this term plays a decisive role in designating those who lead a properly religious life. Being righteous is not viewed as the gift of God. Rather the righteous are those who practise the commandments.

This is not to say that God does not give any help to the righteous. On the contrary, in Sifre Num 135 on Deut 3:26 (p. 181) God's word to Moses, 'Let it suffice you', is interpreted as meaning that God prevents the righteous from committing a grave transgression (*'aberah ḥamurah*). Such a sentiment is also reflected when it is argued that if God is merciful with the righteous in the time of his anger, then he will definitely be so in the time of his good will.[112] It is also stated that God hears the prayers of the righteous.[113]

This help, however, is not construed as making being righteous the gift of God. Being righteous (*tsaddiq*) is the result of man's actions. Salvation, on the other hand, is the gift of God insofar as God's forgiveness on the basis of man's repentance cannot be viewed as having been earned by man. It must be stressed that being *tsaddiq* and salvation are not equivalent concepts. The righteous are those who are properly religious insofar as they live according to the commandments of the law.

3 The noun *tsedeq*

That a close relationship exists in the Tannaitic literature between the righteous one and righteousness is not a mere assumption, for in Sifre Num 133 on 27:1 (p. 176) it is clearly stated that the *tsaddiq* has *tsedeq*.[114] 'R. Nathan says: Scripture teaches you that (with) every righteous person (*tsaddiq*) who (according to scripture) grew up in the bosom of a wicked person (*rasha'*) and did not do according to his deeds, (this is reported) to make known to you how great his righteousness (*tsidqo*) must have been ... '

What is the nature of *tsedeq*? Is it the gift of God or the demand upon man? Does it have a broad or narrow meaning?

Let us begin the discussion of the noun *tsedeq* with the following statistics. In the Tannaitic literature as defined above, there are a total of 70 occurrences of the noun *tsedeq*. Of these 22 are independent, that is, occu in passages other than biblical quotations, and 48 are dependent, that is, form a part of biblical quotations. Of the 48 dependent occurrences, 6 wil not be discussed since the term *tsedeq* in the quotations is irrelevant to the context in which the quotation is found. In other words, in these instances the biblical texts were quoted for reasons other than the fact that they contained the term *tsedeq*. Three of these passages are found in Sifre on Deuteronomy[115] and three in the Mekilta de-Rabbi Ishmael.[116]

The total number of 70 occurrences are distributed as follows among the Tannaitic writings: Sifre on Deuteronomy, 29 (10, 19);[117] Sifra, 14 (5, 9); Mekilta de-Rabbi Ishmael, 12 (5, 7);[118] Tosefta, 12 (1, 11);[119] Sifre on Numbers, 2 (1, 1); Mishnah, 1 (0, 1).

Before turning to the discussion of the meaning of the noun *tsedeq*, it is necessary to deal with the frequency with which this noun occurs in the Tannaitic literature. It has been stated that the whole concept of human righteousness is narrowed down in the Rabbinic literature to the idea of almsgiving.[120] In other words, it is suggested that the term *tsedeq* really plays no significant role in this literature.

As the foregoing statistics show, outside of direct biblical quotations the noun *tsedeq* occurs 22 times in the Tannaitic literature. Of these, 21 occurrences are in the Tannaitic midrashim and one in the Mishnah and Tosefta. Let us first look at the Tannaitic midrashim.

Of the 21 independent occurrences of the noun *tsedeq* in the Tannaitic midrashim, 8 are found in the expression *ger tsedeq* (righteous proselyte). Of the remaining 13, 5 are in the discussion of passages in which the term *tsedeq* occurs in a biblical quotation. Thus it could be argued that there actually are only 8 completely independent references to the noun *tsedeq* as it occurs in an absolute state. Furthermore, these 8 references are found in only three distinct passages.[121] It could be concluded that such a few occurrences cannot be significant.

But this conclusion can easily be refuted. While it is true that the noun *tsedeq* in its absolute state is only found in three passages in which it bears no relationship to the term *tsedeq* of biblical quotations, it is by no means true that only such occurrences are relevant in determining the significance of this term in the Tannaitic literature.

Passages in which the term *tsedeq* in the course of the discussion is given a different meaning from that which it has in the biblical quotation are highly significant.[122] The mere fact that the term *tsedeq* is used at all in the course of the discussion is significant, for if the term had fallen into disuse then another term could have been substituted for it.

Occurrences of *tsedeq* in biblical quotations are also significant when they are used in support of a specific argument. In determining the use, it is possible to see what meaning was bestowed on the term in the Tannaitic period. The 8 cases in which *tsedeq* occurs in the expression *ger tsedeq* are also significant in determining the meaning of the term *tsedeq*.

Although we thus have a significant number of passages in which the term *tsedeq* is used, it is granted that this is not a great number. The reason for this relatively small number is easily discernible. The Tannaitic midrashim are largely limited in their subject matter by the topics which are found in the biblical books upon which they are commenting. It should therefore be noted that in Exodus and Numbers, the books which form the basis for the Mekilta and Sifre on Numbers respectively, the noun *tsedeq* does not occur. Consequently, it is significant that, despite this fact, the expression *ger tsedeq* occurs 5 times in the Mekilta and the noun *tsedeq* occurs once in Sifre on Numbers in a completely independent way.

In Leviticus the noun *tsedeq* occurs twice[123] and both passages are commented upon in Sifra.[124] In addition to these passages the term *tsedeq* occurs in the discussion of Eccles 7:15, a passage in which the term *tsedeq* occurs,[125] and in two additional passages in the expression *ger tsedeq*.[126]

In Deuteronomy the noun *tsedeq* occurs 6 times[127] and all these references are discussed in Sifre on Deuteronomy.[128] In addition there are two passages[129] in which the term *tsedeq* is used in a completely independent way and one passage in which the expression *ger tsedeq* occurs.[130]

It can therefore be concluded that not only are all references to the noun *tsedeq* occurring in the biblical books upon which the Tannaitic midrashim are based commented upon, but in each of the midrashim the use of *tsedeq* goes beyond the subject matter suggested by the biblical material. It should also be noted that the Tannaitic midrashim do not comment on all parts of their respective biblical books. Consequently, the fact that all occurrences of *tsedeq* are commented upon shows that there is absolutely no reticence in the use of this term.

With respect to the seemingly small number of occurrences of *tsedeq*, the example of the use of *tsedaqah* is very informative. It is generally acknowledged that *tsedaqah* is a very significant term in the thought-world of the Tannaim. It should therefore be noted that outside of direct biblical quotations there are only 11 references[131] to this term in the Tannaitic midrashim, that is, 10 fewer than the references to *tsedeq*.

In the Mishnah and Tosefta there is only a single independent reference to the term *tsedeq* and it occurs in the expression *ger tsedeq* in T. Arakin 5.9. In addition, however, there are one and 11 references to the term *tsedeq* in the Mishnah and Tosefta respectively which occur in biblical quotations. Although the term *tsedeq* is by no means absent in the Mishnah and Tosefta, the low frequency of usage may appear peculiar if one is unfamiliar with the character of these writings. These two writings are of a yet more halakic character than the Tannaitic midrashim and it is a well-known fact that halakah deals primarily with specific details rather than with comprehensive concepts. Since righteousness is a very comprehensive concept, it is therefore not surprising that little use is made of it in the Mishnah and Tosefta.

Having established that the total number of occurrences of the term *tsedeq* is quite significant, let us now turn to the meaning of this term. Just as the adjective *tsaddiq* referred to those who led properly religious lives, so the noun *tsedeq* is used adjectivally with much the same meaning. This use of *tsedeq* occurs in the expression *ger tsedeq* which is found 9 times in the Tannaitic literature.

That the term *tsedeq* is indeed used adjectivally in the expression *ger tsedeq* is indicated as follows. In Mek. Kaspa 3 a variant for *ger tsedeq* is *ger tsaddiq*,[132] indicating that *tsedeq* is adjectival. A comparison of the expression *ger tsedeq* with the expression *ger toshab* leads to the same conclusion. In the latter expression, *toshab* is definitely adjectival. The *ger toshab* is the resident alien.[133] Consequently, Lauterbach's translation of *ger tsedeq* as 'righteous proselyte'[134] seems to be correct.

In Mek. Kaspa 3[135] the expression *ger tsedeq* occurs twice. In this saying by R. Jose the Galilean the stress is on the *ger toshab*. Consequently, little can be learned about the meaning of *tsedeq*.

The two occurrences of the expression *ger tsedeq* in Mek. Baḥodesh 7,[136] on the other hand, are relevant to this discussion. Here the term *wegereka* found in Ex 20:10 is under discussion, and it is concluded that *wegereka* refers to the *ger tsedeq* since in Ex 23:12 *weha-ger* refers to the *ger toshab*.

In order to comprehend the significance of the use of the term *tsedeq* we must discuss Ex 20:10 and 23:12. Winter points out that in Ex 23:12 the rationale behind the prohibition to work on the sabbath is that it is to be a day of rest.[137] By saying that in this case *ger* refers to the *ger toshab* it is implied that resting on the sabbath is to be observed even by resident aliens. In Ex 20:10, on the other hand, the rationale is the sanctification of the sabbath. The sanctification of the sabbath is of higher religious significance than the mere resting on the sabbath. Accordingly *ger* cannot refer to a resident alien in this instance. It must refer to the *ger tsedeq* who is fully like a native Israelite. Such an explanation is in harmony with Lauterbach's definition that the *ger toshab* or resident alien is a heathen who has forsworn idolatry and is a potential proselyte whereas the *ger tsedeq* or righteous proselyte is fully like a native Israelite.[138]

The plural form *gere tsedeq* is found in Mek. Nezikin 18.[139] In order to show that the proselytes (*ha-gerim*) are beloved, it is pointed out that 'you find them also among the four groups who respond and speak before Him by whose word the world came into being'.[140] Four groups corresponding to the four responses of Is 44:5 are then listed. The *gere tsedeq* correspond to the statement 'And another shall call himself by the name of Jacob.'[141] Is 44:5 deals with the growth of Israel by way of proselytes.[142] Thus in this passage, as in Mek. Baḥodesh 7, the term *tsedeq* serves the function of showing that a specific category of people are to be regarded fully like native Israelites.

In T. Arakin 5:9 we find the following interpretation of Lev 25:39.

'And if your brother becomes poor beside you, and sells himself to you' (Lev 25:39). (This does) not (mean that he sells himself) to you but to the stranger (*ger*). For it is said: 'And he sells himself' (Lev 25:47). (This means that he does) not (sell himself) to the righteous proselyte (*ger tsedeq*) but to the sojourner (*ger toshab*). For it is said: 'And he sells himself to the sojourner (*ger toshab*)'[143] (Lev 25:47).

The intent of this argument is to show that an Israelite does not sell himself to another Israelite but only to a sojourner. The proof is dependent on the fact that a righteous proselyte (*ger tsedeq*) is fully like a native Israelite. The term *tsedeq* thus is again instrumental in pointing out that a certain type of person is properly religious so that he can be treated like a native Israelite.

In Sifre Deut 278 on 24:14 (p. 296) the phrase *'o miggereka* (Deut 24:14) is interpreted as referring to the *ger tsedeq*, the righteous proselyte. From the context, however, it is impossible to infer the specific meaning of this term.

The 2 remaining occurrences of the expression *ger tsedeq* are found in Sifra Behar parasha 5:1 on Lev 25:35 and in Sifra Behar pereq 8:1 on Lev 25:47. Here the term *ger* is identified with the *ger tsedeq* while the term *toshab* is identified with the stranger (*ger*) who eats *nebelot*, that is, meat that is not kosher. The distinction drawn is between those who do and those who do not obey a certain dietary law. The term chosen to identify the person who does obey the dietary law is *tsedeq*. Thus once again the term *tsedeq* is used to indicate who is properly religious. It should be noted that in all passages the stress is not on salvation but on proper religious behaviour in everyday life.

The noun *tsedeq* is used adjectivally not only to designate persons who lead a properly religious life but also to designate a religiously normative ac In Sifre Deut 354 on 33:19 (p. 416) the expression 'sacrifices of righteousness' found in Deut 33:19 is quoted. Regarding Deut 33:19, 'They shall call the peoples unto the mountain', it is noted that the Gentiles came to Jerusalem and saw that the nation of Israel was better off than they were. The discussion ends as follows: 'How can you say that they do not move from there until they have offered sacrifices? Scripture says: "There shall they offer sacrifices of righteousness (*zibḥe tsedeq*)" (Deut 33:19).'

It is implied in the discussion above that on the basis of the proof text Deut 33:19, 'There shall they offer sacrifices of righteousness', it can be deduced that the Gentiles in question will become proselytes and will offer sacrifices. The latter deduction is obvious. But why can it be deduced that they will become proselytes? The key must lie with the term *tsedeq*. If sacrifices of *righteousness* are offered, this must indicate that the act was performed by *bona fide* religious persons and that biblical rather than heathen sacrifices were involved. Consequently, the Gentiles must have become proselytes. *Tsedeq* is a key term signifying proper religious behaviour defined as Torah observance.

The noun *tsedeq* is also used adjectivally in the description of balances, weights and measures. In Lev 19:36 as quoted in T. Baba Batra 5:7 the expressions *mo'zene tsedeq*, *'abne tsedeq*, *'epat tsedeq* and *hin tsedeq* occur. They should be translated as 'just balances', 'just weights', 'just epha' and 'just hin'. The stress is on honest weights and measures.

Lev 19:36 is also quoted in Sifra Qedoshim pereq 8:7 on Lev 19:36. In this passage the term *tsedeq* occurs 8 times. Six of these occurrences are in direct quotations of Lev 19:36 and 2 are independent. It is self-evident that in these expressions the noun *tsedeq* is used adjectivally.

> 'Just balances'. Make the balances exactly right.[144] 'Just weights'. Make the weights exactly right. 'Just epha'. Make the ephot exactly right. 'Just hin'. Make the hin exactly right. R. Jose ben Judah[145] says: 'But was not hin included in epha?' For it is said: 'And a just epha'. If this is so, why is it said: 'You shall have a just hin.' (It is said because you shall have) a righteous No and a righteous Yes.[146]

The conclusion reached in this discussion is based on a play on words. R. Jose ben Judah argues that the term 'hin' is repeated because in the second case it is not meant to refer to the measure hin but to the Aramaic 'hen'[147] meaning 'yes'. The noun *tsedeq*, being used adjectivally in the genitive position of the construct-genitive relationship, in this case has the meaning of honest.[148] Consequently, *tsedeq* is used to designate honesty in speaking. It can therefore be concluded that the noun *tsedeq* when used adjectivally in the genitive position of construct-genitive expressions functions as a symbol to designate normative religious behaviour or states.

Let us now turn to the substantive use of the term *tsedeq*. In its most comprehensive meaning, the noun *tsedeq* designates all religious teaching which defines normative religious behaviour. This use is evident in Sifre Deut 144 on 16:19 (p. 199).

> Another interpretation: 'For a bribe blinds the eyes of the sages' (Deut 16:19). They say that the unclean is clean and that the clean is unclean.

'And subverts the words of the righteous (*dibre tsaddiqim*)' (Deut 16:19). They say that the forbidden is permitted and the permitted is forbidden. Another interpretation: 'For a bribe blinds the eyes of the sages' (Deut 16:19). And he does not fulfil his obligation until he teaches righteousness in his decision as teacher (*'ad sheyoreh tsedeq behora'ato*).[149] 'And subverts the words of the righteous' (Deut 16:19). He does not fulfil his obligation until he knows what he is saying.

In the passage above, *tsedeq* is a term signifying the correct decisions of the sages which are not distorted by bribery. *Tsedeq* encompasses all religious behaviour concerned with what is clean or unclean, permitted or forbidden.

It should also be noted that the totality of the normative religious teaching known as *tsedeq* is explicitly referred to as the truth. Is 45:19, 'I the Lord speak righteousness (*tsedeq*), I declare things that are right (*mesharim*)', is quoted in both Mek. Bahodesh 1[150] and 5,[151] and is interpreted in terms of truth.

> R. Jose says: Behold it says: 'I have not spoken in secret', etc. (Is 45.19). When I gave the Torah from the very start, I gave it not in the place of a land of darkness, not in a secret place, not in an obscure place . . . . Did I not give it in broad daylight? And thus it says: 'I the Lord speak righteousness, I declare things that are right (ibid.).' Mek. Bahodesh 1.[152]

In the passage above it is stressed that in giving the Torah, God acted above suspicion in every possible way. To clinch the argument Is 45:19 is quoted. In this quotation 'righteousness' is parallel to 'things that are right'. Consequently, *tsedeq* has the meaning of truth. God speaks the truth in the sense that what he says is above reproach and normative.

In Mek. Bahodesh 5 the use of Is 45:19 is even more pointed. Here R. Nathan gives a refutation of the heretics who claim that there are two powers. The argument is clinched with the quotation of Is 45:19. Thus in this case the concept of *tsedeq* is seen as including the central teaching that there is only one power, God.

Having established the meaning of *tsedeq* in its most comprehensive sense, that is, as correct, truthful teaching, let us now consider various other aspects of this term. It should be noted that *tsedeq* is not only something which is external with respect to man. As was pointed out at the beginning of this section, the *tsaddiq* can have *tsedeq*, and there are further passages which show that *tsedeq* is a quality which a person can possess as a result of living according to the correct teaching, that is, *tsedeq*.

This internal aspect of *tsedeq* is strikingly portrayed in Sifra Emor parasha 1:13f on Lev 21:3. Here R. Jose says, 'A man should not defile himself for a (piece of) his father's bone the size of a barley grain.'[153] To

illustrate this point, the following example is given. It is stated that Joseph
b. Paksas had a gangrenous swelling on his leg. When he went for an oper-
ation he told the doctor. 'Let me know when the leg is hanging by a hair.'
The doctor then operated and told him when the leg was hanging by a hair.
While still being technically whole, Joseph called his son, Nehonyah, and
said to him, 'My son, until now you were obligated to attend to me. From
now on go away, for a man should not defile himself for the limb from a
living person, (not even) from his father.'[154] The illustration concludes as
follows: 'And when the matter came to the attention of the sages they said:
"About this one (Joseph b. Paksas) it is said: 'There is a righteous man
(*tsaddiq*) who perishes in his righteousness (*betsidqo*)' (Eccles 7:15)." The
righteous man (*tsaddiq*) perishes but his righteousness (*tsidqo*) remains
with him.'

Zlotnick states that this story shows Joseph's devotion to the law.[155]
This interpretation is particularly brought out in the parallel in Śĕmahot
pereq 4:15, where not only Eccles 7:15 but also Ps 119:109 is given: 'My
soul is continually in my hand; yet have I not forgotten Thy Law.' Indeed,
Joseph's devotion to the law was so great that he did not fear the prospect
of personal hardship on account of it. As Eccles 7:15 implies, not having
his son care for him would lead to the end result that Joseph b. Paksas
would perish. Despite such a prospect, Joseph did not deviate from the
strict interpretation of the law that a man should not defile himself for the
limb of a living person, not even his father. Because of such devotion to the
law the sages noted that Joseph b. Paksas had righteousness (*tsedeq*).
Tsedeq thus refers to a quality which a person possesses as a result of his
strict adherence to the law.

The foregoing interpretation is the one which arises most naturally out
of the text as found in Sifra Emor parasha 1:13f on Lev 21:3 and P. Nazir
55d. On the basis of a variant of Śĕmahot pereq 4:15, however, another
interpretation is possible. Whereas according to Sifra and P. Nazir it is clear
that Joseph b. Paksas acted as he did because he knew that a son should
not defile himself for the limb of his father, on the basis of the variant
reading it appears that it was only *as a result* of this particular incident that
the sages ruled that a man should not defile himself from a living person,
not even from his father.[156]

On the basis of this variant reading Dr A. Baumgarten has suggested that
the righteousness of Joseph b. Paksas was based on the fact that he did
more than the law required. According to this interpretation Joseph b.
Paksas thought that his son would have to defile himself. Joseph b. Paksas
thus acted as he did in order to protect his son from defilement. In order
to prevent this type of self-sacrifice which a father might be tempted to

undergo for his son, the sages ruled that a son should not defile himself for the limb of his father.

The latter interpretation indeed appears to answer the question of Joseph's motivation more appropriately than the former one, but in keeping with the adopted methodology of giving priority to the Tannaitic literature as defined above, preference will be given to the interpretation based on the text of Sifra.

The internal aspect of *tsedeq* is also demonstrated with respect to Moses in Sotah 1:9 and Sifre Num 106 on 12:15 (p. 105). Since both of these passages quote Is 58:8 and refer to the fact that Moses took the bones of Joseph, we will deal only with one of them, namely Sotah 1:9.

> Moses was reckoned worthy to take the bones of Joseph, and none in Israel is greater than he, as it is written, 'And Moses took the bones of Joseph with him' (Ex 13:19). Whom have we greater than Moses, for none other than the Almighty occupied himself with him, as it is written, 'And he buried him in the valley' (Deut 34:6). And not of Moses alone have they spoken thus, but of all the righteous (*kol ha-tsaddiqim*), for it is written, 'And thy righteousness (*tsidqeka*) shall go before thee; the glory of the Lord shall gather thee [in death]' (Is 58:8).[157]

The discussion relevant to our passage starts with Sotah 1:7, 'With what measure a man metes it shall be measured to him again.'[158] In the remainder of 1:7–8 this general statement is illustrated with negative examples, that is, how bad deeds are punished. In 1:9 positive examples are cited. They are introduced by the statement *weken le'inyan ha-tobah*. Blackman translates this as follows: 'And thus also in the matter of a good deed'.[159] This is followed by examples of how good deeds are rewarded in the case of Miriam, Joseph and Moses. In this context *tsedeq* is the quality which a person possesses because he has performed good deeds. The good deed singled out in the case of Moses is that of caring for the bones of Joseph. This is in fact a deed of mercy.[160]

At this point it is necessary to discuss Sifre Deut 277 on 24:13 (p. 295), a passage in which not only the noun *tsedeq* but also the noun *tsedaqah* occurs.

> 'When the sun goes down, you shall restore to him the pledge' (Deut 24:13). It teaches that he (must) return to him the object of the day for the day and the object of the night for the night. (He must return) the mattress for the night and the plough for the day but not the mattress for the day and the plough for the night. 'That he may sleep in his cloak and bless you' (Deut 24:13). It teaches that he commands to bless you. You might conclude that if he blessed you, you are blessed

and if (he did) not (bless you) you are not blessed. (Therefore) scripture says: 'And it shall be righteousness (*tsedaqah*) to you' (Deut 24:13). By yourself you do righteousness (*tsedaqah*). 'And it shall be righteousness (*tsedaqah*) to you' (Deut 24:13). It teaches that righteousness (*ha-tsedaqah*) goes up before the throne of glory and thus it says: 'Righteousness (*tsedeq*) will go before him and make his footsteps a way' (Ps 85:13).[161]

In this passage *tsedeq* and *tsedaqah* are treated as synonyms, for the term *tsedeq* in Ps 85:13 is used by way of proof for the preceding argument in which the term *tsedaqah* occurs. It is argued that *tsedeq/tsedaqah* is not dependent on the action of others. One can do *tsedeq/tsedaqah*, and an example of such action is the returning of the proper objects at the proper time. On the one hand, *tsedeq/tsedaqah* therefore refers to what is right with respect to human action. On the other hand, the passage shows that *tsedeq/tsedaqah* is also the resultant quality which a person possesses once he has completed such action.[162]

What is the effect of having *tsedeq*? Are there any outward manifestations of this quality? The Tannaitic literature shows that there are. In Sifre Deut 334 on 32:44 (p. 384) there are 6 independent references to the term *tsedeq*; that is, the terms *tsidqo* and *betsidqo* each occur 3 times.

'He and Hoshea the son of Nun' (Deut 32:44). Why is (this passage) necessary? Has it not already been said: 'And Moses called Hoshea the son of Nun Joshua' (Num 13:16)?[163] Why does scripture say: 'He and Hoshea the son of Nun' (Deut 32:44)? (It is said) to make known the righteousness of Joshua. I might have thought that he was arrogant when he was appointed at first. (Therefore) scripture says: 'He and Hoshea the son of Nun' (Deut 32:44). Hoshea (was) in his righteousness. Although he was appointed leader over Israel, Hoshea (was still) in his righteousness. Similarly you say: 'And Joseph was in Egypt' (Ex 1:5). But do we not (already) know that Joseph was in Egypt? But (this is said) to make known (to you) the righteousness of Joseph who was tending the flock of his father. Although he was appointed king in Egypt, he (was still) Joseph in his righteousness.[164] Similarly (you say): 'And David was the youngest' (1 Sam 17:14). But do we not (already) know that David was the youngest? But (this is said) to make known (to you) the righteousness of David who was tending the flock of his father. And although he was appointed king over Israel, he was (still) David in his smallness (*beqotno*).

In the examples above, the *tsedeq* of Joshua, Joseph and David was evidenced by the fact that, although they had been appointed to high positions, they nevertheless remained humble. This is especially clear in the case of David where the terms *tsidqo* and *qotno* are used with parallel meanings. One of the outward manifestations of *tsedeq* is therefore humility.

Another manifestation is the ability to do good deeds. Sifre Num 133 on 27:1 (p. 176) states:

> R. Nathan says: Scripture teaches you that (with) every righteous person (*tsaddiq*) who (according to scripture) grew up in the bosom of a wicked person (*rasha'*) and did not do according to his deeds, (this is reported) to make known to you how great his righteousness (*tsidqo*) must have been that he grew up in the bosom of a wicked person (*rasha'*) and did not do according to his deeds. And every wicked person (*rasha'*) who (according to scripture) grew up in the bosom of a righteous person (*tsaddiq*) and did not do according to his deeds (this is reported) to make known to you how great his wickedness (*rish'o*) must have been that he grew up in the bosom of a righteous person (*tsaddiq*) and did not do according to his deeds.

At this point the presentation may appear to be circular. It was argued previously that *tsedeq* was the quality which came as a consequence of the doing of good deeds while now it is suggested that *tsedeq* is a quality which manifests itself by the doing of good deeds. Without doubt *tsedeq* is viewed primarily as the result of rather than the cause for good deeds. However, the person who has *tsedeq* as the consequence of his having done good deeds is viewed as being capable of continuing to do good deeds.

This type of thinking proceeding from result to cause is typical of the Tannaim. For example in Mek. Vayassa' 1[165] it is stated: 'If a man hearkens to one commandment he is given the opportunity to hearken to many commandments. For, it really says: "If you begin to hearken you will continue to hearken."'[166] In this case the result, that is, obeying a commandment, appears to be the cause for being able to obey further commandments. Consequently, the argument from result to cause is simply indicative of the fact that once a person has set out on a certain road it becomes progressively easier to follow that road. In other words, *tsedeq* cannot be viewed as a gift which then becomes the cause for the doing of good deeds.

Not only is *tsedeq* manifested by humility and the doing of good deeds but also by fairness in the judicial process. That *tsedeq* is an essential quality for judges is stated in Sifre Deut 144 on 16:18 (p. 198). In this passage the phrase *mishpat tsedeq* which is found in Deut 16:18 is quoted twice in the following context. '"And they shall judge the people" (Deut 16:18). Without their will. "With judgment of righteousness" (Deut 16:18). But has it not already been said: "You shall not pervert justice" (Deut 16:19)? (Therefore) why does scripture say: "With judgment of righteousness"

(Deut 16:18)? This (is said with respect to) the appointment of the judges.'
This passage raises the question of why the phrase 'with judgment of righteousness' is added; the implication is that this phrase was not really needed since
the topic of the perversion of justice is adequately covered without it. The
proposed answer is that the phrase 'with judgment of righteousness' introduces a new topic, namely, the issue of the 'appointment of judges'. Consequently, *tsedeq* is descriptive of one of the factors which must be taken into
account in the choice of judges.

How does the righteousness of the judge influence his decisions? In
Sifre Deut 16 on 1:16 (pp. 25ff), the term *tsedeq* occurs 3 times in direct
quotations of Deut 1:16 and twice in the course of the discussion of this
verse. The passage begins by quoting Deut 1:16, 'And I charged your judges
at that time, "Hear the cases between your brethren, and judge righteousness."' In the ensuing discussion the emphasis is placed on the need to
examine the differences between the various cases brought before the
judges ensuring that not all cases are treated alike. Deut 1:16 is illustrated
and in a sense even summed up by a saying attributed to the men of the
Great Synagogue, 'Be deliberate in judgement, raise up many disciples, and
make a fence around the Law.'[167]

The discussion then turns to 'and judge righteousness (*ushepaṭṭem
tsedeq*)'.[168]

> 'And judge righteousness.' The righteous in his righteousness (*tsaddiq
> betsidqo*) claims and offers evidence.[169] For example one is wrapped in
> his cloak and the other says: 'It is mine.' One ploughs with his cow and
> the other says: 'It is mine.' One takes possession of his field and the
> other says: 'It is mine.' One dwells in his house and the other says: 'It is
> mine.' Therefore it was said: 'And judge righteousness.' The righteous
> in his righteousness (*tsaddiq betsidqo*) claims and offers evidence.

In the passage above, *tsedeq* refers to the proper type of judgment. The
tsedeq of the *tsaddiq* manifests itself by the fact that all his decisions are
based strictly on evidence. Everything he owns is definitely his on the basis
of clear evidence.

There are a number of other passages which indicate that *tsedeq* is viewed
as an important aspect of the judicial process. In Sifre Deut 294 on 25:15
(p. 313) the term *tsedeq* occurs twice in the quotation of Deut 25:15, 'and
it shall be righteousness to you'. It should be noted that in Deut 25:15
tsedeq is actually used adjectivally insofar as it describes the 'weight' and
'measure': 'A full and just weight you shall have, a full and just measure
you shall have.' In Sifre on Deuteronomy, however, the term *tsedeq* is
divorced from its biblical context and used substantively. Consequently, it

can be argued that this is really an independent use. In its present context the statement 'and it shall be righteousness to you' is used to refer to fair treatment so that justice prevails.

In Ps 58:2(1) quoted in T. Sotah 9:8, in Ps 119:164 quoted in T. Berakoth 6(7):25 and in Lev 19:15 quoted in T. Sanhedrin 6:2 and Sifra Qedoshim pereq 4:4 on Lev 19:15 the term *tsedeq* is again interpreted as referring to proper judgment. From these passages it is clear that *tsedeq* presupposes complete equality of all persons in judgment with respect to such things as the opportunity to speak, uniformity with respect to sitting and standing and the degree of strictness of the judges.

In T. Sanhedrin 6:2 the reference to *tsedeq* in the biblical quotations is especially relevant to the Rabbinic discussion. Danby's translation of this passage is as follows:

> Men must stand when they pronounce sentence, or bear witness, or ask for absolution from vows, or when they remove any one from the status of priesthood or of Israelitish citizenship. The judges may not show forbearance to one man and strictness to another, nor suffer one to stand and another to sit; for it is written: 'In righteousness shalt thou judge thy neighbour' (Lev 19:15).[170]

Righteousness not only requires fairness and equality in judgment but also leniency. This point is made in the following two passages. In Sifra Qedoshim pereq 4:4 on Lev 19:15 the text under discussion is 'With righteousness (*betsedeq*) shall you judge your neighbour' (Lev 19:15). *Betsedeq* is interpreted to mean that all men are to be judged 'in the scale of innocence' (*lekap zekut*). Consequently, 'with righteousness (*betsedeq*)' is taken to be equivalent to 'with mercy'. Judging your neighbour with righteousness means to judge him leniently.

In Sifre Deut 144 on 16:20 (pp. 199f) the partial phrase *tsedeq tirdop* of Deut 16:20 is quoted once and the complete phrase *tsedeq tsedeq tirdop* is quoted three times.

> 'Righteousness you shall pursue' (Deut 16:20). How do we know (that if) one leaves a court (having been declared) innocent, they do not reverse the decision to declare him guilty? Scripture says: 'Righteousness and only righteousness you shall follow' (Deut 16:20). (If) he went out guilty, how do we know that they may reverse the decision to innocence? It is said: 'Righteousness and only righteousness you shall follow' (Deut 16:20). Another interpretation: 'Righteousness and only righteousness you shall follow' (Deut 16:20). Follow the court whose judgment is good; (i.e. follow) the court of Rabban Johanan b. Zakkai and the court of R. Eleazar.

The discussion above centers on the reason for the double occurrence of *tsedeq*. In the first interpretation the problem is resolved by arguing that this refers to two distinct cases; that is, a person who is initially found innocent cannot at a later date be found guilty while a person initially found guilty may later be found innocent.[171] The biblical phrase thus means 'pursue leniency'.

In the second interpretation the double reference to *tsedeq* is said to refer to two specific courts. In this instance the meaning of *tsedeq* is not as clearly brought out as in the first interpretation. It is to be expected, however, that the 'good judgment' is the more lenient one. Consequently, it is probable that the meaning of *tsedeq* is similar in both interpretations.

It should be noted that the term *tsedeq* is not reserved to refer to justice on the human level. It is also used in conjunction with God's activity. In Mek. Shabbata 1,[172] Ps 89:15(14) and 97:2[173] are quoted. In both of these verses the expression *tsedeq umishpat* occurs and it is this expression which is used to support the assertion that God's administration of justice (*din*) did not cease when he rested on the seventh day.

All except two passages in which the noun *tsedeq* occurs have now been considered and in all of these passages *tsedeq* was used with a consistent meaning. It is this meaning which must therefore be called its primary meaning. In its primary meaning the term *tsedeq* refers both to a very comprehensive concept and to the parts which make up the whole. It has both an external and an internal aspect.

In its most comprehensive sense *tsedeq* refers to every aspect of religious teaching which is normative for man's conduct. In other words, *tsedeq* is the norm by which every aspect of man's behaviour including the juridical is to be measured. As such, *tsedeq* is not the gift of God but the demand upon man. In some instances, as in the expression *ger tsedeq*, *tsedeq* takes the form of a symbol signifying adherence to the normative religious practice of Israel.

The foregoing description dealt with the external aspect of *tsedeq*. Once a person has lived according to the external norm of *tsedeq*, he himself is said to possess *tsedeq*. *Tsedeq* then manifests itself as a quality which leads to further acts of *tsedeq*. It is not suggested that one can only perform such acts as a result of possessing *tsedeq*. Rather it is simply implied that once one has successfully set out on a way of conduct it becomes progressively easier to follow that way.

When the English term 'righteousness' is used in this study with reference to the Tannaitic literature, it stands for the primary meaning of *tsedeq* as just defined. It should be noted that this meaning is indeed primary insofar as it covers all except two passages in which the term *tsedeq* occurs.

The two passages in which the meaning of *tsedeq* does not comply with the primary meaning are T. Peah 4:18 and T. Maaser Sheni 5:25. In these passages the term *tsedeq* is used with meanings which are more characteristic of the term *tsedaqah*. These passages will be discussed below in the context of the relevant discussions of the term *tsedaqah*.

It should be noted at this point that these two exceptions are relatively insignificant. In these two passages the references to *tsedeq* are found in biblical quotations only. All independent occurrences of *tsedeq* and the vast majority of dependent occurrences are used in a consistent way in the Tannaitic literature. Consequently, it is not only possible but necessary to refer to a primary meaning of *tsedeq* which is indeed distinctive of this term.

4 The noun *tsedaqah*

The noun *tsedaqah* occurs a total of 80 times in the Tannaitic literature. Of these references 53 are independent and 27 are dependent; that is, they occur outside of and within biblical quotations respectively. Of the 27 dependent occurrences 10 will not be discussed because the term *tsedaqah* in the quotations is irrelevant to the context in which the quotation is found.[174] The 80 occurrences of *tsedaqah* are distributed as follows in the Tannaitic literature: Tosefta, 41 (36, 5);[175] Sifre on Deuteronomy, 16[176] (8, 8); Mekilta de-Rabbi Ishmael, 9 (1, 8); Mishnah, 7 (6, 1);[177] Sifre on Numbers, 5 (1, 4); Sifra, 2 (1, 1).

As was the case with *tsedeq*, so the noun *tsedaqah* is used with varying frequency in the Tannaitic midrashim as opposed to the Mishnah and Tosefta. In the Tannaitic midrashim there are only 11 independent occurrences of the term. Since this term is not found in Exodus, Leviticus and Numbers, it is not surprising that there is only one independent reference to it in each of the midrashim which deal with these biblical books. In Sifre on Deuteronomy there are 8 independent occurrences of the term *tsedaqah*. Four of these occur in the discussion of Deut 24:13 and 33:21, verses in which the term *tsedaqah* occurs.[178] Consequently, the frequency of the use of *tsedaqah* in the Tannaitic midrashim is directly proportional to the frequency with which this term occurs in the relevant biblical books.

In the Mishnah there are 6 and in the Tosefta 36 independent occurrences of the term *tsedaqah*. Why this difference in frequency? The answer is very simple. The term occurs more frequently in the Tosefta than in the Mishna because the Tosefta deals much more with the concept of almsgiving. As a matter of fact, the primary meaning of the term *tsedaqah* in the Tannaitic literature is without doubt that of almsgiving as defined in T. Peah 4:19. In this passage the concepts of almsgiving (*tsedaqah*) and deeds of lovingkindness (*gemilut ḥasadim*) are compared. Moore translates this passage as follows:[179]

Almsgiving and deeds of lovingkindness are equal to all the commandments of the Law. Almsgiving is exercised toward the living, deeds of
lovingkindness toward the living and the dead; almsgiving to the poor,
deeds of lovingkindness to the poor and to the rich; almsgiving is done
with a man's money, deeds of lovingkindness either with money or
personally.[180]

Out of a total of 36 independent occurrences in the Tosefta, the noun
tsedaqah is used 31 times with reference to the giving, receiving or administration of alms. Of these 31 uses, *tsedaqah* occurs 26 times[181] in the
singular absolute state, once[182] in the plural absolute state and 4 times[183]
in the genitive position in the expression *gabba'e tsedaqah*, collectors of
public charity. All these references adhere to the definition of *tsedaqah*
given in T. Peah 4:19.

On the basis of the Tosefta, almsgiving (*tsedaqah*) is of the utmost
importance. Not only are almsgiving and deeds of lovingkindness equal to
all the commandments of the law[184] but according to T. Peah 4:21 they
are a great intercessor and a great peacemaker between Israel and their
Father in Heaven. As far as R. Joshua b. Karḥa is concerned, to refrain from
almsgiving is tantamount to practising idolatry.[185]

Due to the great importance of almsgiving, care must be taken in the
designation of alms. For example, alms must not be collected from those
who eat the fruit of the seventh year[186] nor taken out of the poor-tithe
money.[187] The acceptance of ill-gotten alms can have dire consequences.
For example, it is argued in T. Sotah 14:10 that ever since the Israelites
accepted alms from the Gentiles, they decreased while the Gentiles
increased.

The primary meaning of *tsedaqah*, i.e. almsgiving, also is predominant
in the rest of the Tannaitic literature. Four of the 6 independent references
to *tsedaqah* in the Mishnah definitely refer to almsgiving. In Baba Kamma
10:1 it is noted that none should take alms (*tsedaqah*) from excisemen or
tax-gatherers. In both Demai 3:1 and Kiddushin 4:5 there are discussions
concerning the function of almoners (*gabba'e tsedaqah*), that is, the collectors
of charity in Jewish communities. In Aboth 5:13 it is noted that 'There
are four types of almsgivers (*benotene tsedaqah*).'[188] The passage then goes
on to describe the four types.

Perhaps there could also be a reference to almsgiving in the saying of
Hillel in Aboth 2:7. 'He used to say: . . . the more study of the Law the more
life; the more schooling the more wisdom; the more counsel the more understanding; the more righteousness (*marbeh tsedaqah*) the more peace.'[189]
On the basis of the context, however, it is impossible to arrive at a definite
conclusion as to the meaning of *tsedaqah*. This is reflected in the lack of

uniformity of the various English translations of this passage.[190] A clue to the meaning of *tsedaqah* may be Is 32:17, a possible source for the passage under discussion. It appears that in Is 32:17 *tsedaqah* does not necessarily refer to almsgiving.[191] Consequently, although it is possible that the term *tsedaqah* in Aboth 2:7 could refer to almsgiving, no definite conclusions as to its meaning can be reached.

In the Mekilta the one independent occurrence of the noun *tsedaqah* definitely refers to almsgiving. It is found in Mek. Amalek 4.[192] 'He who made the other ignorant will in the end make him wise. Something similar you find in the matter of giving charity.[193] How so? If the poor man stretches out his hand towards the householder,[194] and the householder gives willingly, then "the Lord giveth light to the eyes of both".'[195]

As was noted previously, of the 8 dependent references in the Mekilta, 4 are not relevant to the context. Of the 4 remaining there is one, Mek. Nezikin 10,[196] in which the term *tsedaqah* of the quotation plays a pivotal role as a proof-text. Without doubt *tsedaqah* refers to almsgiving. 'R. Ishmael says: Come and see how merciful He by whose word the world came into being is to flesh and blood. For a man can redeem himself from the Heavenly judgment by paying money, as it is said . . .'[197] Then among the proof texts Dan 4:27[198] is quoted: 'Therefore, O King, let my counsel be acceptable to thee, and break off thy sins by almsgiving (*betsidqah*).' Von Rad has noted that in Dan 4:27 'there is heralded a decided narrowing and curtailment of the concept of *ts-d-q-h* in so far as . . . the Aramaic *ts-d-q-h* has the meaning of "good works", "almsgiving" . . . '[199]

In Sifre Deut 265 on 23:24(23) (p. 286) there is an independent occurrence of the noun *tsedaqah* the meaning of which cannot be determined. Every part of Deut 23:24 is commented upon. 'With your mouth' is interpreted as meaning *zo tsedaqah*. Since a continuous theme does not run throughout the interpretation of the various parts of the verse, it is impossible to determine the meaning of *tsedaqah* from the context.

In 4 of the 7 remaining independent occurrences in Sifre on Deuteronomy, *tsedaqah* definitely refers to the concept of almsgiving. In Sifre Deut 47 on 11:21 (pp. 105f) Dan 12:3 is quoted: 'And those who turn the many to righteousness (*umatsdiqe*) are like the stars for ever and ever.' In the first two interpretations this verse is seen as referring to the *tsaddiqim*. In the third interpretation it is seen as referring to the *gabba'e tsedaqah*, the collectors of public charity.

In Sifre Deut 108 on 14:27 (p. 169) the welfare of the Levite is under discussion. It is concluded that if other means of support fail, then the Levite is to be supported from alms (*min ha-tsedaqah*).

In Sifre Deut 143 on 16:16 (p. 196) the phrase *min ha-tsedaqah* occurs

in the discussion of Deut 16:16, 'They shall not appear before the Lord
empty-handed.' Since the ensuing discussion deals with money, it is certain
that *tsedaqah* refers to almsgiving.

In Sifre Deut 355 on 33:21 (pp. 418f) two interpretations of Deut 33:21
are given. The first one is as follows.

> 'The righteousness (*tsedaqah*) of the Lord he (Moses) did' (Deut 33:21).
> Is it really so? What righteousness (*tsedaqah*) did Moses do in Israel? Did
> not all the forty years that Israel was in the desert the well rise up for
> them and the manna descend for them and (were not) quails found for
> them and (did not) the clouds of glory cover them? But it says: 'If there
> is among you a poor man . . . (you shall not harden your heart . . .)'
> (Deut 15:7).

The problem underlying the discussion revolves around how Moses could
have done the righteousness of the Lord if, as it appears, the Lord himself
took care of all Israel's wants. The problem is solved with reference to
Deut 15:7 which states that there were poor people among the Israelites.
Consequently, there was the possibility of doing *tsedaqah* and Moses'
tsedaqah must have been evidenced by the fact that he gave alms to the
poor.[200]

It should be noted that in MS. d[201] the term *tsedaqot* occurs instead of
tsedaqah in the statement 'What righteousness did Moses do in Israel?'
Billerbeck gives the following translation based on MS. d: 'Wie, was für
Wohltaten *tsedaqot* (nach Art Jahves) hat er denn den Israeliten erwiesen?'[202]
It appears that the variant reading does capture the intended meaning of
the giving of alms.

Of the 8 dependent occurrences of *tsedaqah* in Sifre on Deuteronomy, 3
are not relevant to the context. Of the 5 remaining references only the one
in Sifre Deut 355 on 33:21 (pp. 418f), discussed immediately above, refers
to almsgiving.

The only independent occurrence of the noun *tsedaqah* in Sifre on
Numbers is found in Sifre Num 42 on 6:26 (p. 47). K. G. Kuhn interprets
tsedaqah in this case as referring to almsgiving. 'Gross ist der Friede, denn
er ist gegeben denen, die Wohltätigkeit üben. Denn es heisst: "Und es wird
das Werk der Wohltätigkeit Friede sein" (Jes 32, 17).'[203] The reason Kuhn
gives for this translation is that ' *-sh-h ts-d-q-h* = Almosen geben'.[204] It is
indeed probable that *tsedaqah* refers to almsgiving in this case. However,
since the context does not explicitly point to this meaning it cannot be
assumed with any degree of certainty. After all, as will be shown below, in
Sifre Deut 277 on 24:13 (p. 295) the phrase *-sh-h ts-d-q-h* has another
meaning.

Of the 4 dependent occurrences of *tsedaqah* in Sifre on Numbers only 2 are relevant to the context in which the quotations are found. The use of *tsedaqah* in the quotation of Is 32:17 in Sifre Num 42 on 6:26 (p. 47) was discussed above and it was concluded that although *tsedaqah* could refer to almsgiving, no absolutely definitive determination of meaning could be made.

In Sifra the one dependent occurrence of *tsedaqah* is not relevant to the context. In the only independent use, which is found in Sifre Ḥobah parasha 12:12 on Lev 5:17, *ha-tsedaqot* means alms. Rabbi argues that if scripture (Deut 19:5) assures protection to the one who accidentally killed somebody, how much more will the person 'who collects alms (*ha-tsedaqot*) and provides for the poor and is charitable be given life'.

In the discussion of the noun *tsedeq* it was noted that there are two passages in which the dependent occurrences of *tsedeq* have meanings which are more characteristic of the noun *tsedaqah*. In T. Peah 4:18 the noun *tsedeq* found in Ps 85:12(11)[205] and 89:15(14) and Is 58:8 refers to almsgiving. In the same passage Deut 24:13 is quoted and the term *tsedaqah* is likewise interpreted as referring to alms. It should be noted that these interpretations occur in a context which specifically deals with the topic of alms, for in T. Peah 4:19 almsgiving (*tsedaqah*) and deeds of lovingkindness (*gemilut hasadim*) are discussed. In T. Maaser Sheni 5:25, Ps 85:12(11) is quoted once again. Here *tsedeq*, although not referring specifically to alms, has a closely related meaning insofar as it refers to God's gifts for man.

Another meaning of *tsedaqah* closely associated with almsgiving is that of mercy. That almsgiving and mercy are indeed closely related is best indicated by T. Peah 4:21, where the occurrence of the term *rahamim* in the quotation of Jer 16:5 is seen to point to the term *tsedaqah*, even though in this case *tsedaqah* has the meaning of almsgiving.[206]

> R. Eleazar said in the name of R. Jose:[207] From where (do we know) that almsgiving (*ha-tsedaqah*) and deeds of lovingkindness (*gemilut hasadim*) are a great intercessor and a great peace(maker) between Israel and their Father in Heaven? Because it says: 'For thus says the Lord: Do not enter the house of mourning, or go (to lament, or bemoan them; for I have taken away my peace from this people, says the Lord, my steadfast love and mercy)' (Jer 16:5). Steadfast love (*hesed*), that is, deeds of lovingkindness (*gemilut hasadim*); and mercy (*rahamim*), that is, almsgiving (*tsedaqah*).

In the passage above the relationship between the concepts of mercy and almsgiving could very well be based on the assumption that one shows mercy by giving alms to the poor. Such reasoning seems to underlie the use of *tsedaqah* in T. Sanhedrin 1:4.

When judgment has been given in a case, justifying him who was in the right, and condemning him who was in the wrong, if it be a poor man who has been condemned the judge sends him away and gives him support out of his own pocket. He is thus found acting with judgment (*din*) to the one and with mercy (*tsedaqah*) to the other.[208]

In the passage above *tsedaqah* definitely has the meaning of mercy; mercy that is put into practice by the giving of money. In the immediately following passage in T. Sanhedrin 1:5, mercy is also used in conjunction with material benefits. In this case, however, mercy is shown by taking away rather than by giving, for *tsedaqah* is based on the taking away of stolen property.

Rabbi says: When judgment has been given in a case, justifying him who was in the right, and condemning him who was in the wrong, kindness (*tsedaqah*) is dealt to him who was in the wrong since what was stolen is taken from him; and judgment is meted out to him who was in the right, since what was his is restored to him.[209]

The use of the noun *tsedaqah* in Mek. Shirata 5[210] is more difficult to classify.

Another interpretation: 'LIKE A STONE', for like stone they hardened their hearts. – But as for Thee, Thy goodness, Thy manifold mercies . . . and it is written, 'By Myself have I sworn, the word is gone forth from My mouth in charity, and shall not come back' (etc.) (Isa 45:23).[211]

Goldin points out that the term *tsedaqah* of Is 45:23 is here quoted with the understanding that it refers to 'the rabbinic sense of charity, love'.[212] This use is an extension of the concept of mercy. Instead of confining mercy to material benefits it is generalized to refer to God's goodness as a whole. After all, it would be inappropriate to depict God as being involved in the human practice of almsgiving. God's gifts for man have to take a more general form.

Let us now consider those passages in which *tsedaqah* has a meaning which overlaps with that of *tsedeq*. We shall start with the overlap in the area of juridical behaviour. It was noted that in Sifra Qedoshim pereq 4:4 on Lev 19:15 and Sifre Deut 144 on 16:20 (pp. 199f) *tsedeq* referred to leniency in judgment. *Tsedaqah* is also used with such a meaning, that is, leniency or mercy that is not necessarily associated with material benefits.

In the second interpretation of Deut 33:21 in Sifre Deut 355 on 33:21 (pp. 418f) it is stated: "'The righteousness (*tsedaqah*) of the Lord he did" (Deut 33:21). It teaches that righteousness (*tsedaqah*) hangs beneath the court under the throne of glory, as it is said: "Thus says the Lord: 'Keep justice, and do righteousness (*tsedaqah*)'" (Is 56:1).' Here Deut 33:21 is interpreted not with respect to Moses as in the first interpretation but with respect to God. It is stated that *tsedaqah* plays a role in God's judgment. On the basis of the proof-text, Is 56:1, it appears that *tsedaqah* is contrasted with justice. The interpretation thus implies that God judges with mercy. In this context Is 56:1 should be translated 'Keep justice and at the same time do mercy.'

Not only is God's justice tempered by mercy but this ideal is held in high esteem with respect to man's administration of justice. This fact is illustrated by T. Sanhedrin 1:3.

> R. Joshua b. Karha said: . . . And it is written of David: 'And David administered (strict) justice (*mishpat*) and mercy (*tsedaqah*)[213] to all his people' (2 Sam 8:15). And is it not the case that wherever there is (strict) justice (*mishpat*) there is no mercy (*tsedaqah*)? And where there is mercy (*tsedaqah*) there is no (strict) justice (*mishpat*)? Then what is (strict) justice (*mishpat*) wherein there is mercy (*tsedaqah*)? Say, that is mediation (*b-y-ts-w-ʾ*).[214]

As the context[215] clearly indicates, the discussion deals with the relative merits of formal judgment according to the strict interpretation of halakah as opposed to informal judgment making use of the concept of mediation in order to arrive at a fair settlement. *Tsedaqah* clearly refers to that type of judgment which is less harsh and consequently more merciful than strict justice.

In three passages the noun *tsedaqah* appears to refer primarily to strict justice, but it is possible that the concept of mercy may also be implicit. Mek. Shirata 1[216] states: 'From strife he fled to return to strife, (everywhere "executing the righteousness of the Lord[217] and His ordinances with Israel" (Deut 33:21). Lo then, because he gave over his life to the pursuit of justice the judges go by his name.'[218]

Similarly in Mek. Nezikin 18[219] the term *tsedaqah* found in the quotation of Is 56:1 has the meaning of justice. Is 56:1 is quoted to give support to the assertion that when one actually executes justice (*din*) one will receive benefits. In Deut 33:21, as quoted in T. Sotah 4:9, *tsedaqah* appears to refer to the ordinances of God.

Let us now consider those passages where the meaning of *tsedaqah* overlaps with that of *tsedeq* in other than juridical behaviour. In Sifre Num 106 on 12:15 (p. 105) there is the following dependent use of *tsedaqah*. 'And the ministering angels praised him (Moses) and said: "The righteousness (*tsidqat*) of the Lord he did, and his judgments with Israel" (Deut 33:21).' In this saying by R. Judah, Deut 33:21 is directly applied to Moses.[220] It is thus implied that man, i.e. Moses, can do the righteousness of the Lord. Consequently, a relationship exists between man's and God's righteousness. In this case *tsedaqah* is understood in terms of the doing of good deeds since the general context deals with the fact that Moses took the bones of Joseph with him. This meaning is also suggested by the use of the verb *q-y-l-s*. Kuhn points out that this verb is here used as a technical term 'für die Ausrufe, mit denen man bei einem Leichenzug die Verdienste und Tugenden des Verstorbenen pries'.[221]

The occurrence of *tsedaqah* in Sifre Deut 277 on 24:13 (p. 295) has already been discussed in the treatment of *tsedeq*. In this passage *tsedaqah* refers to what is right with respect to human conduct and to the quality which a person possesses once he has completed such conduct.

In Aboth 2:2 it can also be established with some certainty that the meaning of *tsedaqah* goes beyond that of almsgiving.

> Rabban Gamaliel the son of R. Judah the Patriarch said: . . . And let all them that labour with the congregation labour with them for the sake of Heaven, for the merit (*zekut*) of their fathers supports them and their righteousness (*tsidqatam*) endures for ever. And as for you [will God say,] I count you worthy of great reward as ye [yourselves] had wrought.[222]

Maimonides makes the following comment regarding those who labour with the congregation.

> For at times, while they are engaged in the needs of the community they will be precluded from practicing a precept. He said that the Lord, may He be blessed, will consider them worthy of recompense as though they had practiced that precept even though they did not practice it, since they were engaged with the community for the sake of Heaven.[223]

It appears that Maimonides implies that *tsedaqah* refers to the practising of precepts. This may only in part reflect the real meaning. In this instance *tsedaqah* may also refer to the quality a person possesses because he has done unselfish work.

The term *tsedaqah* also occurs in a scriptural quotation where it does not have the meaning of almsgiving. In Aboth 5:18, Deut 33:21 is quoted as follows:

> He that leads the many to virtue, through him shall no sin befall; but he that leads the many to sin, to him shall be given no means for repentance. Moses was virtuous and he led the many to virtue; the virtue (*zekut*) of the many depended on him, as it is written, 'He executed the justice (*tsidqat*) of the Lord and his judgements with Israel' (Deut 33:21).[224]

In this passage the terms *zekut* and *tsedaqah* are related insofar as the virtue of the many is dependent on the fact that Moses executed the *righteousness* of the Lord. These terms are not equivalent[225] but rather *zekut* is the result of doing *tsedaqah*. The concept of righteousness (*tsedaqah*) in this case may include the giving of alms but its meaning is definitely more comprehensive than this.

There are two further dependent occurrences in which *tsedaqah* does not refer to almsgiving. In Ez 3:20, as quoted in T. Yom ha-Kippurim 4(5):12, *tsedaqah* appears to refer to proper conduct in the sight of God. In Ez 33:12 as quoted in T. Kiddushin 1:15, *tsedaqah* clearly refers to the quality which a righteous man possesses because he has lived in accordance with a proper norm. As was pointed out in the discussion of T. Kiddushin 1:15 in the context of the adjective *tsaddiq*, *tsedaqah* is not regarded as a soteriological principle. Rather this passage indicates the necessity of repentance.

What general conclusions can be drawn as to the meaning of the noun *tsedaqah* in the Tannaitic literature? Without doubt *tsedaqah* refers primarily to the various aspects of almsgiving. The fact cannot be overlooked, however, that the term *tsedaqah* is at times used in other ways. It does refer to mercy, both in the sense of the showing of kindness through the giving of material benefits and in the sense of the opposite of judgment according to strict justice. It should be noted that the former meaning is characteristic only of *tsedaqah* while the latter meaning is intrinsic to both *tsedaqah* and *tsedeq*. At times *tsedaqah* is also used with reference to proper conduct according to a norm. This meaning is parallel to the primary meaning of *tsedeq*. It should be noted that in this case we are not dealing with a meaning which is equally characteristic of *tsedeq* and *tsedaqah*. Rather *tsedaqah* is used in this case with a meaning which is much more characteristic of *tsedeq*. Yet the fact remains, while the meaning of almsgiving is undoubtedly primary, the term *tsedaqah* is at times used with other meanings. Consequently, care must be taken not to attribute the meaning of almsgiving indiscriminately to *tsedaqah* in the Tannaitic literature.

5 The concept of righteousness in the Tannaitic literature

Having established the meaning of the adjective *tsaddiq* and the nouns *tsedeq* and *tsedaqah*, let us now consider the following questions. How do these individual terms unite to form a concept of righteousness? Of what significance is this concept in Tannaitic thought?

In contrast to the Old Testament where there was no discernible shift of meaning between the masculine noun *tsedeq* and the feminine noun *tsedaqah*, in the Tannaitic literature distinct primary meanings have been attached to these two terms. The noun *tsedeq* is used to denote all aspects of religious teaching which are normative for man's conduct. The person who lives according to the norm of *tsedeq* not only does righteousness (*tsedeq*) but also has righteousness (*tsedeq*). The noun *tsedaqah* is used primarily to designate almsgiving. Since almsgiving is in fact one aspect of normative religious teaching governing proper conduct, *tsedaqah* must be viewed as being included in the concept of *tsedeq*. This is by far the most important aspect in the relationship between these two terms.

There are, however, still other factors which must be taken into account to gain a complete view of the full range of interaction between *tsedeq* and *tsedaqah*. It was pointed out above that there was some overlap in the usage of *tsedeq* and *tsedaqah*. With respect to this overlap it is necessary to differentiate between an overlap resulting from the fact that these two terms are interchangeable in the Old Testament and an overlap not attributable to external constraint. Finally a meaning related to almsgiving must be taken into account.

It was noted previously that in two passages the noun *tsedeq*, as found in biblical quotations, was used with meanings which are more characteristic of *tsedaqah* than of *tsedeq*. Similarly, it was pointed out that *tsedaqah* was at times used with a meaning parallel to the primary meaning of *tsedeq*. In the case of *tsedeq* only dependent occurrences and in the case of *tsedaqah* primarily dependent occurrences were involved. In other words, when the Tannaim made use of the Old Testament for the purpose of proof-texting, they had to deal with a literature which did not assign separate meanings to the terms *tsedeq* and *tsedaqah*. In the process of proof-texting the Tannaim were thus forced to use these terms in the same manner as in the Old Testament. Consequently, the resulting overlap in meaning should not be viewed as significant in determining Tannaitic usage.

With respect to the concept of mercy, on the other hand, the overlap in meaning between *tsedeq* and *tsedaqah* is significant; that is, it is not simply attributable to external constraint. It is part of the normative religious teaching (*tsedeq*) that there be leniency in judgment. Similarly, it is explicitly noted in T. Peah 4:21 that almsgiving and mercy are related. The concept of mercy is thus intrinsic both to *tsedeq* and *tsedaqah*. The special case of mercy involving material benefits, on the other hand, is only associated with the term *tsedaqah* and must therefore be treated as a distinct meaning of *tsedaqah* closely related to almsgiving.

At this point it should be self-evident how the adjective *tsaddiq* is related to *tsedeq* and *tsedaqah*. The righteous one (*tsaddiq*) is the one whose conduct conforms to the norm of *tsedeq*, with *tsedaqah* being an important aspect of this norm.

As far as their primary meanings are concerned, the relationship between the terms *tsedeq*, *tsedaqah* and *tsaddiq* can therefore be summarized as follows. By living according to the intent and content of righteousness (*tsedeq*) - and almsgiving (*tsedaqah*) is included in this - the righteous one (*tsaddiq*) in effect not only does righteousness (*tsedeq*) but also shows that he has righteousness (*tsedeq*).

Having determined the meaning of and the relationship between the righteousness terminology in the Tannaitic literature, let us now see what overall significance the concept of righteousness plays in the thought-world of the Tannaim. In contrast to the Old Testament where it was not absolutely certain whether righteousness (*tsedeq/tsedaqah*) should be viewed as norm or relationship, in the Tannaitic literature righteousness (*tsedeq*) is a norm. As such, righteousness is the demand upon man rather than the salvific gift of God for man. There is no room for an imputed righteousness (*tsedeq*) in the Tannaitic literature.[226]

The function and significance of the concept of righteousness in the Tannaitic literature pertain to behaviour rather than soteriology. In other words, the righteousness terminology (*tsedeq*, *tsedaqah*, *tsaddiq*) is used to denote conduct which is properly religious. The righteous one (*tsaddiq*) is not directly involved in a quest for salvation. Rather, being righteous (*tsaddiq*) refers to following the norm of righteousness (*tsedeq*) which in essence refers to God's will as depicted by his laws given in the covenant. Righteousness (*tsedeq*) pertains to man's status of remaining in the covenant. As such, it is strictly the demand of God upon man.

Although it is not the aim of the present study to consider the soteriological system of the Tannaim, it is nevertheless imperative to allude again to this point, so as not to leave the misleading impression that since righteousness (*tsedeq*) is not the gift of God, then salvation must be seen as being earned in the Tannaitic literature. It must be reiterated that the righteousness terminology is concerned with behaviour rather than with soteriology. In other words, on the basis of the nature of the concept of righteousness no inferences can be drawn as to the nature of salvation in the thought-world of the Tannaim. Righteousness is the demand of God upon man; salvation, on the other hand, is the gift of God for man. As was briefly described above, salvation is concerned with repentance and atonement.[227] It is not earned. Righteousness, in contrast, is earned. By living according to the norm of righteousness (*tsedeq*) the righteous one (*tsaddiq*) demonstrates that he wants to remain in a relationship with God culminating with life in the world to come. Righteousness is concerned with the maintenance of a relationship based on the gift of God.

4

THE MEANING OF *DIKAIOSYNĒ*, *ELEĒMOSYNĒ* AND *DIKAIOS* IN THE GOSPEL OF MATTHEW

1 Introduction

It has been demonstrated that in the Dead Sea Scrolls and the Tannaitic literature the terms *tsedeq*, *tsedaqah* and *tsaddiq* represent the righteousness terminology. In turning to the Gospel of Matthew the question thus emerges: are these Hebrew terms related to the Matthaean righteousness terminology?

As will become evident as this study progresses, *tsedeq* is in fact equivalent to *dikaiosynē*, *tsedaqah* in its meaning of alms to *eleēmosynē* and *tsaddiq* to *dikaios*.[1] While in the final analysis only the foregoing conclusion based on the Gospel of Matthew itself provides a definitive answer to the question posed above, a look at the Greek translation equivalents employed in the LXX for the Hebrew terms under discussion is also illuminating inasmuch as the Septuagintal usage points to trends reflected in the Gospel of Matthew.

It should not be surprising that Matthaean usage corresponds to Septuagintal usage in this case. Not only has the general conclusion been drawn that the 'LXX constitutes the bridge between the OT and the NT' and that it provides the 'vocabulary for the NT writers'[2] but it has also been specifically demonstrated that Matthew[3] made use of the LXX in the writing of his gospel.[4]

In the Hebrew OT there are 115 occurrences of the noun *tsedeq*, 158 of the noun *tsedaqah* and 208 of the adjective *tsaddiq*.[5] Ziesler has noted that out of the total number of occurrences of these three terms 'only about 32 are not represented in LXX by some form of δικαι-'.[6] Ziesler goes on to explain that this number is effectively reduced from 32 to 23 because in some cases the relevant verses do not occur in LXX or the difference is so great that a different Hebrew text must underlie the Greek.[7]

Ziesler comments that in this small number of exceptions 'no trend is perceptible, except the very notable one of using ἐλεημοσύνη or ἔλεος instead of a δικαι- word'.[8] Specifically *eleēmosynē* is used 9 times[9] and *eleos* 3 times[10] for *tsedaqah*. It should be noted that it is only *tsedaqah*, never *tsedeq*, which is translated by *eleēmosynē* and *eleos*.[11]

According to Septuagintal usage, *dikaiosynē* is the primary Greek equivalent for *tsedeq* and *dikaios* for *tsaddiq*.[12] Although the primary Greek equivalent for *tsedaqah* is also *dikaiosynē*, it is significant that the Greek term *eleēmosynē* is used 9 times as a translation equivalent.[13] Consequently it appears advisable that in studying the concept of righteousness in the Gospel of Matthew special attention should be directed to the significance of these three Greek terms.

2 *Dikaiosynē*

The noun *dikaiosynē* occurs 7 times (3:15; 5:6, 10, 20; 6:1, 33; 21:32) in the Gospel of Matthew. It should be noted, however, that some scholars have expressed reservations regarding the use of this term in 6:1. In this passage some MSS. read δικαιοσύνην[14] while others read ἐλεημοσύνην.[15]

Of those scholars who claim that ἐλεημοσύνην represents the better reading, W. Nagel[16] has presented the strongest case. He argues that one should not assume that the great MSS. of the fourth century always give the best NT text. In other words, just because ℵ and B have δικαιοσύνην it cannot be assumed that this is the correct reading. Nagel also argues that Mt 6:1–18 consists of an introductory warning and a concluding instruction. In this overall structure v. 1 is the introductory statement for vv. 2–4. In vv. 2–4 the term *eleēmosynē* is found 3 times. Nagel concludes that ἐλεημοσύνην represents the correct reading because the same term is required in the introductory warning as in the concluding instruction.[17]

The overwhelming majority of New Testament scholars, however, claim that δικαιοσύνην represents the better reading.[18] This conclusion is supported not only by the better manuscript evidence for the reading δικαιοσύνην but also on other grounds. Rather than being an introductory statement for vv. 2–4, v. 1 in actual fact appears to be a heading for vv. 2–18. Consequently, a more inclusive term than ἐλεημοσύνην is required in v. 1. The maxim 'choose the reading which best explains the origin of the others'[19] also supports this conclusion. For example, Zahn[20] has noted that because of the double meaning of *tsedaqah*, *dikaiosynē* in 6:1 could have been understood in the sense of *eleēmosynē* so that the latter was adopted into the text. The reverse process, on the other hand, would be impossible to understand.

On the basis of the foregoing discussion it does appear that δικαιοσύνην represents the best reading in Mt 6:1. The noun *dikaiosynē* thus occurs 7 times in the Gospel of Matthew. Since in the rest of the Synoptic Gospels this noun occurs only once,[21] it has been noted that righteousness (*dikaiosyn* is a characteristically Matthaean term.[22]

A number of scholars explicitly state that all 7 occurrences of *dikaiosynē* in the Gospel of Matthew are redactional.[23] The analysis of the *dikaiosynē*-passages by Strecker[24] and Fiedler[25] indeed provide convincing support for this conclusion. Nevertheless, the only absolutely valid conclusion which can be reached is that the Matthaean use of the term *dikaiosynē* is not based on extant synoptic sources.

Even such a limited conclusion can indeed be of value in this study, for although no absolutely valid conclusion can be reached, differentiations can be made on the basis of varying degrees of probability. Specifically, on the basis of a redaction-critical analysis it is clear that the 7 *dikaiosynē*-passages can be divided into three distinct groups, reflecting varying degrees of redactional probability.

Strecker[26] and Fiedler[27] both indicate that in Mt 5:6 and 6:33 the term *dikaiosynē* is inserted by Matthew by way of interpolation. This is indeed probable; for Lk 6:21 and 12:31 are parallel to Mt 5:6 and 6:33 respectively, the only major variation being the occurrence of the noun *dikaiosynē* in Matthew.

Strecker[28] and Fiedler[29] also agree that in Mt 5:20 and 6:1 not only the occurrence of the noun *dikaiosynē* is redactional but also the context in which this term is found. This conclusion is also probable, for Mt 5:19–23 and 6:1–8 have no synoptic parallels and in addition 5:20 and 6:1 play a significant role in the structure of their respective contexts insofar as they are headings or general statements which introduce what follows.[30]

It is thus highly probable that in 5:20 and 6:1 Matthew had complete freedom in the use of the term *dikaiosynē* and that consequently these passages may best reflect the meaning which Matthew, as the final redactor, attached to this term. By the same token, it appears that in 5:6 and 6:33 Matthew could have experienced great constraint in the use of the term *dikaiosynē* because this term had to be interpolated into a *Vorlage*. As the result of such constraint the meaning which Matthew attached to this term may not be as explicit in these two passages as in 5:20 and 6:1.

The three remaining *dikaiosynē*-passages (3:15, 5:10, 21:32) fall between the two extreme positions mentioned above. The term *dikaiosynē* does not seem to occur in these passages simply by way of interpolation, for 3:14–15, 5:8–10 and 21:28–33 do not have synoptic parallels, yet 3:15, 5:10 and 21:32 do not play as crucial a role in the overall development of their respective contexts as is the case with 5:20 and 6:1.[31]

On the basis of the foregoing redaction-critical considerations it thus appears that the occurrences of *dikaiosynē* in 5:20 and 6:1 may provide the best evidence for the meaning which Matthew attached to this term. Consequently, the following investigation of the meaning of *dikaiosynē* will begin with these two passages.

Matthew 5:20

It has been suggested by many scholars that Mt 5:20 is an introductory statement or heading for 5:21–48.[32] In 5:20 Jesus, in the context of a polemical discussion dealing with the relationship between Judaism and his own teaching, is represented as telling his disciples (5:1-2) and the crowds (7:28), 'For I tell you, unless your righteousness (ὑμῶν ἡ δικαιοσύνη) exceeds that of the scribes and Pharisees, you will never enter the kingdom of heaven.'

In Mt 5:21–48 examples of this greater righteousness are given. These examples are generally referred to as the antitheses. Let us see how the antitheses have been viewed as defining the term *dikaiosynē*.

W. D. Davies argues that 'we cannot speak of the Law being annulled in the antitheses, but only of its being intensified in its demand, or reinterpreted in a higher key'.[33] That Davies views this interpretation of the law as defining the term *dikaiosynē* is clear when he claims that 'Matthew has draped his Lord in the mantle of a teacher of righteousness.'[34]

G. Barth states, 'It is plain that the antitheses are not directed primarily against the Old Testament itself, but against the interpretation of it in the Rabbinate.'[35] Specifically, Mt 5:21–48 'provides a marked radicalising of the demand of God'.[36] On the basis of this interpretation Barth concludes that in 5:20 *dikaiosynē* refers to 'the conduct demanded of the disciples',[37] that is, a conduct reflecting the radicalized demand of God upon discipleship.

Bornkamm also understands Mt 5:21–48 as a radicalizing of the divine command.[38] In contrast to Barth, however, who argues that 5:21–48 does not show that the law which is valid for Matthew is opposed to the Sinaitic Law,[39] Bornkamm argues that the third, fifth and sixth antitheses not only show a sharpening of the law as is the case in the first, second and fourth, but the abolition of the law.[40] Consequently, according to Bornkamm the 'better righteousness'[41] of 5:20 is at least partly concerned with a new law.

Strecker, like Bornkamm, supports the view that the antitheses largely supplant the demands of the Old Testament by way of new regulations.[42] *Dikaiosynē* refers to the sum total of such new commandments.[43]

Fiedler views the antitheses as the commandments of the νόμος.[44] He agrees with Windisch that Matthew sees the Sermon on the Mount as the 'new legislation for the eschatological Kingdom of God'.[45] Fiedler therefore concludes that in 5:20 *dikaiosynē* must be understood as an eschatological possibility which can only be realized by the church (*Gemeinde*) of the Messiah, for the righteousness demanded by the Messiah is radically different from that of the Pharisees.[46]

Which of the foregoing divergent views is in fact the correct one? Do the antitheses reflect a new interpretation of the old law or do they herald the coming of a new law?

In order to answer this question we must differentiate between two levels of meaning. We must attempt to discover how Matthew himself viewed the antitheses and how they could have been understood by his audience.

It is easy to imagine that a saying such as 5:29, 'If your right eye causes you to sin, pluck it out and throw it away', could be viewed as an extremely radicalized demand of God, a demand so qualitatively different from the requirement of the old law that it appears to be part of a new law. It is thus conceivable that a segment of Matthew's audience may have understood 5:21-48 in terms of a marked radicalizing of the demand of God or even in terms of a new law. The scholars who interpret the antitheses in terms of a new law are in a sense justified in their exegesis. They can maintain that, in spite of what Matthew may have intended to communicate, he in effect did communicate something else.

The present study, however, is concerned with the redactional motifs at work in the Gospel of Matthew which bear upon the concept of righteousness. Consequently, for the purpose of this study the crucial point is not how the antitheses were misunderstood by others, even if there was a good basis for misunderstanding, but how Matthew himself understood them.

When the antitheses are viewed from the latter perspective, it becomes evident that Matthew himself viewed them as being representative of a new interpretation of the old law. There are a number of factors which point to this conclusion.

One factor which suggests that the antitheses reflect a new interpretation of the old law is that it appears that Matthew is applying the Rabbinic principle of making a fence around Torah in 5:21-48. Moore explains that this was a hermeneutical principle used to protect the law 'by surrounding it with cautionary rules to halt a man like a danger signal before he gets within breaking distance of the divine statute itself'.[47]

An example of the application of this principle is found in Berakoth 1:1. As Moore explains, 'things which by the letter of the law must be completed before morning (e.g., Lev 7, 15; 22, 30), by rabbinical rule must be done before midnight, "to keep a man far removed from transgression"'.[48] In this example the fence consists of the recommendation that one should do things earlier than required, for then one will definitely have completed them by the required time.

Let us now observe how the principle of making a fence around Torah is applied in Mt 5:21-48. In 5:21-6 the fence consists of the recommendation that one should not even be angry with his brother, for in this way one will definitely obey the commandment 'You shall not kill.'

In 5:27-30 it is suggested that one should not even look at a woman lustfully for in this way one will never reach the stage of breaking the commandment 'You shall not commit adultery.'

In 5:31–2 the problem appears to be the legality of a bill of divorce. On what grounds can a bill of divorce be based? It is implied that a bill of divorce should be based solely on the grounds of unchastity. The fence in this case consists of the suggestion that in order to prevent somebody else from marrying a not properly divorced woman (even though she may have a certificate of divorce) and thus committing adultery, one should not divorce one's wife on any questionable grounds but only for the gravest possible reason, that is, unchastity.

In 5:33–7 it is argued that in order not to break the commandment 'You shall not swear falsely' it is best not to swear at all.

In 5:38–42 the underlying problem is the uncertainty which is necessarily involved in the application of the principle 'an eye for an eye and a tooth for a tooth'. Can one ever be sure that one has done *exactly* that which has been demanded? The implicit answer is, No! Consequently, depending on the situation, it is best not to retaliate at all or to do more than is required.

In 5:43–7 the dilemma which is to be resolved is the uncertainty of defining who in fact is one's neighbour and who one's enemy. Since one can never be absolutely certain, it is thought to be best to treat everybody as one's neighbour.

That the principle of making a fence around Torah underlies 5:21–48 is not only suggested by the passage itself but is consistent with the context in which this passage is found. Mt 5:19 warns against the relaxing of 'one of the least of these commandments'. Manson explains that the verb λύω refers to relaxing in the sense of 'one who permits less than the Law requires either by allowing what it forbids or by exempting men from some of its positive requirements'.[49] The logical antidote to the practice of the relaxing of the commandments would be to make a fence around Torah.

It was noted above that by an outsider the saying in 5:29, 'If your right eye causes you to sin, pluck it out and throw it away', could easily be understood as pointing to a new law rather than to a new interpretation of an old law. How could Matthew himself have viewed this statement?

It is probable that Matthew did not view this saying in a literal way but conceived of it as a hortatory device employed to demonstrate the gravity of the situation discussed in 5:27–30. On the other hand, it should also be taken into account that the discussion of the Tannaitic literature has shown that it was not unheard of that a person would not shirk hardship in the course of the meticulous observance of the law, For example, Sifra Emor parasha 1:14 on Lev 21:3 shows that Joseph b. Paksas was praised for his righteousness (*tsedeq*) because despite the prospect of personal hardship he did not deviate from the strict observance of the law. Consequently, although it is conceivable that Mt 5:29 could be interpreted as pointing to a new law, this is by no means the only reasonable interpretation. This saying, too, can be seen in the context of making a fence around the old law.

Another factor which indicates that Matthew viewed the antitheses as representing a new interpretation of the old law is found in 5:17–18. Here it is stated that Jesus has not come to abolish the law and that 'not an iota, not a dot, will pass from the law until all is accomplished'. Although a number of points in 5:17–18 are difficult to interpret, the point relevant to our discussion is clear. This passage definitely announces that Jesus does not intend to discard the old law and establish a new law.

It could conceivably be argued that Matthew is inconsistent; that is, he portrays Jesus as being an adherent of the old law and then, under the pretence of being true to the tradition, in actual fact initiating a new law. This type of interpretation appears rather forced when it can be demonstrated that 5:21–48 is easily understood in a way which is in direct harmony with the intention of 5:17–18.

On the basis of the foregoing discussion it is necessary to conclude that from Matthew's perspective the antitheses reflect not a new law but a new interpretation of the existing law. This new interpretation of the law should not be viewed as a radicalized view of the law. Rather this new interpretation of the law is representative of an extremely meticulous observance of the law.[50] I would suggest that if this type of interpretation does not correspond directly to the hermeneutical principle of making a fence around Torah, it has at least been strongly influenced by this particular principle.

As was shown above, the term *dikaiosynē* in Mt 5:20 is defined by the antitheses. Consequently, the righteousness that is to exceed that of the scribes and Pharisees is a righteousness that is representative of an extremely meticulous observance of the law, an observance that is based on an interpretation reminiscent of the principle of making a fence around Torah.

That the term 'righteousness' can indeed be used in conjunction with the principle of making a fence around Torah is supported by examples from both the Tannaitic literature and the Dead Sea Scrolls.

In Sifre Deut 16 on 1:16 (p. 25) the statement 'Hear the cases between your brethren, and judge righteousness' is discussed and the conclusion is reached that the saying by the men of the Great Synagogue, 'Be deliberate in judgment, raise up many disciples, and make a fence around the law', is applicable to the act of judging righteousness.

In 1QS 10:25 it is implied that in order to preserve faith and strong judgment in accordance with the righteousness (*tsedaqah*) of God, it is necessary to fence in knowledge within a firm boundary. Leaney has suggested that the author of this passage may be referring to the principle of making a fence around Torah.[51]

On the basis of the foregoing discussion it is thus clear that on the level of Matthew's own intention – in my opinion an intention stated clearly enough to have been properly understood by a large part of his audience – the term 'righteousness' (*dikaiosyne*) in 5:20 refers to the conduct demanded of the disciples,[52] a conduct characterized by the meticulous observance of the law. The genitive ὑμῶν clearly shows that 5:20 deals with man's righteousness. Yet there is no scholarly consensus whether it is man's righteousness in the sense that it is demanded of man by God or in the sense that it is God's gift for man.

Many scholars suggest that 5:20 deals exclusively with righteousness as the demand of God upon man.[53] Others claim that in this passage righteousness must be viewed as both God's demand upon man and God's eschatological gift for man. For example, Fiedler claims that 5:20 refers back to 3:15 with the effect that it is only possible for men to do righteousness because the Messiah has fulfilled all righteousness.[54]

The views of various other scholars are confusing insofar as it is not clear whether they think that in Matthew the double meaning of demand and gift is applicable to each *dikaiosyne*-passage or whether these are separate meanings applicable only to specific passages. In other words, it is not clear whether they view *dikaiosyne* as having a uniform meaning in the Gospel of Matthew.

For example, Barth notes, on the one hand, that in 5:20 *dikaiosyne* refers to 'the conduct demanded of the disciples'[55] while, on the other hand, he argues that on the basis of 3:15 it is clear that for Matthew 'righteousness is at the same time a demand and an eschatological gift'.[56]

Similarly, Ziesler's position is unclear. On the one hand, he lists Mt 3:15; 5:6, 10, 20; 6:1, 33 as 'cases where "righteousness" means Christian behaviour',[57] and specifically with respect to the occurrence of *dikaiosyne* in 5:20 he states that 'There is no suggestion that it is anything but man's activity, unless one supposes that 5.6 implies that it is also God's gift.'[58] On the other hand, he states that in 5:6 righteousness is viewed as a divine gift[59] and thus generalizes that for Matthew 'Righteousness is thus both demand and eschatological gift.'[60]

Although the exact position of some scholars with respect to the meaning of *dikaiosyne* as the gift of God cannot be ascertained, it is nevertheless clear in all the interpretations that it is only on the basis of other *dikaiosyne*-passages that Mt 5:20 is given such a meaning. Consequently, a final decision as to whether or not the term *dikaiosyne* is used with reference to the gift of God in the Gospel of Matthew must be postponed until all the *dikaiosyne*-passages have been examined.

It must be pointed out, however, that there are additional factors which cast doubt on the possibility of the term *dikaiosynē* in 5:20 referring to righteousness as the gift of God. In this verse it is implied that not only the disciples but also the scribes and Pharisees have righteousness. Consequently, if *dikaiosynē* is to refer to the gift of God, then this meaning must apply both to the righteousness of the disciples and to that of the scribes and Pharisees. Since the whole point of 5:20 is that the righteousness of the scribes and Pharisees is not sufficient to enter the kingdom of heaven, it is quite unlikely that their righteousness is based on the gift of God.[61]

It could conceivably be argued that in 5:20 a qualitative distinction is made between two kinds of righteousness, the righteousness of the Pharisees being related solely to the demand of God while the greater righteousness is seen as the gift of God. While it is true that a qualitative distinction is inherent in 5:20, this distinction is not in terms of demand versus gift but in terms of adherence to two distinct norms of conduct which are based on different interpretations of the same general law. The greater righteousness is based on a very meticulous observance of the law.

It should be noted, however, that the meaning of 5:20 is not exhausted by a qualitative distinction. The terms περισσεύσῃ and πλεῖον also point to a quantitative distinction. Banks has pointed out with respect to the use of *dikaiosynē* in 5:20 that 'the comparative construction in which it occurs can lexically be understood in a quantitative, not a qualitative sense'.[62] While it is true that exegesis cannot limit itself to lexical understanding, it would be surprising if the two terms just mentioned were used without any reference to a quantitative distinction.

That the contrast between the righteousness of the disciples and that of the scribes and Pharisees should be viewed not only in qualitative but also in quantitative terms is supported by Mt 5:48: 'You, therefore, must be perfect, as your heavenly Father is perfect.'

Some commentators suggest that the term 'perfect' (τέλειος) should be defined by its immediate context. Since 5:43-7 deals with the concept of love, it has therefore been suggested that 5:48 refers to perfection in love.[63]

It appears, however, that the term τέλειος governs more than its immediate context. As was noted previously, 5:20 is a heading for vv. 21-48. In the latter passage vv. 21-47 give examples of the greater righteousness. Verse 48 functions as a concluding statement for vv. 21-47. Zahn is correct in stating that with the idea of perfection the climax of the discourse is reached.[64]

Mt 5:48 thus appears to be a restatement of 5:20. By the greater righteousness Matthew really points toward perfection, and the idea of perfection in turn applies to all the examples in vv. 21-47.

That 5:21–48 was indeed understood in this way by an author in the early centuries is shown by the Didache. Didache 1:4 states, 'If any man smite thee on the right cheek, turn to him the other cheek also, and thou wilt be perfect.'[65] Here the author of the Didache seems to have combined Mt 5:39 and 48. In other words, the tradition in the Didache shows that the concept of perfection in 5:48 was understood as governing more than just the teaching about love.

Another indication that τέλειος refers to all the examples is provided by the choice of the word τέλειος itself. It should be noted that the parallel passage in Lk 6:36 states, 'Be merciful, even as your Father is merciful.' It appears that Luke rather than Matthew preserves the traditional reading.[66] Thus τέλειος is redactional. Why did Matthew make this redactional change? The reason seems to be that he wanted a concluding statement for 5:21–47 and only the use of the adjective τέλειος rather than οἰκτίρμων could contribute to this purpose.

Having established the function of the term 'perfect' in its broader framework, let us now consider its meaning. A number of commentators have suggested that τέλειος refers solely to wholeness.[67] This suggestion, however, seems to be based not so much on an actual interpretation of the Gospel of Matthew as on the supposition that Matthew's usage reflects that of the LXX.

In the Gospel of Matthew τέλειος refers to more than wholeness. It should be noted that the term τέλειος in 5:48 is immediately linked with the term περισσόν in 5:47. Being perfect involves doing more than others, for v. 47 states, 'And if you salute only your brethren, what more are you doing than others?' In this context περισσόν and consequently τέλειος definitely point not only to a qualitative distinction but also to a quantitative one.

That perfection in 5:48 can indeed be understood in a quantitative rather than merely in the qualitative sense of wholeness is borne out by the Didache. It was shown above that Didache 1:4 combined Mt 5:39 and 48, thus reflecting the Matthaean use of τέλειος. In Didache 6:2 the meaning of this adjective became very clear: 'For if thou canst bear the whole yoke of the Lord, thou wilt be perfect, but if thou canst not, do what thou canst.'[68] Here τέλειος refers to the attainment of the highest rank according to a specific standard.

The similarity between the concept of perfection in the Gospel of Matthew and in the Dead Sea Scrolls should also be noted. W. D. Davies has commented as follows upon the use of τέλειος in Mt 5:48. 'In the DSS the Hebrew equivalent or its cognates occur frequently, and it may be urged that the usage of the DSS illumines that of Matthew. Thus DSD [1QS]

I:13 which reads: "To direct their strength according to the perfection of His ways" recalls directly Matthew 5:48.'[69] Davies explains further that 'In several passages degrees of perfection appear to be recognized. Thus DSD V:24 implies that there is a yearly examination to ascertain the degree of perfection achieved.'[70]

Although the qualitative meaning of wholeness should by no means be ruled out in Mt 5:48, it is evident that there is also a quantitative meaning. In 5:48 perfection not only refers to conduct according to a norm which is qualitatively different from another norm but also the quantitative idea of the attainment of the highest rank. In addition to the foregoing arguments this fact is also borne out by the Matthaean use of all ($\pi\tilde{\alpha}\varsigma$).

Mt 28:20 states that the disciples are to teach 'them to observe *all* that I have commanded you'; 3:15 states that Jesus told John, 'for thus it is fitting for us to fulfil *all* righteousness'; 5:18 states, 'till heaven and earth pass away, not an iota, not a dot, will pass from the law until *all* is accomplished'. The use of $\pi\tilde{\alpha}\varsigma$ appears to be redactional in all three cases[71] and these passages refer to activity which is measured in a quantitative sense. Consequently, the use of $\pi\tilde{\alpha}\varsigma$ further corroborates the conclusion that Mt 5:20 and 48 have a quantitative force.[72]

We are now able to reach a conclusion as to the meaning of *dikaiosynē* in 5:20. *Dikaiosynē* is a term which refers to conduct according to a norm which in this case is the law.[73] Both the disciples and the scribes and Pharisees have righteousness insofar as both groups live according to the demands of the law. This, however, does not mean that the righteousness of the two groups is identical. Jesus demands that the righteousness of the disciples is to exceed that of the scribes and Pharisees. This does not mean that the disciples are to live according to a different law but that they are to live according to a different interpretation of the law, namely, an extremely meticulous and strict interpretation which appears to be based on a principle related to making a fence around Torah. The goal of this type of conduct is perfection. In this case perfection is not only to be understood in the qualitative sense of observing a different norm based on a more meticulous observance of the law, but also in the sense of the attainment of the highest rank. The disciples are to observe everything that Jesus commanded.

Matthew 6:1

The expression $\tau\grave{\eta}\nu\ \delta\iota\kappa\alpha\iota\sigma\sigma\acute{\nu}\nu\eta\nu\ \acute{\nu}\mu\tilde{\omega}\nu$ in 6:1 is very similar to the expression $\acute{\nu}\mu\tilde{\omega}\nu\ \acute{\eta}\ \delta\iota\kappa\alpha\iota\sigma\sigma\acute{\nu}\nu\eta$ which is found in 5:20. Since 6:1 just like 5:20 refers to the righteousness of the disciples it is obvious that 6:1 refers back to 5:20.[74]

The function of 6:1 with respect to its context is also similar to that of 5:20. Just as 5:20 was a heading for 5:21–48, so 6:1 is generally thought of as a heading for 6:2–18.[75] Consequently, just as the meaning of *dikaiosynē* in 5:20 could be determined on the basis of vv. 21–48, so the meaning of this term in 6:1 can be determined on the basis of vv. 2–18. Indeed, a continuous argument is presented in 6:1–18.

Mt 6:1 is concerned with the motives underlying the doing of righteousness. The disciples are warned not to practise their righteousness in order to be seen by men, for such action will preclude receiving a reward from God. Following this warning, three illustrations of the doing of righteousness are given. These are the giving of alms (vv. 2–4), praying (vv. 5–15) and fasting (vv. 16–18).[76] It thus seems that the doing of righteousness in 6:1 refers to the practical side of man's religion.[77] In 6:1 *dikaiosynē* is thus a very comprehensive term. W. D. Davies's suggestion that *dikaiosynē* should be translated as 'religion'[78] in this case is certainly fitting.

It was mentioned above that 6:1 refers back to 5:20. What is the exact nature of this relationship? Schniewind[79] has suggested that in 5:20 righteousness is seen with reference to the interpretation of the law while in 6:1 the righteousness which one does in everyday life is judged. Billerbeck[80] has proposed that 5:20 deals with the nature of true righteousness while 6:1 deals with the pitfalls of practising righteousness. The latter suggestion is persuasive, especially since 5:19 stresses that teaching and doing must always go hand in hand.[81] The rationale behind 6:1 thus appears to be that even if one knows the nature of true righteousness, one will not receive a reward unless one adheres to the proper practice of righteousness.[82] Theory and practice must go in hand in hand.[83] Taken together, 5:20 and 6:1 thus show that *dikaiosynē* is a very comprehensive term, encompassing both the theoretical and practical aspects of the right conduct of man.

Whereas most commentators agree that in Mt 6:1 righteousness is viewed in terms of God's demand upon man, there are some who claim that even here righteousness is God's gift to man. For example, Fiedler states that 6:1 should be viewed in the light of the Old Testament teaching that man can only do righteousness because God does righteousness and imputes it to man.[84] This conclusion is unwarranted, for there are absolutely no indications in the text itself which would suggest an interpretation in terms of this Old Testament teaching. Mt 6:1 states clearly that man can do righteousness. There is no reference to the gift of God.

The occurrences of the term *dikaiosynē* in 5:20 and 6:1 were discussed first because on the basis of redaction-critical considerations it appeared that in these passages Matthew had the greatest amount of freedom in the use of this term. The foregoing investigation has shown that it is indeed possible to gain a precise definition of this term on the basis of these two passages.

Let us now turn to those *dikaiosynē*-passages in which it appears that Matthew's use of this term was much more restricted. It is most logical to start with 6:33 since this passage occurs in a context which is still governed by the same general framework as that in which 5:20 and 6:1 are found.

Matthew 6:33

It was noted above that Mt 6:1 is a heading which governs vv. 2-18. In actual fact, this is correct only as far as the first part of 6:1 is concerned; namely, the three illustrations in vv. 2-18 refer to 6:1a. Mt 6:1b, on the other hand, deals with the giving of rewards, and this theme is taken up in vv. 19-33.[85] In this passage the discussions concerning wealth and anxiety serve to illustrate the point that one's primary concern should be with future rather than present rewards.

With this background as to the general structure of chapter 6, let us now turn to v. 33 in particular. It is generally assumed that v. 33 refers back to v. 32 so that αὐτοῦ in the phrase τὴν δικαιοσύνην αὐτοῦ is governed by the expression ὁ πατὴρ ὑμῶν ὁ οὐράνιος.[86] Although it is generally acknowledged that 6:33 deals with the concept of the righteousness of God, there is no consensus as to the meaning of this concept in this particular context.

Some commentators have argued that God's righteousness here refers to his vindicating activity, particularly as this pertains to the Kingdom.[87] This interpretation is by no means obvious from the context. Hill has pointed out that 'This interpretation would necessitate understanding the Kingdom as wholly eschatological.'[88]

Mt 6:33 specifically exhorts the disciples to *seek* God's righteousness. It is thus clear that this passage does not deal with God's righteousness *per se*. Rather it deals with God's righteousness insofar as it is the norm governing man's conduct. The disciples are encouraged to live according to the righteousness of God. The point of contention in the interpretation of this relationship is whether righteousness is to be viewed as God's gift or as a demand upon man.

Although they do not agree as to the degree of involvement, the majority of commentators suggest that the idea of righteousness as being a gift of God is included in 6:33. Some scholars state that in this instance righteousness is both demand and eschatological gift,[89] while others claim that it is to be viewed primarily as the gift of God.[90] Fiedler even claims that 6:33 provides unequivocal proof that Matthew adopted the Old Testament idea of interpreting the *tsedaqah* of God as meaning salvation (*Heil*).[91]

The main proof on which this view is based hinges on the meaning of the verb προστεθήσεται. For example, Ziesler argues that 'προστεθήσεται points to righteousness as God's gift and not only the object of man's search.'[92] This proof is not convincing, for, as was shown above, it appears that in 6:33 only the phrase καὶ τὴν δικαιοσύνην αὐτοῦ is redactional.[93] The verb προστεθήσεται, on the other hand, is not redactional.[94] Since this verb formed part of the *Vorlage* it is unwarranted to base Matthew's understanding of righteousness on it.

To find the meaning of *dikaiosynē* in 6:33 we must ask the question: why did the redactor interpolate this expression? In order to answer this question it is necessary to look again at the structure of chapters 5 and 6.

It was noted that in chapter 5, v. 20 was a heading for vv. 21–48 with v. 48 forming the culmination to the train of thought started in v. 20. In chapter 6 a similar structure exists. Mt 6:1 is a heading which governs and in turn is made explicit by vv. 2–33, with v. 33 representing the climax of the discourse.[95]

While 6:1 stated the negative side of the argument – that is, if the disciples practise their righteousness before men they will not receive a reward – 6:33 states the positive side – that is, if they do seek God's righteousness then they will receive a reward. Since it has already been shown that a close relationship exists between 5:20 and 6:1, it is thus clear that this relationship extends to 6:33.[96] Mt 5:20–6:33 comprises a continuous argument.

It was shown above that 5:48 and 6:33 perform similar functions as far as their roles in the structure of their respective chapters are concerned. It should also be noted that this parallelism even extends to a similarity of meaning.[97] In both verses the disciples are urged to imitate God. Seeking God's righteousness (6:33) is essentially the same as being perfect as God is perfect (5:48). Consequently, just as in 5:20, 48 and 6:1 righteousness/perfection was not thought of as the gift of God, so in 6:33 it is not viewed in this way. Trilling is correct in stating that 6:33 is so bound up in the general thought of the Sermon on the Mount that it is out of the question to interpret *dikaiosynē* in the Pauline sense of God's righteousness through which man is justified.[98]

God's righteousness in 6:33 must be understood as a norm for man's conduct. It is 'righteousness of life in agreement with the will of God.'[99]

Such an understanding of God's righteousness is not peculiar to Matthew. It is clear that in James 1:20 God's righteousness is not the righteousness which is freely imputed to man but that righteousness which is demanded of man.[100]

As was shown above, in the Damascus Document the stress is never on God's righteousness *per se*. For example, in CD 20:29–31 God's righteousness in the form of his judgment and ordinances is seen as governing man's conduct. In other words, God's righteousness is seen in the context of the norm for man's behaviour. It is in this sense that man is to imitate God.

It should also be noted that in Sifre Deut 49 on 11:22[101] it is stated that man can be righteous (*tsaddiq*) just as God is righteous (*tsaddiq*). Just as in Mt 6:33 man is urged to imitate God's righteousness, so this passage tells us that man can indeed be righteous just as God is righteous.

On the basis of the preceding discussion it is possible to conclude that the meaning of *dikaiosynē* in 6:33 corresponds to that in 5:20 and 6:1. In all three passages righteousness is seen as the demand of God upon man rather than God's gift to man. Rather than contradicting the meaning of *dikaiosynē* in 5:20 and 6:1, 6:33 simply makes the meaning more explicit. On the basis of 5:20 and 6:1 it was clear that the norm for the disciples' conduct was a certain interpretation of the law. On the basis of 6:33 it is now clear that this interpretation is nothing less than God's righteousness or, in other words, God's own interpretation.

Matthew 3:15

It has been shown that in Mt 5:20, 6:1 and 6:33 righteousness refers to man's conduct according to a specific interpretation of the law. It is a demand upon man. It is not the gift of God. With respect to the latter, 3:15[102] is crucial, for G. Barth claims, 'That righteousness is at the same time a demand and an eschatological gift has its basis here.'[103] Barth's argument is as follows:

> In the context of Matthew's Gospel a special emphasis lies upon πᾶσαν; it has to do with the whole will of God, with the whole righteousness. But this righteousness is not understood legally; Jesus fulfils it precisely in that he, as the Messiah-'judge-of-the-worlds', humbles himself and enters into the ranks of sinners, acts for sinners. The unity of righteousness and mercy demonstrated above has its Christological basis here.[104]

Does 3:15 really teach this or is Barth reading this passage in the light of the baptismal teaching of Rom 6? It appears that Barth anticipated such criticism, for he attacks Bartsch for doing the latter.

> H. W. Bartsch ('Die Taufe im NT', *Ev Th*, 1948/49, pp. 89f.) goes too far, however, when he deduces: 'The baptism is not only a pointer to the atoning deed of Christ that was to follow, but is the sacramental execution of his death and resurrection.' That is to import the baptismal teaching of Rom 6 into Matthew. Matt 3.15 does not say that Jesus now, in his baptism, fulfils all obedience which he has ever to accomplish.[105]

Although Barth does not interpret Mt 3:15 as crassly in the light of Paul's view of baptism as does Bartsch, he nevertheless interprets this verse in a

Pauline sense, for Barth goes beyond the supposition that the baptism is 'only a pointer to the atoning deed of Christ that was to follow'[106] when he states that 'there is contained in the baptism of Jesus that he does this for sinners, that he fulfils all righteousness for them'.[107]

This interpretation clearly imposes Pauline conceptions on 3:15, for it is in tension with this text. It must be noted that 3:15 reads: 'οὕτως γὰρ πρέπον ἐστὶν ἡμῖν πληρῶσαι πᾶσαν δικαιοσύνην'. Barth himself explains that ἡμῖν 'can hardly be understood as a plural of majesty; it rather links Jesus and the Baptist'.[108] Consequently, not only Jesus but also John should be seen as fulfilling all righteousness for sinners. This fact points to a weakness in Barth's interpretation, for the explanation that 'the Baptist is a Christological organ'[109] hardly explains this discrepancy.

Of the many other scholars who in effect paulinize 3:15 we shall deal only with Fiedler and Cullmann since they go into more detail than the others.[110] Fiedler states that in 3:15 *dikaiosynē* is a term embracing the total demand of the will of God.[111] He then goes on to make the assertion that the only parallel to such a concept is found in connection with the expectation concerning the activity of the Messiah which is not only found in the Old Testament but generally in Judaism.[112]

Fiedler therefore concludes: 'Das "Erfüllen aller Gerechtigkeit", das Jesus als die eine Forderung Gottes an ihn selbst und an den Täufer Johannes erkennt, das er erkennt als die Forderung, die das ganze Wollen Gottes über seinem Wege und also auch über seiner Taufe bezeichnet, ist nichts anderes als die besondere Aufgabe des Messias und seines "Vorläufers".'[113]

Fiedler argues that because *dikaiosynē* in 3:15 is associated with the activity of the Messiah it refers not only to the demand made by God upon man but also to the eschatological gift of God.[114]

This interpretation has two major weaknesses which render it invalid. Fiedler's claim that a general belief existed in Palestinian Judaism to the effect that the Messiah was to fulfil the entire will of God ('all righteousness' is not supported by the evidence presented.[115] Even if the claim were substantiated, Fiedler's assertion that there is no parallel for this comprehensive meaning of *dikaiosynē* other than that in which this term is used in conjunction with the activity of the Messiah would nevertheless be incorrect. As has been shown in the discussion of the Dead Sea Scrolls and the Tannaitic literature, there are instances where *tsedeq* has such a comprehensive meaning and is not used in a messianic context.[116] Fiedler also makes the methodological mistake of looking outside the Gospel of Matthew for an interpretation of 3:15 when in actual fact the clear meaning of *dikaiosynē* as found in Mt 5:20 and 6:1 is sufficient for an interpretation of this passage.

O. Cullmann writes with respect to 3:15: 'The Baptism of Jesus is related to δικαιοσύνη, not only his own but also that of the whole people. The word πᾶσαν is probably to be underlined here. Jesus' reply, which exegetes have always found difficult to explain, acquires a concrete meaning: Jesus will effect a general forgiveness.'[117]

Hill notes that Cullmann's view 'involves a Pauline understanding of *dikaiosynē* and of *pasan* ("for all")'[118] and it is indeed suggestive that Cullmann does not support this interpretation using the Gospel of Matthew but using the other gospels and Paul.

Cullmann explains that on the basis of Mk 10:38 and Lk 12:50 it is clear that for Jesus the verb βαπτίζω has the meaning 'die'.[119] It should be noted that the major textual variation between Mt 20:20-8 and Mk 10:35-45 is that Matthew does not contain the two references to the theme of baptism found in Mark. Also Mt 10:34 is parallel to Lk 12:51 but Matthew does not have the reference to baptism which is found in Lk 12:50. Consequently, rather than supporting the interpretation that Mt 3:15 points to the fact that Jesus will effect a general forgiveness, Mk 10:38 and Lk 12:50 cast doubt on such an interpretation, for these two passages may very well have been purposely omitted by Matthew.

Cullmann's claim that the baptismal doctrine of Rom 6:1ff is traceable throughout the whole New Testament and 'that Christian Baptism in the New Testament is participation in the death and resurrection of Christ'[120] also does not relate directly to Mt 3:15. Neither does Jn 1:29, 'Behold, the Lamb of God, who takes away the sins of the world!' necessarily reflect Matthew's view of baptism.[121]

Thus the plain fact remains that in order to show that righteousness in Mt 3:15 is to be seen in the general sense of the gift of God, proof must be derived from sources extraneous to the Gospel of Matthew. This type of argumentation is used despite the possibility that such proof-texts may have been intentionally omitted by Matthew or that such proof is directly in conflict with the elements in the text such as the use of the plural pronoun ἡμῖν. Rather than starting with an outside explanation it would appear to be more logical to resort to such a procedure only after other methods of exegesis have proven unsuccessful. Before basing an interpretation on sources outside the Gospel of Matthew it is necessary to ascertain whether the immediate context or other passages in Matthew can lead to a satisfactory explanation.

On the basis of the story line in Mt 3:13-17 it is obvious that the act of baptism must be included in the meaning of the expression 'to fulfil all righteousness'. Some exegetes have even suggested that the meaning of *dikaiosynē* is exclusively concerned with the act of baptism so that instead of δικαιοσύνη the text should read δικαίωμα.[122] Although it is clear that the act of baptism is stressed, the reference to all (πᾶσαν)[123] righteousness in 3:15 suggests a more inclusive meaning for *dikaiosynē*. The act of baptism is just one aspect of the righteousness which Jesus and John are to fulfil.

It is thus possible to conclude that in 3:15 righteousness does not refer to the gift of God[124] but to God's demand upon man. John and Jesus are to carry out the total will of God. They are 'to leave nothing undone that has been revealed as the righteous will of God'.[125] Righteousness is the norm for the conduct of John the Baptist and Jesus.[126]

Matthew 21:32

Mt 3:15 is not the only passage in the Gospel of Matthew where the term *dikaiosynē* is used in conjunction with John the Baptist. A similar use is found in 21:32. Indeed, a number of commentators have observed a relationship between these two passages,[127] and it would thus be logical to continue this study of the *dikaiosynē*-passages by turning to 21:32.

Mt 21:32 states: 'For John came to you in the way of righteousness (ἐν ὁδῷ δικαιοσύνης), and you did not believe him.' Some commentators have suggested that the expression 'the way of righteousness' is a technical term. J. A. T. Robinson, for example, writes: 'Just as both the covenanters (1QS ix, 18) and the Christians (Acts ix, 2) knew themselves as "the way", and dwelt strongly on the two ways (1QS iii, 13–iv, 26; Didache i–vi; Matthew vii, 13f.), so "the way of righteousness" may well have been the popular name for John's movement.'[128]

Fiedler claims that Mt 21:32 will always remain a *crux interpretum* unless one delves into the background of the expression 'the way of righteousness'.[129] He attempts to show that on the basis of the Old Testament and a number of Jewish-Palestinian writings[130] it is clear that 'the ways of righteousness' are the ways which correspond to proper conduct in the sight of God. However, insofar as righteousness is the goal of these ways, it is understood not simply as an achievement of man but as the way of salvation (*Heil*).[131] Fiedler thus concludes that in 21:32 the way of righteousness is the way upon which righteousness and salvation (*Heil*) are won.[132]

Fiedler's interpretation of 21:32 in the light of specific texts drawn from the Old Testament and a number of Jewish-Palestinian writings is not convincing. If it were true that the expression 'the way of righteousness' was a well-defined formulaic term, then such an interpretation might be justified. But Fiedler himself admits that it is only possible to speak of a formulaic term with respect to the LXX version of Proverbs.[133] It should be noted that in Prov 8:20; 12:28; 16:17, 31; 17:23 ὁδός is in the plural, while in 21:16, 21 it is in the singular. Consequently, even Fiedler's assertion that we are dealing with a formulaic term in the LXX version of

Proverbs is suspect. It should also be noted that while the evidence in Proverbs is five to two in favour of the plural, in Mt 21:32 the singular is found.[134] These facts militate against the validity of interpreting 21:32 in terms of Proverbs.

It should be noted that in his analysis of the Old Testament and the Jewish-Palestinian literature, Fiedler does not distinguish between the nouns *tsedeq* and *tsedaqah*. Therefore his general conclusion that righteousness in the expression 'the way of righteousness' means '*Heil*' is suspect. Since Mt 21:32 itself does not in any way imply that righteousness is the gift of God, it seems that Fiedler's analysis is simply an attempt to attribute this meaning to the Matthaean use of the term.

The foregoing discussion has shown that although expressions similar to 'the way of righteousness' exist, these expressions by no means provide the basis for a definitive interpretation of 21:32. We must turn to the Gospel of Matthew itself in order to understand the meaning of this expression.

There is no reason to suppose that in 21:32 the meaning of the term *dikaiosynē* is not essentially the same as in the four *dikaiosynē*-passages just discussed. Here, as in the other passages, *dikaiosynē* refers to conduct which is in agreement with the will of God.

This interpretation is indeed suggested by two factors other than the argument of the continuity of meaning. First, Lk 7:30, a passage parallel to Mt 21:32, states, 'but the Pharisees and the lawyers rejected the purpose of God (τὴν βουλὴν τοῦ θεοῦ) for themselves'. The expression 'the way of righteousness' is thus parallel to 'the purpose of God'. If, as has been proposed, righteousness refers to the will of God, then these two verses of the same tradition do in fact carry the same meaning.

Secondly, it should not be overlooked that Mt 21:31 uses the expression 'the will of his father'. It is therefore possible that the concept of the will of God may govern v. 32.[135]

A large number of scholars agree that righteousness refers to conduct which is in agreement with the will of God. There is, however, disagreement amongst them whether ὁδός is to be viewed as a way of life or as a subject of preaching. In other words, does it refer to the conduct of John the Baptist or to the content of his message?

W. Michaelis writes, 'The construction ἦλθεν ἐν ὁδῷ demands that ὁδός be referred to the Baptist himself. What is meant is that he came to you in the way of righteousness, as a righteous man, and yet you did not believe him.'[136] On the other hand, Ziesler states, 'Probably ἐν here means "with", and the whole phrase means "with the message of righteousness", i.e. the message of the standard which God demands of men, the life of obedience to the divine will.'[137]

The fact that Mt 21:32 states, 'you did not believe him' indicates that John the Baptist presented a message which was refused. This would support the premise that ὁδός refers to the subject of John's preaching. One must not forget, however, that Mt 5:19 stresses that teaching and doing must not be separated. Accordingly, it is possible that not only the idea of John's message but also that of his conduct is connoted in 21:32. John practised what he preached.[138]

Matthew 5:6

Whereas Barth[139] claims that Mt 3:15 is the decisive passage showing that righteousness should be viewed not only as a demand but also as an eschatological gift, Fiedler appears to attach such a significance to 5:6. He claims that in this passage righteousness refers solely to the eschatological gift of God.[140] It is a 'fremde Gerechtigkeit'.[141] Indeed a number of exegetes claim that in 5:6 *dikaiosynē* is regarded as a gift which God gives to those who ask for it.[142]

Some commentators suggest that in Mt 5:6 *dikaiosynē* means justification. For example, Bultmann writes, 'By those who "hunger and thirst after righteousness", Mt 5:6 obviously does not mean those who "ever striving, endeavour" to attain ethical perfection, but those who long to have God pronounce the verdict "righteous" as His decision over them in judgment.'[143]

Another interpretation of 5:6 which is similar to those mentioned above inasmuch as it too views *dikaiosynē* as God's rather than man's activity is suggested by C. H. Dodd. He argues that if this saying is put back into 'its presumed original Aramaic'[144] then *tsedaqta'* or *tsidqa'*, the equivalent to δικαιοσύνη, could refer to God's vindicating activity with respect to his elect.[145]

There is, however, by no means a general consensus of scholars that *dikaiosynē* in 5:6 refers solely to God's activity. There are exegetes who suggest that this passage refers to both the demand and gift of God. For example, Manson writes with respect to the meaning of *dikaiosynē* in 5:6, 'It is the fulfilment by man of God's will *and* the fulfilment by God of His own purposes of grace and mercy.'[146]

All of the foregoing interpretations are at variance with the meaning of the term 'righteousness' as found in the *dikaiosynē*-passages discussed thus far. Are these interpretations incorrect or does the meaning of the term *dikaiosynē* in actual fact vary within the Gospel of Matthew?

A detailed investigation shows that the interpretations of 5:6 discussed thus far are misleading. It should be noted that the interpretations discussed above are not in agreement with each other. Why? It was noted previously that it is extremely probable that in 5:6 the term *dikaiosynē* was inserted by Matthew by way of interpolation. Matthew thus experienced great constraint in the use of this term.

In dealing with the meaning of this interpolated term, the question must be asked: should the meaning be derived from the immediate context, which after all is not redactional but belongs to the *Vorlage*, or should the meaning be derived from the larger context of the whole gospel?

The interpretations given above are based on the former method of interpretation. The immediate context mentions 'those who hunger and thirst', and it is argued that one hungers and thirsts for something which one hopes to receive. Consequently, righteousness is seen specifically as the gift of God or at least as referring to God's action.

Mt 5:7 appears to substantiate such an interpretation for it is stated that the merciful shall obtain mercy. However, not all the beatitudes presuppose a direct correspondence in kind between the characteristics of the persons named and their reward. According to 5:7 the meek do not obtain meekness nor do the pure in heart in 5:8 receive purity. Consequently, it cannot be taken for granted that in 5:6 the ones who hunger for righteousness will obtain righteousness as a gift. This verse only states that they will be satisfied. The satisfaction could come about through any number of ways. It is indeed possible that those who hunger and thirst to fulfil the demand of God upon man will receive a reward which will indeed satisfy them. This reward does not have to be salvation, for as the other beatitudes show there are many other possible rewards. Thus the interpretations of 5:6 by the various scholars listed above which are based on the immediate context are by no means without difficulties.

Let us now see what results are obtained when the use of the term *dikaiosynē* in 5:6 is viewed in the broader context of Matthew's thought. Whereas 5:6 reads, 'Blessed are those who hunger and thirst for righteousness, for they shall be satisfied', the parallel passage in Lk 6:21 reads, 'Blessed are you that hunger now, for you shall be satisfied.' Why does Matthew, in comparison to Luke, include an expanded saying of the same tradition in his gospel?

Hill answers this question when he states, 'Matthew expands the shorter form in the interest of clarification.'[147] The saying in Lk 6:21 is vague. The object of the hunger is unspecified. Matthew, in order to clarify this saying, adds the term 'righteousness'.

What effect does this clarification have? Weiss makes the astute observation that this term is added to make this passage subordinate to Mt 5:20.[148] This suggestion is very convincing. The concept of righteousness plays a significant role not only in 5:20 but also in 6:1 and 33, two passages directly related to 5:20. It is indeed fitting that this concept should be used to govern and define the object of the hunger. Consequently, just as *dikaiosynē* in 5:20 and 6:1, 33 refers to man's conduct in accordance with the will of God, so it probably has the same meaning in 5:6. Since there are no compelling reasons to suggest that the term *dikaiosynē* must have different meanings in 5:6 and 5:20, it is reasonable to assume that Matthew used this term in a consistent way.[149] After all, in the Gospel of Matthew *dikaiosynē* appears to be a significant redactional concept and one should assume unity unless there are compelling signs to the contrary.

Matthew 5:10

In 5:10 righteousness is regarded as a cause for persecution.[150] In this passage it is clear that righteousness refers to something which a person has, for one is usually persecuted for one's own action.[151] Even Fiedler, who has attempted to interpret all the foregoing *dikaiosynē*-passages as referring to the gift of God, notes that there appears to be a contradiction between 5:6 and 5:10, since 5:10 refers to something which a person has.[152]

For a solution to this seeming contradiction, Fiedler draws attention to the three following factors. He first of all suggests that it should not be expected that there must be uniformity of usage among the 7 occurrences of the term *dikaiosynē* in the Gospel of Matthew.[153]

Secondly, Fiedler notes that the interpretation given by W. Michaelis could be correct: 'Weil sie als Gerechte gelten, auch wenn sie selbst nach 5,6 sich nicht so ansehen können, werden sie verfolgt, unschuldig zwar, aber doch nicht ohne Grund.'[154]

Thirdly, Fiedler argues that it may be possible that 5:10 refers to persons who were persecuted for a righteousness which they did not possess. The people had no righteousness but knew that they could expect everything on the basis of the eschatological gift of God. This angered those who thought that they had righteousness and consequently the latter persecuted the former.[155]

Fiedler concludes that the third suggestion leads to the correct understanding of 5:10. Consequently, there is no contradiction between 5:6 and 5:10 after all. According to 5:10 a person has righteousness only in the sense that it has been given to him as the gift of God.[156]

What Fiedler has in actual fact done is interpret Mt 5:10 in terms of the meaning which he attached to 5:6. Since it has been shown that the term *dikaiosynē* in 5:6 probably does not refer to the gift of God, this proof is unconvincing.

The majority of scholars agree that in 5:10 righteousness refers to man's conduct, that is to say, to the demand rather than the gift of God.[157]

All seven *dikaiosynē*-passages in the Gospel of Matthew have now been analysed, and it is possible to conclude that Matthew's usage of the term *dikaiosynē* is consistent. In all seven passages righteousness is seen as God's demand upon man. Righteousness refers to proper conduct before God.

3 *Eleēmosynē*

As was discussed above, Ziesler has shown that 'the LXX translators considered δικαι- to represent *ts-d-q* adequately',[158] for there are only 23 exceptions to such usage. With respect to the exceptions, Ziesler has found that 'no trend is perceptible, except the very notable one of using ἐλεημοσύνη or ἔλεος instead of a δικαι- word'.[159] *Eleēmosynē* is used 9 times, and *eleos* 3 times, for *tsedaqah*. It should be noted that *eleēmosynē* and *eleos* never stand for *tsedeq*.

Ziesler warns that on the basis of these facts it would be precarious 'to conclude that δικαιοσύνη cannot bear the "gracious" connotation of *tsedaqah*'.[160] After all, *dikaiosynē* is used 9 times in the LXX to render the term *hesed*.[161] Ziesler especially points out that in Prov 20:28 *hesed* 'occurs twice with the same meaning, but once is rendered ἐλεημοσύνη and once δικαιοσύνη'.[162]

On the basis of this evidence Ziesler reaches the conclusion that 'it is clear that δικαιοσύνη and ἐλεημοσύνη can be used interchangeably for *ts-d-q* and *ch-s-d*'.[163]

Dodd, on the other hand, states with respect to the usage in the Septuagint, 'Thus two aspects of *tsedeq* are polarized into δικαιοσύνη and ἐλεημοσύνη. In place of the comprehensive virtue of *tsedaqah*, we have justice on the one hand, mercy on the other.'[164]

To substantiate this conclusion, Dodd cites the following examples. In Dan 4:27(24) *tsedaqah*, referring to human benevolence, is translated by *eleēmosynē* in the LXX.[165] In Ps 23(24):5; Deut 6:25, 24:13; Ps 102(103):6, and Ps 32(33):5, *tsedaqah*, referring to the gracious activity of God, is again rendered by *eleēmosynē* in the LXX.[166]

Which of these two opposing views is in fact the correct one? It should be noted that the 9 cases cited by Ziesler are in the category of exceptions, for Hatch has shown that in the LXX *hesed* is generally rendered by *eleēmosynē* or *eleos*.[167] In addition it must be noted that in the Old Testament the terms *tsedeq* and *tsedaqah* are used almost interchangeably. Consequently, the fact that in some instances *dikaiosynē* and *eleēmosynē* are used interchangeably in the LXX may simply reflect the usage in the Hebrew Old Testament.

The view promulgated by Dodd, on the other hand, appears to be significant insofar as it isolates the beginning of a trend. As was shown above, in the Dead Sea Scrolls and the Tannaitic literature, although there was some overlap it was nevertheless clear that the terms *tsedeq* and *tsedaqah* were generally used with distinct meanings. In both literatures *tsedeq* was used primarily to refer to man's conduct while *tsedaqah* was used to designate benevolent activity, namely God's gracious, saving activity in the Dead Sea Scrolls and alms in the Tannaitic literature.

With respect to the usage in the LXX of rendering *tsedaqah* by *eleēmosynē*, Ziesler himself notes that this shows 'that the Rabbinic tendency to give *tsedaqah* the meaning "benevolence", "charity" or even "almsgiving", was extant as early as this'.[168] As a matter of fact, it appears that not only this specific trend but also the more general one that 'two aspects of *tsedeq* are polarized into δικαιοσύνη and ἐλεημοσύνη'[169] is indeed evident in the LXX. Despite Ziesler's claim to the contrary, it does appear that the usage of the LXX points to the trend that δικαιοσύνη tends not to bear 'the "gracious" connotation of *tsedaqah*'.[170]

Let us now see how the Matthaean use of the term *eleēmosynē* relates to the Septuagintal usage. This term occurs 3 times in the Gospel of Matthew, i.e. Mt 6:2, 3, 4. In all three cases *eleēmosynē* is used to refer to almsgiving.[171] It is thus clear that the Matthaean use of *eleēmosynē* is equivalent to the way *tsedaqah* is used in the Tannaitic literature.[172]

The discussion of Mt 6:1 showed that the doing of righteousness (*dikaiosynē*) included almsgiving, praying and fasting. Consequently, there is a relationship between the usage of the terms *eleēmosynē* and *dikaiosynē*; namely, the giving of alms is simply one aspect of doing righteousness. Similarly, in the Tannaitic literature, almsgiving (*tsedaqah*) is included in the doing of righteousness (*tsedeq*).

As has been shown, in the Gospel of Matthew the meanings of the terms *dikaiosynē* and *eleēmosynē* are distinct and well defined. *Dikaiosynē* refers strictly to the demand of God upon man, never to the gift of God. Matthaean usage thus reflects the trend visible in the LXX, namely that *dikaiosynē* tends not to bear the gracious connotation of *tsedaqah*. The gracious connotation of *tsedaqah*, however, is visible in the use of the term *eleēmosynē*, although only in the limited sense of almsgiving. While the doing of *dikaiosynē* includes *eleēmosynē*, there is no reference to God's saving, gracious activity but only to man's gracious activity in the form of almsgiving.

Does Matthew completely neglect the concept of God's gracious, saving activity which was expressed by the Hebrew term *tsedaqah*? It was noted that in the LXX the term *eleos* was used 3 times to translate *tsedaqah*.[173] Let us see how Matthew used this term.

The noun *eleos* occurs 3 times in the Gospel of Matthew. In 9:13 and 12:7 it occurs in the quotation of Hos 6:6, 'I desire mercy and not sacrifice.' This quotation is used in both instances with the implication that the

Pharisees have not shown mercy to others. In Mt 23:23 it is explicitly stated that the scribes and Pharisees have neglected mercy. In all three cases the noun *eleos* is used not with respect to Gòd's saving, gracious activity but with respect to God's demand that men should show mercy toward one another.

The verb *eleeō*, on the other hand, is used with reference to God's saving, gracious activity, at least insofar as such activity is centered in Jesus. For example, in Mt 9:27, 15:22, 17:15, 20:30f this verb is used in the pleas of various people imploring Jesus to have mercy on them. Thus Matthew does not neglect the theme of God's saving, gracious activity. What is clear, however, is that Matthew does not use righteousness terminology such as *dikaiosynē* and the subordinate term *eleēmosynē* to express this theme.

4 *Dikaios*

There are 17 occurrences of the adjective *dikaios* in the Gospel of Matthew.[174] In Mark and Luke, on the other hand, there are only 2 and 11 occurrences respectively. Of the 17 cases in Matthew there is only a single instance where the Matthaean usage is parallel to Mark and/or Luke, namely Mt 9:13 (= Mk 2:17 = Lk 5:32), 'For I came not to call the righteous, but sinners.'

Of the 16 occurrences which have no synoptic parallels, 6 are found in completely unique Matthaean pericopae,[175] 6 in uniquely Matthaean material occurring in pericopae having synoptic parallels,[176] and 4 in passages where the immediate context in which the adjective is found has a synoptic parallel.[177] Consequently, there are only 4 occurrences of the adjective *dikaios* which lend themselves to redaction-critical analysis.

Lk 10:24 refers to 'prophets and kings' while Mt 13:17 refers to 'prophets and righteous men'. Lk 11:47 mentions the 'tombs of the prophets' while Mt 23:29 refers not only to the latter but also to the 'monuments of the righteous'. Lk 11:50 refers to the 'blood of all the prophets' while Mt 23:35 refers to 'all the righteous blood' ($\pi\tilde{\alpha}\nu$ $\alpha\tilde{\iota}\mu\alpha$ $\delta\iota\kappa\alpha\iota o\nu$). Lk 11:51 refers to the 'blood of Abel' while Mt 23:35 has the phrase $\dot{\alpha}\pi\dot{o}$ $\tau o\tilde{\upsilon}$ $\alpha\tilde{\iota}\mu\alpha\tau o\varsigma$ "$A\beta\epsilon\lambda$ $\tau o\tilde{\upsilon}$ $\delta\iota\kappa\alpha\iota o\upsilon$. This phrase has been translated as either 'from the blood of innocent Abel'[178] or 'from the blood of Abel the righteous'.[179] The latter translation appears to express the real intention of the text most clearly.[180]

On the basis of these 4 uses of the adjective *dikaios*, a redactional trend can be isolated; namely, when referring to those who in the past were properly religious, Matthew likes to use the designation 'righteous' (*dikaios*).

Let us now attempt to classify the 17 occurrences of the adjective *dikaios* in the Gospel of Matthew. As was shown above, Matthew uses this term to describe those who were properly religious in the past or, as Ziesler has noted, 'the pious, God-fearing, upright people of the OT'.[181] The occurrences of *dikaios* in 13:17 and 23:29, 35 (twice), belong to this category.[182] Ziesler also includes 10:41 in this category.[183] In the latter passage, however, the reference is to the present. Consequently, the pious of the Old Testament can hardly be included.

The adjective *dikaios* is also used to describe a certain group of religious contemporaries of Jesus and/or Matthew, namely those who observed the law but were not necessarily properly religious as far as the teaching of Jesus was concerned. Ziesler suggests that in 1:19, 5:45, 9:13 and 23:28 *dikaios* means 'obeying the law'.[184] This is certainly true in the case of 1:19, for Joseph is righteous because he acted according to the teaching of the law.[185]

With respect to 5:45 Ziesler notes that 'it is disputable whether righteous under the old or the new covenant is intended'.[186] He is probably right, however, in placing it in this category rather than the 'Christian righteous' category.

In 9:13 *dikaios* again refers to the observance of the law. This verse implies that the Pharisees are righteous and on the basis of 5:20 we know that the Pharisees have a righteousness which is obtained by obedience to the law.[187] The meaning of *dikaios* in 23:28 is quite similar to that in 9:13. As Descamps has pointed out, φαίνεσθε could imply an external rather than a false righteousness.[188] Consequently, here as in 9:13 the Pharisees are viewed as being righteous in much the same sense.

In addition to the four passages just discussed, the occurrences of *dikaios* in 10:41 and 27:19 also belong to this category. With respect to 10:41, Montefiore has suggested that 'the righteous' may refer to the whole body of Christians.[189] Ziesler, on the other hand, does not classify 10:41 in the category of the 'Christian righteous'.[190] Ziesler's view is to be preferred, for it appears that in this passage a distinction is made between the righteous and the disciples. The latter are those who are properly religious in the Christian sense.

The reference to Jesus as being righteous, found in 27:19, also belongs to the category referring to properly religious contemporaries who are not necessarily Christian. After all, it is stated that the wife of Pilate referred to Jesus as 'that righteous one' (τῷ δικαίῳ ἐκείνῳ). This in effect means that in the eyes of a nonbeliever Jesus appeared to be a properly religious person with reference to contemporary religious standards. Such a statement may also have implied that, being properly religious, Jesus must be innocent of the charges levied against him.[191]

Interpretations of 27:19 to the effect that 'Jesus is for Matthew *the* exemplary Just One!'[192] or that this verse shows that the passion of Jesus should be viewed from the perspective of the suffering righteous one[193] read a significance into this verse which in no way harmonizes with the general usage of the term *dikaios* in the Gospel of Matthew. Even discussing 27:19 under the special heading 'Christ as Righteous' rather than 'Man as Righteous', as Ziesler has done,[194] is not justified.

In the passages discussed up to this point the adjective *dikaios* has not been used specifically to designate those who are properly religious in the sense that they followed the teachings of Jesus. Let us now turn to those passages which Ziesler claims deal with the 'Christian righteous', namely 'those who live in obedience to Jesus, and so receive his verdict of approval'.[195] The passages which Ziesler lists as belonging to this category are 13:43, 49; 25:37, 46.

It should be noted that rather than referring to the past or the writer's contemporary situation, as was the case with the passages discussed up to this point, these passages all refer to the future. Specifically, these four passages refer to the future judgment and the hope of eternal life.

It is not to be denied that in these passages the righteous are indeed the 'Christian righteous' as defined by Ziesler. This fact is especially obvious in the case of 25:46 where the righteous (οἱ δίκαιοι) are said to enter eternal life as opposed to eternal punishment.

It is to be expected that with respect to the writer's past, there are no references to the Christian righteous. It is indeed perplexing, however, that the expression *dikaios* is used only with reference to the Christian righteous of the future and not of the present. What is the reason behind this peculiar usage?

Bultmann has noted that 'it is impossible to avoid thinking that Matt. 25:31–46 derives from Jewish tradition'.[196] This conclusion is indeed convincing. In the discussion of the Tannaitic literature it was seen that those who were to inherit life in the world to come were known as the righteous. In the four passages under discussion Matthew does not emphasize that those who are properly religious in the Christian sense are to be known as the righteous, but rather, using traditional Jewish teaching, Matthew emphasizes that the properly religious will inherit eternal life. Thus no extraordinary significance should be attached to the fact that in a few passages dealing with the future hope of eternal life, the righteous happen to be the Christian righteous.

It is therefore possible to conclude that in the Gospel of Matthew the term *dikaios* is not used with the express purpose of designating those who are properly religious in the sense that they follow the teaching of Jesus. The righteous are basically those who obey the law. This does not mean that one who is properly religious in the Christian sense could not also be referred to as being righteous. It does mean, however, that in the Gospel of Matthew the term *dikaios* is not a preferred technical term for those who are properly religious in the Christian sense.

That *dikaios* is indeed not such a technical term is supported by the way it is used in Mt 20:4, 'You go into the vineyard too, and whatever is right (δίκαιον) I will give you.' Here *dikaios* is not used to define the religious status of a person. As Ziesler points out, in this case *dikaios* refers to a just or proper payment.[197] Schrenk also notes that 20:4 is among those passages in which *dikaios* follows everyday usage and does not reflect any new or distinctive early Christian understanding.[198]

5

THE RELATIVE SIGNIFICANCE OF THE CONCEPT
OF RIGHTEOUSNESS IN THE GOSPEL OF MATTHEW

Having analysed the meaning of the component terms of the concept of righteousness, we are now in a position to discuss the question: what relative significance is attached to the use of the concept of righteousness in the Gospel of Matthew?

In the previous chapter it was demonstrated that the terms *dikaiosynē*, *dikaios* and *eleēmosynē*, insofar as the latter is included in the doing of *dikaiosynē*, are used to describe the demand of God upon man to live according to a certain norm, the law. Although the nature of the law never changes,[1] the possibility of varying interpretations of the law is taken into account. Consequently, there are degrees of righteousness, the righteousness that exceeds that of the scribes and Pharisees being that which corresponds to the interpretation of the law given by Jesus.

It should be noted that even the reference to God's righteousness in Mt 6:33 does not provide an exception to this general meaning of righteousness. God's righteousness is seen primarily as a norm for man's conduct. Consequently, the view expressed by Ziesler,[2] Schrenk,[3] Fiedler[4] and Bornkamm,[5] for example, that the concept of righteousness plays a significant role in Matthew's theology insofar as it relates both to the demand made upon man and God's eschatological gift for man, is not supported by the present study.

If this view does not have a foundation in the actual text of the Gospel of Matthew, why has it been promulgated by a large number of scholars? This writer has come to the following conclusion as to the basis of this view. Whether consciously or unconsciously, these scholars have read the Gospel of Matthew in the light of the Pauline writings. In other words, they have paulinized the Matthaean concept of righteousness.

It is generally accepted that righteousness is one of the primary soteriological terms in the Pauline writings and that this term refers solely to the gift of God for man. Indeed, this view is so well established that it has led to the assumption that righteousness in the Gospel of Matthew must have the same function and meaning as it has in the Pauline writings. To effect such an agreement, it is argued that the Matthaean concept of righteousness includes the idea that righteousness is not only God's demand upon man but also God's gift for man.

Having reached such a conclusion, it is recognized by some scholars that the component parts of this double meaning are in fact in tension. In order to resolve this tension it is generally assumed that the idea of the gift is the more important component. In other words, it is concluded that the gift must precede the demand. This solution is essentially proposed by Ziesler,[6] Schrenk,[7] Fiedler[8] and Kertelge.[9] It should be noted that this solution is based on the value judgment that in Christianity the gift should precede the demand. In other words, a pseudo-problem has been given an arbitrary answer.

Stuhlmacher, on the other hand, having created the same problem as the scholars just discussed, at least treats it as a real problem. He admits that there is a theological problem with respect to Matthew's teaching about righteousness.[10] The problem is the imbalance between the aspects of righteousness as divine gift and human action. Stuhlmacher concludes that because of this imbalance in the Matthaean concept of righteousness it was impossible for Matthew unmistakably to lend expression to a *sola gratia*.

Is Stuhlmacher's conclusion valid? After all, if, simply on the basis of an imbalance between the gift and demand aspects of righteousness, Stuhlmacher comes to the conclusion that Matthew could not lend a clear expression to a *sola gratia* view of salvation, how much more would this hold true if Stuhlmacher had realized that the Matthaean concept of righteousness deals solely with God's demand rather than gift?

Does this mean that the Pauline and Matthaean concepts of *salvation* are diametrically opposed to each other? That in effect Paul teaches justification by faith while Matthew teaches justification by man's own better righteousness?[11]

No! Matthew does teach that salvation is the gift of God. It has already been pointed out that the verb *eleeō* is used with reference to God's saving, gracious activity through the ministry of Jesus.[12] But the clearest statement in the Gospel of Matthew to the effect that salvation is the gift of God is found in 1:21. This passage, which has no synoptic parallel, states, 'and you shall call his name Jesus, for he will save his people from their sins'.

The idea that salvation is made possible because of the gift of God through Jesus is also evident in 26:28. Compared to Mk 14:24, Mt 26:28 adds the phrase 'εἰς ἄφεσιν ἁμαρτιῶν'. Matthew thus makes it absolutely clear that the blood of the covenant which is poured out for many is indeed poured out 'for the forgiveness of sins'. Because of this emphasis on the salvific role of Jesus it is understandable why Matthew, like Mark, has incorporated into his gospel the teaching that 'the Son of man came . . . to give his life as a ransom for many'.[13]

Passages such as the ones just mentioned show beyond doubt that Matthew views salvation as the gift of God. In contrast to Paul, however, who expresses this idea using the concept of righteousness, Matthew expresses this idea without reference to the concept of righteousness.

It is therefore clear that Paul and Matthew are not in conflict as to the teaching that salvation is the gift of God. *The apparent conflict is artificially created when, instead of comparing the Pauline and Matthaean concepts of salvation, their respective concepts of righteousness are contrasted.*

As suggested previously, the interpretation of the Matthaean concept of righteousness as having the double meaning of demand and gift rested on the conscious or unconscious desire to make the Matthaean teaching concerning the nature of salvation compatible with that of Paul. It is now clear that despite their disagreement concerning the meaning of the term *dikaiosynē*, Paul and Matthew agree that salvation is the gift of God. Consequently, the theological reason underlying the attempt to bring the meaning of the Matthaean righteousness terminology into agreement with that of Paul has been obviated.

Not all scholars, however, attributed a double meaning to the Matthaean understanding of righteousness. The foregoing discussion has shown that some commentators, notably Strecker,[14] do consistently interpret *dikaiosynē* as referring to the demand rather than to the gift of God. What overall significance does Strecker attach to this concept in the Gospel of Matthew?

The title of Strecker's book, *Der Weg der Gerechtigkeit*, is indeed descriptive of the importance which Strecker attaches to the concept of righteousness in the Gospel of Matthew. The Gospel of Matthew shows the way of righteousness insofar as all major aspects of Matthew's theology are related to this concept. Strecker states that discipleship must be seen as the realization of the *dikaiosynē*-demand.[15] Baptism is the first step which imposes the obligation upon the church (*Gemeinde*) to put righteousness into practice in the same way as was done by its earthly Lord.[16] Indeed, the exalted Lord is present precisely where the demand of righteousness is proclaimed and put into practice by the post-Easter church.[17]

Does the concept of righteousness really play such a decisive role? It appears not. Strecker overstates the importance of the concept of righteousness in the Gospel of Matthew. Other ideas such as the gift of salvation are also prominent. Since the Matthaean concept of righteousness does not include this teaching, it cannot be viewed as being an all-encompassing concept in the Gospel of Matthew.

That Matthew indeed does not view the concept of righteousness in this manner is especially clear when one considers his terminology designating those who are properly religious in the Christian sense. The discussion of the terms *dikaiosynē* and *dikaios* has shown that these two terms are closely related. The former refers to a type of conduct and the latter to the person who participates in that conduct. It was also noted that Matthew at no point stresses that the people who are properly religious in the Christian sense are to be known as 'the righteous'. This negative conclusion is supported by the positive conclusion that Matthew does have a designation for those who are properly religious in the Christian sense, namely 'disciple'.

It has often been argued that in the Gospel of Matthew the term 'disciple' (μαθητής) is a technical term referring strictly to the Twelve (οἱ δώδεκα).[18] M. Sheridan deviates from this absolute interpretation. He admits that while 'Matthew has restricted the usage of the term disciple exclusively to the twelve'[19] it is nevertheless true that 'the twelve can represent or be an example for the Christian community'.[20]

A thorough examination of the Gospel of Matthew reveals that the term 'disciple' is used to refer not only to the Twelve but to all believers. Even Strecker, who claims that this term refers only to the Twelve, acknowledges a few passages which at first appear to negate this conclusion.[21]

Let us look at these passages. Strecker maintains that if 8:21 is seen apart from its context then the term 'disciple' could refer to one of the Twelve.[22] Yet the fact remains that, when 8:21 is seen within its context, the expression ἕτερος δὲ τῶν μαθητῶν implies that the scribe mentioned in v. 19 is a disciple, and it is unlikely that the scribe was one of the Twelve. It is probable that he was a follower of Jesus, a Christian.

It should be noted that the parallel passage in Luke is not as explicit. The scribe of Mt 8:19 is simply 'someone' (τις) in Lk 9:57, and 'another of his disciples' in Mt 8:21 is simply 'another' (ἕτερον) in Lk 9:59. It is possible that Matthew added the term 'disciple' to make clear that both of the persons under discussion were followers of Jesus, namely Christians.

With respect to Mt 10:24f Strecker admits that the term 'disciples' is used in a very general sense.[23] He points out, however, that this saying is of a pre-Matthaean origin (cf. Lk 6:40) and thus not relevant to the point under discussion.

Since Mt 10:24f has a synoptic parallel in Lk 6:40, it is indeed true that this saying rests on traditional material. Yet the fact that Mt 10:24f presents this material in a form much expanded in comparison to Lk 6:40 may indicate that the view expressed in Mt 10:24f is redactionally significant.

Strecker's interpretation of Mt 10:42 is even less convincing than his interpretations of 8:21 and 10:24f. Mt 10:42 and Mk 9:41 seem to originate from a single source. There is, however, one major discrepancy between these two accounts. Mk 9:41 reads, 'because you bear the name of Christ (ἐν ὀνόματι ὅτι Χριστοῦ ἐστε)' while Mt 10:42 reads, 'because he is a disciple (εἰς ὄνομα μαθητοῦ)'. Strecker states that it cannot be substantiated that the expression εἰς ὄνομα μαθητοῦ originates with the redactor.[24] While absolute certainty can never be attained with respect to redactional activity, the most logical explanation of the textual discrepancy between Mt 10:42 and Mk 9:41 is nevertheless in terms of Matthaean redactional activity. As far as Matthew is concerned, bearing the name of Christ, i.e. being a properly religious person in the Christian sense, is best expressed by the inclusive term 'disciple'.[25]

The use of the verb μαθητεύω indicates that the term 'disciple' has a very inclusive meaning. This verb occurs in Mt 13:52, 27:57 and 28:19.[26] In 28:19 Jesus is represented as saying to the eleven disciples (οἱ δὲ ἕνδεκα μαθηταί, v. 16): 'Go therefore and make disciples (μαθητεύσατε) of all nations.'[27] In this passage no distinction is made between the close circle of the eleven disciples and all the disciples of the future. Just as Jesus made disciples, so the disciples themselves are to make disciples.[28] In other words, the followers of Jesus, present and future, are known as disciples.

In order to adhere to the view that the term 'disciples' refers only to the Twelve, Strecker and Albright and Mann resort to some very curious explanations. Strecker admits that there is no difference between the noun μαθητής and the verb μαθητεύω as far as meaning is concerned.[29] There is, however, a distinction as far as use is concerned. The verb is never used with reference to the Twelve, thus showing that the noun is reserved to designate them.[30]

Strecker's conclusion is unwarranted, for Mt 13:52 shows that the verb is in fact used to designate the narrow circle of the Twelve. Albright and Mann interpret this passage as follows: 'The verbal form of Matt xiii 52, bearing in mind its context, might very properly be translated by a phrase which gave the narrower meaning of "disciple": "the scribe who has been made a disciple of the kingdom ... "'[31] With respect to 27:57 and 28:19, on the other hand, Albright and Mann note that the use of the verbal form may indicate a wider use of the noun 'disciple'. However, they favour the possibility 'that the evangelist here used the verb form precisely in order to avoid a noun which for him had specialized meanings.'[32] They therefore suggest the translation 'a rich man of Arimathea, named Joseph, who had been taught by Jesus'[33] for 27:57 and 'teach all nations'[34] for 28:19.

Having suggested such a translation in the introduction to their book, Albright and Mann then promptly go ahead and give a different translation in the main part of their book. For the actual translation of 28:19f they give 'Therefore go and make disciples of all peoples . . . teaching them to observe . . .'[35]

What underlies this change of view? The reason is obvious. When v. 19 is translated by itself, the translation of μαθητεύσατε as 'teach all nations' seems appropriate. Yet when v. 19 is seen in conjunction with the verb διδάσκοντες in v. 20, this translation is not possible. After all, it would be strange indeed if both the verbs μαθητεύω and διδάσκω were to be treated as meaning 'to teach'.

These attempts to discover distinctions in the meaning and/or use of the noun and the verb are indeed problematic. The facts are best explained if the noun and verb are viewed as referring to a single concept. Just as in some cases the noun is definitely used to refer to the disciples in a very inclusive sense, so the verb shows that disciples are people in general who have accepted (13:52, 27:57) or will accept (28:19) the teaching of Jesus.[36]

With the understanding that the term 'disciple' refers to those who are properly religious in the Christian sense, let us now specifically see how this term relates to the term *dikaios*. As was noted above, Matthew does not suggest that the followers of Jesus are to be known as 'the righteous'. It will now be shown that Matthew indicates that in some contexts the use of this term is indeed inappropriate. This fact is expressed most clearly in 18:13 and 27:57.

In the parable 'The Lost Sheep', Lk 15:7 states that 'there will be more joy in heaven over one sinner who repents than over ninety-nine righteous persons (δικαίοις) who need no repentance'. Mt 18:13, on the other hand, reads, 'he rejoices over it more than the ninety-nine that never went astray'. J. Jeremias has pointed out that this parable has an entirely different audience in Luke and in Matthew.[37] In Luke it is addressed to Jesus' opponents while in Matthew it is directed to his disciples. Jeremias states that there can be no doubt that Luke has preserved the original situation.[38]

Why does Luke refer to the righteous while Matthew does not? The answer is obvious. In dialogue with Jesus's opponents the term *dikaios* is appropriate. In a discussion with the disciples, that is, within the context of those who are properly religious in the Christian sense, the term *dikaios*, which primarily refers to those who are properly religious in a Jewish sense, has no place.

In the pericope of the burial of Jesus, Lk 23:50 states that 'Joseph from the Jewish town of Arimathea' was a 'righteous man (δίκαιος)'. Mt 27:57, on the other hand, states that he was a disciple (ἐμαθητεύθη).[39] It is probable that in order to show that Joseph of Arimathea was properly religious in a Christian sense, Matthew could not refer to him as being righteous but rather as being a disciple.

There is no doubt that these factors indicate that Matthew wanted to make a clear-cut terminological distinction between properly religious Jews and followers of Jesus. Those who led properly religious lives according to Jewish standards were designated as 'the righteous' while those who followed the teaching of Jesus were designated as 'disciples'.

How thoroughgoing is this terminological distinction in the Gospel of Matthew? Does it relate only to the distinction between the names of the followers or also to the norm governing the behaviour of these two distinct groups? In other words, is the saying in 5:20, that the righteousness of the disciples must exceed that of the scribes and Pharisees, representative of Matthew's view of what it means to be a disciple?

Let us first of all put this question into its proper perspective. It has been demonstrated that although the Matthaean concept of righteousness does not include the idea that *righteousness* is the gift of God, this does not mean that Matthew teaches that *salvation* is a human achievement. On the contrary, the Matthaean teaching that Jesus came to save sinners and that consequently salvation is the gift of God is unequivocally stated.

That the disciples are saved sinners is also clear. Barth has pointed out that Mt 18 shows that disciples are not those who rely upon their works but those who are empty before God and thus cleave to his grace.[40] The parable 'The Lost Sheep' especially shows that 'The disciples are thus the weak and lowly, helpless as regards their own salvation.'[41]

Consequently, if it does not refer to the gift of salvation, it must be concluded that the concept of righteousness cannot be representative of Matthew's view of what it means to be a disciple. At this point it should be recalled that in the Tannaitic literature and the Damascus Document, righteousness (*tsedeq*) also just referred to proper conduct and not to the gift of salvation. This aspect of Matthaean usage is thus not unique. As a result, the question under discussion must be limited to the conduct of the disciples. In other words, is *dikaiosynē* the key term designating the conduct expected of disciples?

This question is answered positively by Strecker,[42] Bornkamm[43] and Ziesler.[44] It is undoubtedly true that Matthew places great stress on the importance of proper conduct. For example, Matthew emphasizes the bearing of fruit[45] and draws attention to the fact that the final judgment will involve the criterion of works.[46] Yet is *dikaiosynē* the term Matthew prefers above all others to designate such proper conduct?

If one simply looks at the Sermon on the Mount, then this question could possibly be answered positively with the qualification that in 5:20 the reference is not simply to righteousness but to a greater righteousness. Yet when one looks at the gospel as a whole, one is forced to answer it negatively.

Let us look at 28:19-20. It has been argued that 28:18-20 provides the
key to the understanding of the whole gospel.[47] Whether or not this conclusion is entirely true is debatable. On the other hand, it cannot be denied
that the hand of the redactor is clearly visible in 28:16-20.[48]

In this very important passage at the end of the Gospel of Matthew, the
theme of proper conduct is stressed. Mt 28:20 states that the disciples
should teach the future disciples of all nations 'to observe all' that Jesus has
commanded. The righteousness terminology is not used in this important
proclamation.

Neither is the righteousness terminology used in 12:46-50, a passage
which points to the essence of what it means to be a disciple. Barth has
interpreted this passage with great clarity.

> To be a disciple means for Matthew doing the will of God. This is shown
> especially by the alteration he has made to the apothegm about true
> kinsmen (Mark 3.31-35 = Matt. 12.46-50). In Mark, Jesus looks round
> about upon the ὄχλος and says: whosoever does the will of God is my
> brother . . . In Matthew Jesus stretched forth his hand towards his dis-
> ciples: *They* are my brethren, *for* whosoever does the will of God . . .
> The differentiation from the multitude is clear: the will of God is actually
> done in discipleship.[49]

Barth is right in his conclusion that in 12:46-50 (= Mk 3:31-5) to be a
disciple means to do the will of God. It should be noted that 3:35 is the
only passage in the Gospel of Mark which refers to the will of God. Also in
the Gospel of Luke there is only one explicit reference to the will of God.
This reference is found in 22:42 where Jesus in his prayer in Gethsemane
is portrayed as saying 'not my will, but thine, be done'.[50] This saying is
reflected in Mt 26:42.

The Gospels of Mark and Luke thus each have only a single reference to
the will of God. Matthew, on the other hand, not only parallels the sayings
of Mark and Luke but has three additional references in 6:10, 7:21 and
18:14.[51]

In 6:10 Jesus tells the disciples that they should pray to their Father:
'Thy will be done.' In 18:14, in the parable 'The Lost Sheep', an example
of the will of God is given: 'So it is not the will of my Father who is in
heaven that one of these little ones should perish.' In 7:21 Jesus is reported
as having said that only 'he who does the will of my Father who is in heaven
will enter the kingdom of heaven.

These examples indicate that of the synoptic writers, it is Matthew who
puts the greatest emphasis on the doing of God's will.[52] Indeed, it must be
concluded that for Matthew the terminology which expresses the essence
of discipleship is *doing the will of God.*

What is the relationship between the expressions 'God's will' and 'righteousness'? In the discussion of the *dikaiosynē*-passages it was noted that righteousness referred to the demand of God upon man to live according to the law. In some instances conduct according to the law was essentially seen as conduct according to the will of God. Does this mean that righteousness and doing the will of God are parallel concepts? Is Hare right in stating that 'For Matthew δικαιοσύνη is the abstract noun which corresponds to the phrase ποιεῖν τὸ θέλημα τοῦ πατρός'?[53]

In one sense Hare is right; in another sense he is wrong. Righteousness and doing the will of the Father, though not identical in meaning, are related in meaning. They are not, however, related in use. Matthew's religious self-understanding as a member of the church[54] is that of a disciple doing the will of the Father and not that of a righteous person doing righteousness. The term *dikaiosynē* is reserved strictly for contexts in which Jesus[55] is involved in polemical situations and/or is dealing with non-disciples or audiences comprising both disciples and non-disciples.

In 3:15 and 21:32 the term *dikaiosynē* occurs in the context of the discussions with and about John the Baptist. John the Baptist is not treated as a disciple. In addition it should be noted that 21:32 occurs in a polemical context. Jesus's saying about the way of righteousness is directed to 'the chief priests and the Pharisees' (21:45). It is specifically stated that the chief priests and Pharisees perceived that Jesus was speaking about them in the parables found in 21:28–43.

The other *dikaiosynē*-passages, i.e. 5:6, 10, 20; 6:1, 33, all occur in the Sermon on the Mount which is directed not only to the disciples but to the crowds in general. The nature of the audience is clearly described at the end of the Sermon on the Mount. Mt 7:28 states: 'And when Jesus finished these sayings, the crowds were astonished at his teaching.'

In addition it should be noted that in two of the *dikaiosynē*-passages in the Sermon on the Mount a particular segment of Jewish society is brought into focus. In 5:20 it is said that the righteousness[56] of the disciples must exceed that of the scribes and Pharisees. The warning in 6:1 that one should not practise one's righteousness before men is given with reference to the conduct of the hypocrites (6:2, 5, 16). From 23:13, 15, 23, 25, 27, 29 we know that Matthew identifies the hypocrites with the scribes and Pharisees. Although Jesus is not portrayed in these passages as carrying on a direct polemical dialogue with a specific group of scribes and Pharisees, it is nevertheless clear that he is contrasting the teaching and practice of Judaism with his own teaching. It is in this polemical sense that the use of the term *dikaiosynē* must be seen.

As far as Matthew is concerned, *dikaiosynē* thus appears to be a crucial term in Jesus's polemical encounter with the contemporary religious leaders of the Jews, notably the Pharisees. The expression 'the will of God', on the other hand, is used in contexts dealing with those who are religious in a Christian sense.

The saying in Mt 12:50, 'For whoever does the will of my Father in heaven is my brother, and sister, and mother', is directed specifically to the disciples (12:49). The reference in the Lord's Prayer (6:10) is also directed to the disciples, since this is to be the prayer of the followers of Jesus. The expression 'Thy will be done' occurs not only in the Lord's Prayer but also in the prayer of Jesus in Gethsemane (26:42).

As was noted above, the reference to the will of God in the parable of 'The Lost Sheep' is made within the context of those who are properly religious in a Christian sense.[57]

The reference to the will of God in 7:21 illustrates the distinction between the use of this expression and *dikaiosynē* even more clearly than the passages just discussed. The distinction is especially evident when 7:21 is contrasted with 5:20. Mt 5:20 deals with an implied polemical situation. Jesus contrasts the disciples with the scribes and Pharisees. In this polemical context righteousness is seen as the criterion for entrance into the kingdom of heaven. In 7:21, on the other hand, the immediate context does not refer to the religious leaders of the Jews. In this context doing 'the will of my Father who is in heaven' is seen as the criterion for entrance into the kingdom of heaven. It is therefore evident that Matthew applies the expressions *righteousness* and *doing the will of God* to distinctly different contexts.

We are now in a position to answer the question previously posed: is *dikaiosynē* the key term designating the conduct of the disciples? with a decisive No! It must be reiterated that the rejection of the term *dikaiosynē* does not imply a rejection of the concept represented by this term. As a matter of fact, Matthew stresses proper conduct. Mt 5:20, for example, shows that the conduct of the disciples is to be governed by an extremely meticulous and strict interpretation of the law. Indeed, the goal of this type of conduct is to be perfection. The disciples are to observe everything that Jesus commanded. It is, however, only in polemical contexts or in situations where the true followers of Jesus, i.e. the disciples, form only part of a larger group that the term *dikaiosynē* is used. In situations involving only disciples, Matthew employs the expression 'the will of God'.

Thus Matthew is consistent in his terminological distinction. Properly religious Jews are the righteous whose conduct is governed by righteousness. Properly religious followers of Jesus are disciples whose conduct is governed by the will of God. It is only in explicit or implied polemical contexts in which Jesus is portrayed as contrasting his own teaching with that of Judaism that the righteousness that exceeds that of the scribes and Pharisees is seen as the criterion for entrance into the kingdom of heaven.

With respect to the expression 'the will of God', a further point is noteworthy. There is a difference not only in function but also in meaning between the expressions 'will of God' and 'righteousness'. These two expressions are only related, not identical in meaning. Specifically, the former is more inclusive in meaning than the latter; that is, the concept of righteousness refers exclusively to the demand of God upon man. The expression 'the will of God', on the other hand, is used to refer not only to the demand of God upon man but also to the gift of God for man. The latter use is evident in 18:14 where it is stated that 'it is not the will of my Father who is in heaven that one of these little ones should perish'.

It thus appears that in making the terminological distinction between righteous persons doing righteousness and disciples doing the will of God, Matthew in effect provided not only a clear-cut distinction between properly religious Jews and followers of Jesus but also a concept, i.e. the will of God, which was able to refer to the whole teaching of Jesus, namely proper conduct and soteriology.

Now we are ready to answer the question posed at the beginning of this chapter: what relative significance is attached to the use of the concept of righteousness in the Gospel of Matthew?

It is clear that the ideas expressed by the conceptual terms 'righteous/ righteousness' are not as crucial to the overall message expressed by the Gospel of Matthew as are the ideas expressed by the terms 'disciple/will of God'. In non-polemical contexts dealing exclusively with those who are properly religious in a Christian sense, that is, with those who are members of the church, the concept of righteousness is not used. The concept of righteousness does not pervade Matthaean theology. For example, it plays no crucial role in the Matthaean view of the nature of salvation. Matthew's religious self-understanding is that of a *disciple* doing the *will of God* as distinct from that of a righteous person doing righteousness.

6

THE PROVISIONAL FUNCTION OF THE
MATTHAEAN CONCEPT OF RIGHTEOUSNESS

In the preceding chapter it was shown that the concept of righteousness does not play a crucial role in Matthew's self-understanding as a follower of Jesus. While the Gospel of Matthew clearly indicates that salvation is the gift of God, righteousness is seen only as the demand of God made upon man. Those who are properly religious in a Christian sense are not 'the righteous'. They are 'disciples'. The essence of discipleship is not expressed as 'righteousness' but as 'doing the will of God'.

Having seen the limitations of the use of the concept of righteousness in the Gospel of Matthew, let us now consider the positive side of its use more closely. Why in fact does Matthew make use of the concept of righteousness in his gospel?

It is the conclusion of this study that the concept of righteousness is used in the Gospel of Matthew to provide a point of contact between the religious understanding of first-century Palestinian Jews and the teaching of Jesus as Matthew understood it. In other words, the concept of righteousness is used as a teaching principle leading from the known (contemporary Jewish teaching) to the unknown (the teaching of Jesus).

The concept of righteousness thus is cast in the role of a provisional concept. As a provisional concept it can only facilitate the bridging of a gap in understanding. It is the nature of such a provisional concept that it can never fully express the view to which it points. Consequently, once the way to the new understanding has been shown, the provisional concept is discarded.

Such a process indeed occurs in the Gospel of Matthew. In the previous chapter it was shown that in this gospel the term *dikaiosynē* is reserved strictly for contexts in which Jesus is involved in polemical situations and/ or is dealing with non-disciples or audiences comprising both disciples and non-disciples. In non-polemical contexts dealing exclusively with those who are properly religious in a Christian sense, the concept of righteousness is not used.

In addition to these observations the appropriateness of the use of the

116

concept of righteousness with respect to John the Baptist should be noted. In 3:15 and 21:32 the term *dikaiosyne* occurs in the context of discussions respectively with and about John the Baptist. On the basis of 3:3 and 11 it is clear that John the Baptist is cast into the role of a transitional figure. His function is not to proclaim the entire message of Jesus but only to prepare his way. It is only logical that a provisional concept such as the concept of righteousness be used in the description of such a transitional figure as John the Baptist.

The passage which most clearly denotes the provisional nature of the concept of righteousness is 5:20. It should not be surprising that this passage plays such a role, for the redaction-critical analysis of the seven *dikaiosyne*-passages indicated that 5:20 is one of two passages in which Matthew appears to have had the greatest amount of freedom in the use of the term *dikaiosyne*.[1]

In 5:20 it is implied that both the scribes/Pharisees and the disciples have righteousness. However, the inadequacy of this concept to define the essence of Jesus' teaching is obvious, for the use of *dikaiosyne* is qualified by the stipulation that the righteousness of the disciples must exceed that of the scribes and Pharisees.

The inadequacy of the concept of righteousness to designate the criterion for entrance into the kingdom of heaven (5:20) is also shown in the ensuing discussion. The climax of the train of thought begun in 5:20 is found in 5:48.[2] In this verse the righteousness terminology is abandoned in favour of that of perfection, 'You, therefore, must be perfect, as your heavenly Father is perfect.'

Mt 6:33 was also shown to be an integral part of the structure which included 5:20 and 48. In this passage the term *dikaiosyne* is again qualified, the tacit assumption being that this term by itself did not carry the meaning that needed to be expressed. The righteousness that was to exceed that of the scribes and Pharisees now becomes the righteousness of God.

It is in 7:21, a passage which in contrast to 5:20 is not found in a direct polemical setting involving the scribes and Pharisees, that the transition from the provisional to an absolute concept occurs. While in 5:20 the greater righteousness was the criterion for entrance into the kingdom of heaven, in 7:21 doing the will of God is seen as the criterion. As was demonstrated in the preceding chapter, the concept of salvation is included in the will of God but not in the concept of righteousness.

It is clear that the concept of righteousness by itself was inadequate to express the essence of the teaching of Jesus. This concept was employed solely to provide a vehicle by which the teaching of Jesus could be explained.

Since Matthew uses the concept of righteousness to establish a point of contact between the teaching of Jesus and contemporary religious under-standing, it is to be taken for granted that he thought that this concept was suitable for such a task. It now remains to be seen whether this claim can be substantiated on the basis of external evidence. Does Matthew in fact use the concept of righteousness in a manner that could be understood by his contemporaries?

If no extant literature can be found which indeed uses the concept of righteousness with a meaning parallel to that found in the Gospel of Matthew, then the conclusion presented in this chapter could be called into question. If, on the other hand, there is external evidence for such a meaning, then the proposed conclusion will be substantiated.

In the course of this study a number of similarities between the meaning of the righteousness terminology in the Gospel of Matthew and that of the Dead Sea Scrolls and the Tannaitic literature were noted. This was done primarily to show that certain interpretations were indeed plausible.

At this point it would not serve a useful purpose to list the numerous parallels to which attention has not been drawn. Although such a study may be interesting for its own sake, and on the basis of the facts supplied in chapters 2 and 3 could readily be undertaken, it would not contribute to a decisive answer to the question at hand: does Matthew use the concept of righteousness in a manner that could be understood by his contemporaries?

This question cannot be answered by listing specific similarities. Although there are indeed numerous similarities between the use of the righteousness terminology of the Gospel of Matthew and that of the Dead Sea Scrolls and Tannaitic literature, it could be the case that the differences are so great as to render the similarities meaningless. The question at hand can only be answered on the basis of a comparison of general trends.

Let us therefore look at the terms *eleēmosynē*, *dikaios* and *dikaiosynē* using the methodology outlined above. In the Gospel of Matthew the term *eleēmosynē* consistently refers to almsgiving. Almsgiving in turn is viewed as one aspect of the doing of righteousness (*dikaiosynē*).

In the Tannaitic literature the primary meaning of *tsedaqah* is almsgiving. The use of *tsedaqah* in the Tannaitic literature, however, is not quite as consistent as that of *eleēmosynē* in the Gospel of Matthew. As was shown above, in a few instances the meaning of *tsedaqah* overlapped with that of *tsedeq*. This should not be surprising since the Tannaitic literature is not as homogeneous a body of literature as is the Gospel of Matthew. Nevertheless the primary meaning of *tsedaqah* in the Tannaitic literature is without doubt that of almsgiving.

As in the Gospel of Matthew, so also in the Tannaitic literature, alms-giving is considered to be one among various aspects of the doing of righteousness (*tsedeq*). Matthaean usage of the term *eleēmosynē* obviously corresponds directly to the Tannaitic idea of almsgiving (*tsedaqah*).

That there is no definite proof[3] of the term *tsedaqah* ever referring to almsgiving in the Dead Sea Scrolls does not cast doubt on the foregoing conclusion, especially since there is no evidence that it cannot have such a meaning. The giving of alms is simply not a topic that is stressed in the Dead Sea Scrolls. The parallel between the Gospel of Matthew and the Tannaitic literature is so clear that it cannot be discounted by any argument based on omission. The Matthaean usage of the term *eleēmosynē* can readily be understood in terms of the Tannaitic usage.

One of the most obvious conclusions emerging from the study of the concept of righteousness in the Tannaitic literature was that the term righteous (*tsaddiq*) played an essential role in the definition of those who are properly religious. By far the primary term for the one leading a properly religious life was *tsaddiq*. It should be noted further that to be righteous, to be properly religious, meant to practise the law.

Of the Dead Sea Scrolls the Damascus Document (CD) especially uses the adjective *tsaddiq* as the primary designation for those who are properly religious. As in the Tannaitic literature, the criterion is also observance of the law. In CD, however, the law is not defined as the Mosaic law but as the law of the New Covenant which was made in the Land of Damascus. Nevertheless, in CD as in the Tannaitic literature, the righteous are the properly religious as seen in terms of proper observance of a norm, namely a specific body of law.

This usage corresponds directly with the way the adjective *dikaios* is used in the Gospel of Matthew. As was demonstrated above, Matthew uses this term as the primary designation for those who are considered properly religious in a Jewish sense, namely those who live according to normative religious standards which are based on contemporary interpretation of the law. There is no doubt that the meaning which Matthew attaches to the term *dikaios* could readily be understood in terms of the usage attached to the term *tsaddiq* in the Tannaitic literature and CD.

Not even the Matthaean usage of calling Joseph (1:19) and Jesus (27:19) *dikaios* is in conflict with Tannaitic usage. While it is true that the term *tsaddiq* is mainly used to refer to specific persons living prior to the Tannaitic period, there are instances where this term is applied to persons living during the Tannaitic period. In Mek. Nezikin 18 on Ex 22:22 (III, p. 142; p. 313) R. Simeon and R. Ishmael are said to be *tsaddiq* and in Sifra Emor parasha 1:14 on Lev 21:3 the same is said about Joseph b. Paksas. While it is true that in these cases this is done by way of biblical quotation, it is nevertheless done. Consequently, the Matthaean usage of calling Joseph and Jesus *dikaios* is in harmony with Tannaitic usage.

The noun *dikaiosynē* is used consistently by Matthew to refer to God's demand upon man to live according to a specific norm, the law. Even God's righteousness is seen primarily as a norm for man's conduct in 6:33. The person who lives according to the norm of righteousness in effect has righteousness.[4]

This meaning of the term *dikaiosynē* is in essential agreement with the meaning of the term *tsedeq* in the Tannaitic literature and the Dead Sea Scrolls.[5] There, too, righteousness (*tsedeq*) has both an external and internal aspect insofar as it refers to the norm for man's conduct and the quality a person possesses once he has lived according to this norm. Also *tsedeq* is seen as the demand of God rather than the gift of God. In other words, in both instances righteousness refers to proper conduct rather than to the gift of salvation.

All differences between the meanings of *dikaiosynē* and *tsedeq* in the respective bodies of literature under discussion are minor and directly attributable to the different natures of these bodies of literature. Since the Gospel of Matthew represents a more homogeneous type of literature than the Dead Sea Scrolls and the Tannaitic literature, it might well be expected that its usage of the righteousness terminology would be more consistent. This is indeed the case. Whereas the term *dikaiosynē* is used consistently as described above, the term *tsedeq*, while undoubtedly having a primary meaning parallel to *dikaiosynē*, is in a few passages used with other meanings. In T. Peah 4:18 and T. Maaser Sheni 5:25, *tsedeq*, as found in biblical quotations, is used to refer to almsgiving. This inconsistency in meaning can be traced back to the use of the Old Testament in which the terms *tsedeq* and *tsedaqah* are used interchangeably. In three passages in the Dead Sea Scrolls, i.e. 1QS 10:11, 1QH 11:18 and 1QM 18:8, the term *tsedeq* refers to God's saving, gracious activity, a meaning generally reserved for the term *tsedaqah*.[6] This inconsistency is due largely to the fact that in hymnic materials such as the Thanksgiving Hymns and the Hymn in 1QS 10:9–11:22 traditional modes of expression are easily perpetuated. In this instance it is once again the interchangeability of the terms *tsedeq* and *tsedaqah* as found in the Old Testament which is involved.

Although these exceptions should not be overlooked, neither should their significance be exaggerated. It must be kept in mind that these are indeed in the category of exceptions. The primary meaning of *tsedeq* is without doubt primary in every sense of the word. *Tsedeq* refers to the norm for man's conduct. It is this primary meaning of *tsedeq* which is reflected in the Matthaean use of the term *dikaiosynē*. Thus the trend established in the Tannaitic literature and the Dead Sea Scrolls to differentiate between the terms *tsedeq* and *tsedaqah* is directly reflected in the Gospel of Matthew. *Dikaiosynē* reflects only the meaning of *tsedeq*.

Of course owing to the fact that the combined writings of the Tannaitic literature and the Dead Sea Scrolls compose an enormously larger body of literature than the Gospel of Matthew, it cannot be expected that every aspect of *tsedeq* dealt with in the Tannaitic literature and the Dead Sea Scrolls will be reflected in the Gospel of Matthew. In the Tannaitic literature, for example, juridical behaviour including the idea of leniency in judgment is included in the concept of *tsedeq*. In the Gospel of Matthew this idea is not directly linked to the concept of *dikaiosynē*. This does not mean, however, that correct juridical behaviour was excluded from the Matthaean concept of righteousness. We must simply accept the fact that Matthew only dealt with those aspects which best served his immediate concerns. He was not exhaustive in his presentation of the concept of righteousness.

The conclusion can now be drawn that Matthew uses the concept of righteousness in a way that directly reflects the usage of the Tannaitic literature and the Dead Sea Scrolls. The terms *dikaios* and *tsaddiq* both refer to those who are properly religious in a Jewish sense. The meaning of *eleēmosynē* is identical with the primary meaning of *tsedaqah*, that is, almsgiving. The meaning of *dikaiosynē* directly reflects the main thrust of the primary meaning of *tsedeq*.

Could the Matthaean concept of righteousness be understood by Matthew's audience? Could the agreement in the use of the righteousness terminology between the Gospel of Matthew and the Tannaitic literature/ Dead Sea Scrolls simply be coincidental? Or does this agreement presuppose that the Gospel of Matthew was written in an intellectual milieu similar to that of the Tannaitic literature/Dead Sea Scrolls?

The foregoing comparison justifies the conclusion that the Matthaean concept of righteousness as explicated in the present study was relevant to Matthew's audience. Indeed, the points of contact are so striking as to leave no doubt that with respect to the use of this concept the Gospel of Matthew presupposes an intellectual milieu similar to that of the Jewish-Palestinian writings known as the Tannaitic literature and the Dead Sea Scrolls. By using the concept of righteousness Matthew found a point of contact between the religious understanding of first-century Palestinian Jews and the teaching of Jesus. Matthew could point out that just as Judaism required righteousness, so the teaching of Jesus required righteousness, that is, proper conduct according to the law. Although Jesus required a greater righteousness it was nevertheless a type of righteousness. The greater righteousness, however, composed only part of the teaching of Jesus. The greater righteousness did not specify the means of salvation. For followers of Jesus, salvation came by means of Jesus. He saved people from their sins. The means of salvation for followers of Jesus was thus radically different from that of properly religious Jews who did not attach such a significance to Jesus. The concept of righteousness was unable to express fully the teaching of Jesus as Matthew understood it.

In order to differentiate between the teaching of Judaism and Jesus it was necessary to make a terminological distinction. The term *righteousness* was discarded in favour of the expression *will of God* which included not only the concept of the greater righteousness but also salvation by means of Jesus. The person who lived according to the greater righteousness *and* was saved by means of Jesus was defined by Matthew as being a disciple. After all, such a person was not properly religious in a Jewish sense. Consequently, the designation *righteous one* was discarded in favour of *disciple*.

Thus it is clearly evident that the Jewish righteousness terminology was suitable to refer to a part of the teaching of Jesus. In a sense the righteousness terminology provided the common denominator between the teaching of Judaism and Jesus. It served as a useful point of contact. It could not, however, be used to express the whole teaching of Jesus. Consequently, it could play only a provisional role and in the end had to be discarded. The concept of righteousness is a means to an end rather than the end itself in the Gospel of Matthew.

Were Matthew's contemporaries prepared for the shift from the righteous/righteousness terminology to that of disciple/will of God? In other words, are there parallels for shifts in terminology based on diverging religious understanding?

With respect to this question it is instructive to look at two of the writings constituting the Dead Sea Scrolls, namely the Damascus Document and the Manual of Discipline. Both of these writings betray a sectarian character insofar as their religious understanding differs from that of mainstream Judaism of that time. In the Damascus Document, however, no terminological distinction is made *vis à vis* the mainstream of Judaism. Those who are properly religious are known as the righteous and their conduct is governed by righteousness. The sectarian viewpoint becomes evident only in the definition of righteousness. Rather than referring to the covenant made at Sinai, righteousness is defined in the Damascus Document as referring to the New Covenant made in the Land of Damascus. Thus the righteousness terminology is kept but the basis for righteousness is redefined.

In the Manual of Discipline, on the other hand, one aspect of the righteousness terminology is completely absent while a different significance is attributed to another. In 1QS the term *tsaddiq* is not found and the term *tsedeq* is placed in a subordinate position relative to the term *'emet*. Those who are properly religious are referred to primarily as the sons of truth or light.

They are distinguished by the fact that their conduct corresponds to the truth (*'emet*). Hence in 1QS a religious viewpoint differing from mainstream religious teaching is expressed by means of terminological distinctions. Consequently, not only the meaning of the Matthaean concept of righteousness, but even the shift to another concept is paralleled in the Jewish Palestinian background literature.

Thus to view the Matthaean concept of righteousness from the Pauline perspective is completely to misunderstand Matthew's intention in the use of this concept. The Matthaean concept of righteousness, in contrast to the Pauline one, is not a primary Christian theological concept. The Matthaean concept of righteousness is essentially a Jewish concept, used in a provisional way to provide a point of contact between contemporary Jewish religious understanding and the teaching of Jesus as Matthew understood it.

NOTES

Chapter 1. The problem of the meaning and significance of the Matthaean concept of righteousness

1   *Der Weg der Gerechtigkeit. Untersuchungen zur Theologie des Matthäus* (FRLANT 82; 3rd rev. edn; Göttingen, 1971).

2   'Der Begriff δικαιοσύνη im Matthäus-Evangelium, auf seine Grundlagen untersucht' (2 vols.: Ph.D. dissertation, Martin-Luther-Universität, Halle-Wittenberg, 1957). This dissertation, unpublished except for the article 'Δικαιοσύνη in der diaspora-jüdischen und intertestamentarischen Literatur', *JStJ* 1 (1970), 120–43, is discussed by J. Rohde, *Rediscovering the Teaching of the Evangelists*, ET by Dorothea M. Barton (London, 1968), pp. 90f. The significance of Fiedler's study lies in the fact that the interpretation of righteousness as the gift of God has been taken to its logical extreme. As such this dissertation rounds out the spectrum of possible interpretations which must be taken into account in the present study.

3   See esp. *Weg*, pp. 157f, 179f, 187.

4   See esp. 'Der Begriff', I, pp. 104–51.

5   *The Meaning of Righteousness in Paul* (SNTS Monograph Series, 20; Cambridge, 1972), p. 144. Cf. K. Kertelge, *'Rechtfertigung' bei Paulus* (NTAb NF 3; 2nd edn; Münster, 1971), pp. 46f, who states that Mt 5:20 and 6:1 must be seen in the light of 5:6; B. W. Bacon, *Studies in Matthew* (New York, 1930). p. 134: 'As has been acutely observed the term δικαιοσύνη in Mt can in most cases be best rendered "Salvation".'

6   E. Schweizer, *The Good News According to Matthew*, ET by D. E. Green (London, 1976), p. 55, notes that in Mt 5:20 righteousness 'undoubtedly refers to human actions according to the norm of what God's righteousness requires' while in 6:33 it is 'probably to be understood as a gracious gift, given by God in his mercy'.

7   *Das Evangelium des Matthäus* (Meyers Kommentar Sonderband; Göttingen, 1956). Cf. J. Schniewind, *Das Evangelium nach Matthäus* (NTD 2; Göttingen, 1950).

8   E.g. statements such as the following are made without any recourse to proof: K. Tagawa, 'People and Community in the Gospel of Matthew', *NTS* 16 (1970), 149f; 'It is well known, for example, that δικαιοσύνη is one of the fundamental concepts in Matthew.' Cf. R. Banks, 'Matthew's Understanding of the Law: Authenticity and Interpretation in Matthew 5:17-20', *JBL* 93 (1974), 242; H. Frankemölle, 'Die Makarismen (Mt 5, 1-12; Lk 6, 20-23). Motive und Umfang der redaktionellen Komposition', *BZ* 15 (1971), 71.

9 'Der Begriff', I, p. 4.
10 *Ibid.*
11 *'Rechtfertigung' bei Paulus*, p. 47.
12 *Gerechtigkeit Gottes bei Paulus* (FRLANT 87; 2nd rev. edn; Göttingen, 1966), pp. 190f. Cf. A. Sand, 'Die Polemik gegen "Gesetzlosigkeit" im Evangelium nach Matthäus und bei Paulus', *BZ* 14 (1970), 113; 'Während Matthäus zu den Forderungen des Gesetzes ein positives Verhältnis hat und überzeugt ist, dass durch das Tun des Gesetzes es dem Menschen möglich ist, die von Gott geforderte Gerechtigkeit zu erlangen, steht Paulus dem Gesetz ablehnend gegenüber.'
13 Until the late 1940s the view of the Gospel of Matthew as exhibiting a Jewish-Christian character and being intended for Jewish Christians was generally accepted. With the appearance of an article by K. W. Clark, 'The Gentile Bias in Saint Matthew', *JBL* 66 (1947), 165–72, this view was seriously questioned. The Gentile-Christian character of the Gospel of Matthew was also advocated by P. Nepper-Christensen, *Das Matthäusevangelium, ein judenchristliches Evangelium?* (AThD 1; Aarhus, 1958). However, it was not until the publication of studies by W. Trilling, *Das wahre Israel. Studien zur Theologie des Matthäus-Evangeliums* (StANT 10; 3rd rev. edn; München, 1964), and G. Strecker, *Der Weg der Gerechtigkeit*, in 1959 and 1962 respectively, that the hypothesis stressing a final Gentile-Christian redaction of the Gospel of Matthew was systematically proposed.
14 See ch. 2, sect. 1.
15 *Righteousness*, p. 112.
16 *Ibid.*
17 Thus H. L. Strack, *Introduction to the Talmud and Midrash* (1931; rpt New York, 1969), p. 218.
18 *Righteousness*, pp. 112–27.
19 *Ibid.*, p. 10 n. 2.
20 'Der Begriff', I, pp. 80–7.
21 H. L. Strack and P. Billerbeck, *Kommentar zum Neuen Testament aus Talmud und Midrasch* (4 vols.; 1926; rpt München, 1974).
22 See ch. 3, sect. 1, for the extent of the Tannaitic literature deemed reliable for this study.
23 Fiedler, 'Der Begriff', II, p. 97 n. 2, explains that he has dealt only with the nouns because of limitations of space.
24 It occurs twice: Mt 11:19 = Lk 7:35; Mt 12:37.
25 For a summary of existing studies see H. H. Schmid, *Gerechtigkeit als Weltordnung* (Beiträge zur historischen Theologie 40; Tübingen, 1968), pp. 182–6, and Ziesler, *Righteousness*, pp. 17–46.
26 *Righteousness*, pp. 22–32.
27 *Ibid.*, p. 22 n.2.
28 *Ibid.*, pp. 23f.
29 *Ibid.*, p. 24.
30 *Ibid.*, pp. 24f.
31 *Ibid.*, pp. 25f.
32 *Ibid.*, p. 26.
33 *Ibid.*, pp. 26f.
34 *Ibid.*, p. 27.

35   *Ibid.*, p. 28.
36   *Ibid.*, pp. 28f.
37   *Ibid.*, p. 29.
38   *Ibid.*, p. 30.
39   *Ibid.*, pp. 30f.
40   *Ibid.*, p. 31.
41   *Ibid.*
42   *Ibid.*, pp. 31f.
43   *Ibid.*, pp. 24f.
44   G. A. F. Knight, *A Christian Theology of the Old Testament* (London, 1959), p. 245 n. 1.
45   *Righteousness*, p. 32.
46   'The Concept of Law in the OT', *TDNT*, II (1964), p. 175 n. 2.
47   *Ibid.* Cf. Schmid, *Gerechtigkeit*, pp. 177–9, who refers to *tsedeq/tsedaqah* as to a single concept.
48   *Righteousness*, p. 30.
49   *Ibid.*, p. 27.
50   *Ibid.*, p. 25 n. 2.
51   *Old Testament Theology*, ET by D. M. G. Stalker (2 vols.; Edinburgh, 1962), I, p. 383.
52   *Righteousness*, p. 29.
53   *Theology*, I, p. 372.
54   Schmid, *Gerechtigkeit*, p. 178.
55   *Ibid.*, p. 179.
56   *Theology*, I, p. 373.
57   *TDNT*, II, p. 175.
58   *Theology*, I, pp. 370f.
59   *Ibid.*, p. 377.
60   *TDNT*, II, pp. 174–8.
61   *Righteousness*, p. 38.

Chapter 2. *Tsedeq*, *Tsedaqah* and *Tsaddiq* in the Dead Sea Scrolls

1   M. D. Goulder, *Midrash and Lection in Matthew* (London, 1974), has questioned this view. Goulder states that he has 'found no considerable passage' (p. 474) in the Gospel of Matthew which seems to require a non-Marcan written or oral source. Among the 'considerable passages' he does not include the narratives concerning Pilate's wife and the fish and the stater (*ibid.*). It should also be noted that Goulder leaves room for yet other non-Marcan traditions in the Matthaean community. 'The names of Joseph, Mary's husband, and Caiaphas the high priest, were not in Mark; and Chorazin and Barabbas' name Jesus may be due to tradition also' (*ibid.*). Thus even Goulder is forced to admit that Matthew had at least some traditional materials in addition to Mark before him and 'adapting Mark by midrash and through lection' (p. 475) can be regarded as a particular way of carrying on redactional activity. Goulder has therefore not refuted the basis of *Redaktionsgeschichte*.

2   Bo Reicke, 'Die Ta'āmire-Schriften und die Damaskus-Fragmente', *StTh* 2 (1949), 63, suggests that like all writings from the ancient Near East, these writings too did not come into being all at once but 'recht langsam, auf Grund einer anfänglich mündlichen Entwicklung'.

3   M. Burrows, 'The Discipline Manual of the Judean Covenanters', *OSt* 8 (1950), 162, notes with respect to 1QS, 'it was composed in what may be called "scrapbook fashion". Separate and independent bodies of material seem to have been copied on the same scroll in the order in which they came into the copyist's hands, much as we may suppose the books of the Old Testament prophets were put together.'

4   J. L. Teicher, 'The Damascus Fragments and the Origin of the Jewish Christian Sect', *JJS* 2 (1951), 115f.

5   For a discussion of the problem of dating see esp. H. A. Butler, 'The Chronological Sequence of the Scrolls of Qumran Cave One', *RQ* 2 (1960), 533-9; I. Rabinowitz, 'Sequence and Dates of the Extra-Biblical Dead Sea Scroll Texts and "Damascus" Fragments', *VT* 3 (1953), 175-85.

6   Cf. Y. Yadin, *The Message of the Scrolls* (New York, 1957), p. 161. Some scholars have attempted to give a more exact date. E.g. A. Dupont-Sommer, *The Essene Writings from Qumran*, ET by G. Vermes (Oxford, 1961), p. 340, agrees with R. de Vaux that the date of the concealing of the scrolls was June A.D. 68.

7   *Essene Writings*, p. 340.

8   G. Vermes, *The Dead Sea Scrolls in English* (rev. edn; Harmondsworth, 1968), p. 71.

9   *Ibid.*, p. 123.

10 *Gott und Belial. Traditionsgeschichtliche Untersuchungen zum Dualismus in den Texten aus Qumran* (StUNT 6; Göttingen, 1969).

11 'Sequence and Dates', p. 178.

12 *Der Lehrer der Gerechtigkeit* (StUNT 2; Göttingen, 1963), pp. 169-73. Cf. J. Becker, *Das Heil Gottes. Heils- und Sündenbegriffe in den Qumrantexten und im Neuen Testament* (StUNT 3; Göttingen, 1964), pp. 50-6; S. Holm-Nielsen, *Hodayot. Psalms from Qumran* (AThD 2; Aarhus, 1960), pp. 319ff; J. Maier, *Die Texte vom Toten Meer* (2 vols.; München, 1960), II, p. 63.

13 For a discussion of strata in 1QS see Osten-Sacken, *Gott und Belial*, p. 239; Claus-Hunno Hunzinger, 'Beobachtungen zur Entwicklung der Disziplinarordnung der Gemeinde von Qumran', in H. Bardtke (ed.), *Qumran-Probleme* (Berlin, 1963), pp. 231-47; E. F. Sutcliffe, 'The First Fifteen Members of the Qumran community. A Note on 1QS 8:1ff.', *JSS* 4 (1959), 134-8; P. Wernberg-Møller, *The Manual of Discipline* (StTDJ 1; Leiden, 1957), pp. 56 n. 49, 111 n. 73; Becker, *Heil Gottes*, pp. 39-42; Maier, *Die Texte vom Toten Meer*, I, p. 21; J. Murphy-O'Connor, 'La genèse littéraire de la Régle de la Communauté', *RB* 76 (1969), 528-49.

14 Claus-Hunno Hunzinger, 'Fragmente einer älteren Fassung des Buches Milḥamā aus Höhle 4 von Qumrān', *ZAW* 69 (1957), 131-51, has compared 1QM with 4QM^a (70 fragments discovered in 1952 in cave 4) and concludes, 'Wir hätten dann in 4QM^a eine Kopie des alten, nicht-qumranischen Textes des Buches Milḥamā vor uns, während 1QM eine sozusagen "qumränisierte" Fassung darstelle.' See also Becker, *Heil Gottes*, pp. 43-50; J. van der Ploeg, 'Zur literarischen Komposition der Kriegsrolle', in H. Bardtke (ed.), *Qumran-Probleme* (Berlin, 1963), p. 293.

15 Thus Becker, *Heil Gottes*, pp. 56f; H. W. Huppenbauer, 'Zur Eschatologie der Damaskusschrift', *RQ* 4 (1964), 567f; Rabinowitz, 'Sequence and Dates', p. 175 n. 2.

16 While the Damascus Document is generally included among the Dead Sea
   Scrolls, it should be noted that only fragments of this writing were found
   in the caves of Qumran. The Damascus Document is also known as the
   Zadokite Document.

17 S. Schechter, *Fragments of a Zadokite Work* (Documents of Jewish Sectaries
   1; Cambridge, 1910; rpt n.p., 1970).

18 Yadin, *The Message of the Scrolls*, p. 122.

19 M. Burrows, *More Light on the Dead Sea Scrolls* (New York, 1958), pp.
   254f; cf. Reicke, 'Die Ta'āmire-Schriften und die Damaskus-Fragmente',
   p. 63; 'Die Ta'āmire Gemeinde und die Damaskus-Sekte . . . können aber
   kaum identisch sein, wegen der geographischen Verhältnisse.'

20 See H. H. Rowley, 'Some Traces of the History of the Qumran Sect', *ThZ*
   13 (1957), 535ff.

21 'The Chronological Sequence of the Scrolls of Qumran Cave One', p. 535.
   Other scholars who claim that CD is earlier than 1QS are Rowley, *op. cit.*,
   p. 539; B. Otzen, 'Die neugefundenen hebräischen Sektenschriften und die
   Testamente der zwölf Patriarchen', *StTh* 7 (1953), 141.

22 Thus W. H. Brownlee, 'A Comparison of the Covenanters of the Dead Sea
   Scrolls with Pre-Christian Jewish Sects', *BA* 13 (1950), 53; Burrows, 'The
   Discipline Manual', p. 184; F. M. Cross, jun., *The Ancient Library of
   Qumran and Modern Biblical Studies* (Garden City, N.Y., 1958), p. 60 n.
   46; Rabinowitz, 'Sequence and Dates', p. 185; M. H. Segal, 'The Habakkuk
   "Commentary" and the Damascus Fragments', *JBL* 70 (1951), 132f;
   Vermes, *Dead Sea Scrolls*, pp. 71, 95.

23 Thus Cross, *The Ancient Library of Qumran*, p. 60 n. 46; J. van der Ploeg,
   *The Excavations at Qumran. A Survey of the Judean Brotherhood and its
   Ideas*, ET by K. Smyth (London, 1958), pp. 147f.

24 Maier, *Die Texte vom Toten Meer*, II, p. 63, notes that the majority of
   scholars support the idea that the hymns in 1QH stem from a single author,
   the Teacher of Righteousness. Maier argues, however, that it has not been
   proved that there is a single author. J. Licht, 'The Doctrine of the Thanksgiving Scroll', *IEJ* 6 (1956), 2, argues for a single author of 1QH not on the
   basis of the authorship of the Teacher of Righteousness but for the following
   reason: 'This very monotony, however, proves on closer inspection to be its
   true unity, for insofar as we can judge now, DST is the work of one man
   developing what is almost a single theme in a long series of variations.'

25 *The Faith of Qumran*, ET by E. T. Sander (Philadelphia, 1963), p. v.

26 *Righteousness*, pp. 85–94.

27 *Ibid.* Ziesler points out that Ephesians (p. 153) and the Pastoral Epistles (p.
   154) should not be used as material for Pauline theology. He also notes
   possible problems with respect to the authorship of Philippians (p. 148 n. 1),
   Colossians and Thessalonians (p. 152 n. 4).

28 *'Rechtfertigung' bei Paulus*, pp. 28–33.

29 *Ibid.*, p. 28 n. 62, Kertelge refers to Becker, *Heil Gottes*, pp. 120, 126, 149f.

30 It is not implied that the analogy between the Gospel of Matthew and the
   various Dead Sea Scrolls holds in all details.

31 'Der Begriff', I, pp. 72–80.

32 This nomenclature is the one found in *Gesenius' Hebrew Grammar*, 2nd
   English edn, ET by A. E. Cowley (Oxford, 1910), pp. 416f. J. Weingreen,

'The Construct-Genitive Relation in Hebrew Syntax', *VT* 4 (1954), 51, suggests that in this case the genitive really has the effect of an adjective and notes that an earlier edition of *Gesenius' Hebrew Grammar*, ET by B. Davies (London, 1869), p. 265, refers to this kind of genitive as expressing the idea of an adjective.

33 J. Weingreen, 'The Title Moreh Sedek', *JSS* 6 (1961), 169. There are a number of other scholars who also treat *tsedeq* adjectivally. For example, M. Black, *The Scrolls and Christian Origins* (London, 1961), p. 20, talks about the so-called Teacher of Righteousness and argues that 'The title itself appears to mean the "true (legitimate) teacher", in contradistinction to a "false teacher".' W. H. Brownlee, 'The Habakkuk Commentary', in M. Burrows (ed.), *The Dead Sea Scrolls of St. Mark's Monastery*, I (New Haven, 1950), p. xix, writes, 'His chief interest was in the Righteous Teacher (or Teacher of Righteousness)', but in the remainder of his exposition he uses the title 'Righteous Teacher' exclusively. Cross, *The Ancient Library of Qumran*, p. 83 n. 3, prefers the translation 'Righteous Teacher', for he says that *tsedeq* is not an objective genitive. He does, however, admit that the 'Righteous Teacher' teaches righteousness.

34 Weingreen, 'The Title Moreh Sedek', pp. 168f. He notes that in 2 Chron 15:3, for example, *tsedeq* is equivalent to *'emet*. It is interesting to note that G. Jeremias, *Lehrer*, pp. 312f, uses the OT, i.e. esp. Hos 10:12, as proof that *tsedeq* is to be understood as an objective genitive in the title *moreh tsedeq*.

35 Weingreen, 'The Title Moreh Sedek', p. 169, refers to expressions such as *g-r ts-d-q*, *k-h-n ts-d-q*, and *m-sh-y-h ts-d-q*.

36 *Ibid.*, p. 166; 'It is, in fact, not unusual to find the title Môrēh Ṣedek printed on the official notepaper of a contemporary rabbi, as the formal attestation of his full rabbinic qualification to act as judge.'

37 The majority of scholars favour the view that *tsedeq* is an objective genitive, e.g. F. F. Bruce, *The Teacher of Righteousness in the Qumran Texts* (London, 1956), p. 7; M. Burrows, *The Dead Sea Scrolls* (New York, 1955), p. 349; Dupont-Sommer, *Essene Writings*, pp. 358ff; G. Jeremias, *Lehrer*, pp. 308–16; E. Lohse, *Die Texte aus Qumran. Hebräisch und Deutsch* (2nd rev. edn; Darmstadt, 1971), who uses the translation 'Lehrer der Gerechtigkeit', e.g. CD 1:11, p. 67; Vermes, *Dead Sea Scrolls*, pp. 58ff.

38 So C. Rabin, *The Zadokite Documents* (2nd rev. edn; Oxford, 1958), p. 22. Cf. G. Jeremias, *Lehrer*, p. 312; 'bis auftreten wird, der am Ende der Zeit Gerechtigkeit lehren wird'; Vermes, *Dead Sea Scrolls*, p. 103; 'until he comes who shall teach righteousness at the end of days'.

39 Cf. G. Jeremias, *Lehrer*, p. 312. 'An dieser Stelle kann *ts-d-q* nur das Object der Lehre sein.'

40 The following three editions of the text all agree as to the reading: A. M. Habermann, *The Scrolls from the Judean Desert* (Tel Aviv, 1959), p. 80; Lohse, *Texte*, p. 76; Rabin, *The Zadokite Documents*, p. 23.

41 L. Finkelstein, *Sifre on Deuteronomy* (1939; rpt New York, 1969), p. 199.

42 *Lehrer*, pp. 313f. Jeremias also notes that it is generally acknowledged that the title *moreh (ha-)tsedeq* is probably based on Hos 10:12 and Joel 2:23, and that not only in Hos 10:12 but also in Joel 2:23 *tsedeq/tsedaqah* can only be understood as being objective.

43 *Texte*, pp. 67, 77, 107. Cf. Maier, *Die Texte vom Toten Meer*, I, pp. 47, 54,

70, and Dupont-Sommer, *Essene Writings*, pp. 122, 131, 141, who translates both expressions as 'Teacher of Righteousness'.

44   Thus Rabin, *The Zadokite Documents*, pp. 3, 23; Dupont-Sommer, *Essene Writings*, p. 131 n. 6. For the view that these expressions refer to different persons see L. Ginzberg, *An Unknown Jewish Sect* (New York, 1976), p. 220; 'This very substitution of *y-w-r-h h-ts-d-q* here, for the usual *m-w-r-h ts-d-q* in our document, alludes to the distinction between the status of Elijah and that of other teachers of the law.' Cf. A. S. van der Woude, *Die messianischen Vorstellungen der Gemeinde von Qumrân* (Studia Semitica Neerlandica; Assen, 1957), pp. 72ff, who states that CD 1:11 refers to the historical Teacher of Righteousness and CD 6:11 to Elijah.

45   I could not detect a significant difference in meaning between expressions in which *tsedeq* did or did not have the definite article.

46   For a more detailed discussion of this passage see below in this section. The use of the definite article also suggests the translation 'three kinds of righteousness'.

47   It must be noted that although the best English translation of the verb *y-r-h* is 'to teach', this translation in actual fact does not bring out the full meaning of this verb. Weingreen, 'The Title Moreh Sedek', p. 173, has pointed out that in Rabbinic Hebrew the use of the hiph'il form *moreh* did not imply the involvement of a teacher or guide but that 'the significance of this word is not instructive but legal'. Weingreen admits, however, that it is hard to find an English equivalent and in fact he does not offer an English translation of this title.

48   The primary argument in favour of the translation 'Righteous Teacher' is the analogy to the expression *moreh ha-yahid* (CD 20:1) which can be translated as 'Unique Teacher'. Cf. Dupont-Sommer, *Essene Writings*, p. 139. Although such a meaning is probable, it is by no means certain. Lohse, *Texte*, p. 105, has suggested the translation 'der Lehrer der Gemeinschaft' on the basis of the emendation *moreh ha-yahad*.

49   Translation by Vermes, *Dead Sea Scrolls*, p. 97.

50   With respect to the esoteric factor in the teaching see G. Jeremias, *Lehrer*, pp. 314f.

51   See also CD 20:29, *huqqe ha-berit*, precepts of the covenant.

52   The New Covenant, *ha-berit ha-hadashah*, is mentioned in CD 6:19, 8:21, 19:33f, 20:12.

53   *An Unknown Jewish Sect*, p. 209 n. 1; 'When governed by *h-w-r-h*, *ts-d-q* means that which is true or right, in our document the true interpretation of the Torah.' This view is supported by Black, *The Scrolls and Christian Origins*, p. 19, who gives 'true Doctor of the Law' as a possible translation of *moreh tsedeq*, and by T.H. Gaster, *The Dead Sea Scriptures. In English Translation with Introduction and Notes* (Garden City, N.Y., 1956), p. 61, who translates the title *moreh tsedeq* in CD 1:11 as 'one who could teach the Law correctly'.

54   Weingreen, 'The Title Moreh Sedek', p. 173, points out that the term *moreh* 'was used to designate the rabbinic function, which was not merely to expound the Tôrâ, but to apply and enforce Halakhic decisions'. Consequently, it is not only the term *tsedeq* which implies that the Teacher of Righteousness was associated with the law.

55 Rabin, The *Zadokite Documents*, p. 42, indicates that this is the Teacher of Righteousness mentioned in CD 20:32.

56 *Righteousness*, p. 88.

57 A. R. C. Leaney, *The Rule of Qumran and its Meaning* (New Testament Library; London, 1966), p. 128, suggests that this formula of confession is borrowed from a fixed ritual and may ultimately be based on 1 Kings 8:47. Wernberg-Møller, *Manual of Discipline*, p. 51 n. 52, agrees that this confession is based on 1 Kings 8:47 but points out that in CD 20:28–30 the ceremonial character of the confession does not appear as it does in 1QS 1:24–6.

58 In this case *tsedeq* may not be an objective genitive and could be translated adjectivally. In actual fact, however, there is little difference in meaning between the expressions 'ordinances of righteousness' and 'righteous ordinances'. Since the concept of righteousness is stressed in the Damascus Document the former translation is to be preferred in the interest of clarity.

59 Cf. Dupont-Sommer, *Essene Writings*, p. 131 nn. 5, 6; Rabin, *The Zadokite Documents*, p. 23 n. 11; Ziesler, *Righteousness*, p. 92.

60 *Righteousness*, p. 89.

61 CD 1:19, 20; 4:7; 11:21; 20:20.

62 I follow the suggestion of K. G. Kuhn, *Konkordanz zu den Qumrantexten* (Göttingen, 1960), p. 185 n. 1, that *ts-d-q-m* stands for *ts-d-y-q-y-m*. Cf. Lohse, *Texte*, p. 90, *tsaddiqim* and Rabin, *The Zadokite Documents*, p. 58, who gives the translation 'prayer of the righteous', thus treating *ts-d-q-m* adjectivally, but Habermann, *The Scrolls*, p. 85, who reads *tsidqam*.

63 Thus R. Kittel (ed.), *Biblia Hebraica* (7th rev. edn; Stuttgart, 1968). Schechter, *Fragments of a Zadokite Work*, p. 82 n. 3, notes that there is a discrepancy between the reading *yesharim* of Prov 15:8 and *ts-d-q-m* in our text.

64 Schechter, *op. cit.*, p. 82 n. 3.

65 CD 2:13.

66 CD 20:2. The adjective *yashar* also occurs in 3:6, 8:7 and 19:20 but in this case it does not refer to persons.

67 CD 20:2, 5, 7.

68 CD 7:5–8:21 of MS. A is parallel to 19:1–34 of MS. B. Consequently, the reference to *tsedaqah* in 8:14 and 19:27 must be counted as a single occurrence.

69 *Righteousness*, pp. 89f.

70 Fiedler, 'Der Begriff', I, pp. 73f. Fiedler's analysis consists primarily of the assertion that CD 1:11, 6:11 and 20:32 are based on Hos 10:12; CD 1:1 on Is 51:7; CD 8:14 (19:27) on Deut 9:5; CD 20:11, 33 on Deut 4:8; CD 1:16 and 20:17 on OT thought in general. He fails, however, to see how the term *tsedeq* is actually used in the context of CD.

71 The statistics in this study are generally based on Kuhn's *Konkordanz*. With respect to 1QS 1:26, however, I have not followed Kuhn's reading of *w-ts-d-y-[q* but that of Lohse, *Texte*, p. 6, *watsede*[*q*, and Habermann, *The Scrolls*, p. 61, *watsedeq*. Since 1QS 1:24–6 and CD 20:28–30 are parallel and the reading in CD 20:29 is definitely *tsedeq*, Kuhn's reading in 1QS 1:26 is doubtful not only on textual but also on contextual grounds.

72 A number of scholars suggest that the Teacher of Righteousness is to be regarded as the author of various parts of 1QS. E.g. Leaney, *Rule of Qumran*,

p. 115, suggests that the Teacher of Righteousness is the author of 1QS 10:1–11:22. Dupont-Sommer, *Essene Writings*, pp. 71f, suggests that even though the Teacher of Righteousness is not explicitly mentioned in 1QS, this writing may basically derive from him. R. Schnackenburg, 'Die Erwartung des "Propheten" nach dem Neuen Testament und den Qumran-Texten', *TU* 73 (1959), 635, on the other hand, explains, 'In 1QS, wo der "Lehrer der Gerechtigkeit" noch nicht genannt wird, wartet man auf den Propheten und die beiden Messias, ähnlich nach den Testimonia.' Rowley, 'Some Traces of the History of the Qumran Sect', p. 539, argues that 1QS could not have been written by the Teacher of Righteousness.

73 This number includes 1QS 1:26 (see n. 71 above) and 1QS 9:14. For 1QS 9:14 Habermann, *The Scrolls*, p. 69, reads *b-n-y h-ts-d-w-q*; Leaney, *Rule of Qumran*, p. 231, gives the translation 'the sons of Zadok' and explains that in this case this is a title for the whole community. However, the expression 'sons of Zadok' most naturally refers to the priesthood. Consequently, it has been suggested that *b-n-y h-ts-d-w-q* really stands for *bene ha-tsedeq*; thus Lohse, *Texte*, p. 34 n. d; Kuhn, *Konkordanz*, p. 185 n. 2; W. H. Brownlee, 'The Dead Sea Manual of Discipline', *BASOR* Supplementary Studies 10–12 (1951), 37 n. 24. This emendation is supported by the discovery in cave 4 of a new MS. of 1QS. J. T. Milik, 'Recensions', *RB* 67 (1960), 414, notes with respect to 1QS 9:14 that MS. S[e] reads 'bny hṣdq lpy rwhwh.' Wernberg-Møller, *Manual of Discipline*, p. 90 n. 12 (cf. his '*Tsedeq*, *Tsaddiq* and *Tsedaqah* in the Zadokite Fragments (CDC), the Manual of Discipline (DSD) and the Habakkuk-Commentary (DSH)', *VT* 3 (1953), 310f), suggests that an emendation is not necessary when the transcription is corrected to *b-n-y h-ts-d-y-q*, for in the Samaritan dialect this would be equivalent to *b-n-y h-ts-d-q*.

74 1QS 1:26; 4:24; 10:11; 11:15, 16.

75 1QS 1:13; 2:24; 3:1, 20, 22; 4:2, 4, 9; 9:5, 14, 17.

76 1QS 10:26.

77 Dupont-Sommer, *Essene Writings*, p. 80.

78 Leaney, *Rule of Qumran*, p. 144.

79 Dupont-Sommer, *Essene Writings*, p. 93.

80 *Ibid.*, p. 78.

81 G. Jeremias, *Lehrer*, pp. 309f, argues that in 1QS 1:13, 4:9 and 9:5 *tsedeq* is used adjectivally.

82 Ziesler, *Righteousness*, pp. 88–90, has 15 instead of 17 references because he does not include 1QS 1:26 and 9:14.

83 1QS 2:24; 4:9, 24; 9:5; 11:16.

84 1QS 3:20, 22; 4:2.

85 1QS 9:17; 10:26.

86 1QS 3:1; 4:4.

87 1QS 1:13.

88 1QS 10:11; 11:15 (both legal and gracious).

89 Fiedler, 'Der Begriff', II, p. 77 n. 116, claims that *tsedeq* refers specifically to God's righteousness only in 1QS 1:13 and 11:15.

90 Cf. Ziesler, *Righteousness*, pp. 88f; Leaney, *Rule of Qumran*, p. 246; Kertelge, '*Rechtfertigung' bei Paulus*, p. 32.

91 *Righteousness*, p. 89 n. 1.

92 Cf. *ibid.*, pp. 88–90.

93   *Ibid.*, pp. 89f. Ziesler suggests that in 1QS 5:4 and 8:2 *tsedaqah* refers to
      the behaviour of the covenant people. With the possible exception of 4QS1
      (39) 1:18 where *tsedaqah* is used to refer to the graciousness of angels,
      Ziesler claims that there is no passage in the Dead Sea Scrolls where *tsedaqah*
      has the connotation of benevolence in the sense of almsgiving. He agrees
      with C. F. D. Moule who suggested to him privately 'that as a monastic
      group, eschewing private property, having a common life which would
      render "charity" unnecessary within the sect, and having small concern with
      the material welfare of outsiders, the covenanters would have little scope
      for almsgiving' (*ibid.*, p. 90 n. 5). However, even though the social con-
      ditions reflected in 1QS and CD are admittedly different, it should never-
      theless be noted that CD 14:13ff specifically deals with funds allotted to
      charity.
94   *Righteousness*, pp. 88f. It should be noted that 8 of the 9 occurrences are
      found in the Hymn, i.e. 1QS 10:9–11:22.
95   Up to this point the translation is that of Leaney, *Rule of Qumran*, p. 235.
      The rest of the translation is that of Dupont-Sommer, *Essene Writings*,
      p. 100.
96   Leaney, *Rule of Qumran*, p. 236, designates 1QS 10:8b–11:15a as the
      Hymn and 11:15b–22 as the Benediction. Dupont-Sommer, *Essene Writings*,
      p. 70, refers to 1QS 10:1–11:22 as the Hymn.
97   Cf. Becker, *Heil Gottes*, pp. 39–42. Leaney, *Rule of Qumran*, p. 115, suggests
      that the author of 1QS 10:1–11:22 is the same as the author of 1QH.
98   'Der Begriff', I, p. 75.
99   Cf. *ibid.*, II, p. 81 n. 126; G. Jeremias, *Lehrer*, p. 311, points out that an
      original *'emet* was replaced by a *tsedeq* in 1QH 2:4.
100   1QS 1:26; 2:24; 4:2, 24; 9:17. Cf. G. Jeremias, *Lehrer*, p. 314.
101   CD 3:15; 20:29f, 31. Cf. G. Jeremias, *Lehrer*, p. 314.
102   Translated as 'Seher der Wahrheit' by Lohse, *Texte*, p. 69; cf. Rabin, *The
      Zadokite Documents*, p. 8. The translations of Dupont-Sommer, *Essene
      Writings*, p. 124, 'He showed the truth', and Vermes, *Dead Sea Scrolls*,
      p. 98, 'He proclaimed the truth', are not as accurate.
103   CD 3:15; 20:29f, 31.
104   1QS 3:20, 22; 4:2, 4, 9, 24.
105   Dupont-Sommer, *Essene Writings*, p. 82.
106   *Rule of Qumran*, p. 37.
107   *Ibid.* For the importance of this section see also Dupont-Sommer, *Essene
      Writings*, p. 77 n. 3; Black, *The Scrolls and Christian Origins*, p. 131; Yadin,
      The Message of the Scrolls, p. 117.
108   *Rule of Qumran*, p. 46.
109   1QS 3:20, 22; 9:14. With respect to 9:14 see n. 73 above.
110   *Bene 'emet*, 1QS 4:5, 6.
111   *Bene 'or*, 1QS 1:9; 2:16; 3:13, 24, 25.
112   *Bene 'awel*, 1QS 3:21; *'anshe ha-'awel*, 1QS 5:2, 10; 8:13; 9:17.
113   *Bene hoshek*, 1QS 1:10.
114   D. Barthélemy and J. T. Milik, *DJD*, I. *Qumran Cave I* (Oxford, 1955),
      p. 78, F 8–10, line 6, *m-w-r-y h-ts-d-q*. J. T. Milik, 'Fragments d'un midrash
      de Michée dans les manuscrits de Qumran', *RB* 59 (1952), 415, argues that
      the reading *m-w-r-y* instead of *m-w-r-h* is an intentional 'intensification du

nom du Maître, par le pluriel'. But G. Jeremias, *Lehrer*, p. 147, is probably right in asserting that *m-w-r-y* is simply an orthographic variant for *m-w-r-h*. He points to the similar usage in 1QM 19:3 (*'-w-sh-y* for *'-w-sh-h*) and 1QH 7:17 (*m-h-s-y* for *m-h-s-h*).

115 Cf. Dupont-Sommer, *Essene Writings*, p. 278; G. Jeremias, *Lehrer*, p. 147.

116 Lohse, *Texte*, p. 258.

117 *Ibid.*, p. 246.

118 Dupont-Sommer, *Essene Writings*, p. 315.

119 1QSb 2:26, 3:24, 5:26.

120 1QSb 1:2, 2:28, 3:24.

121 Dupont-Sommer, *Essene Writings*, p. 110 n. 1, shows that there must have been at least a sixth column.

122 There are further references to words connected with the root *ts-d-q* in the following passages. The noun *tsedeq* occurs in 1Q27 1:5, 6 (*DJD*, I, p. 103 (Leaney, *Rule of Qumran*, p. 156, notes that in 1:6 there is a personification of righteousness)), 1Q36 15:2 (*DJD*, I, p. 139) and 25:4 (*DJD*, I, p. 141). In 4QS1 (39) I, i, 18 the expression *d-b-r-y ts-d-q* occurs (J. Strugnell, 'The Angelic Liturgy at Qumrân, 4Q Serek Šîrôt 'Ôlat Haššabbāt', *VT* 7 (suppl.) (1960), 322). The expression *'-t-h '-d-w-n-y h-ts-d-q-h* occurs in 4QDibHam 6:3 (M. Baillet, 'Un recueil liturgique de Qumrân, Grotte 4: les paroles des luminaires', *RB* 68 (1961), 210). The adjective *tsaddiq* occurs in 1Q34 F 3, 1:2, 3, 5 (*DJD*, I, p. 153); 1Q51 1:3 (*DJD*, I, p. 145).

123 The meaning of the remaining reference to *tsedeq* in 1QH 2:4 is uncertain because of lacunae in the text.

124 In 1QH 1:30, 2:13f, 4:40 and 16:4f *tsedeq* and *'emet* have parallel meanings and 1QH 2:4 shows that they could be used interchangeably since an original *'emet* is replaced by a *tsedeq* in this passage.

125 Cf. G. Morawe, *Aufbau und Abgrenzung der Loblieder von Qumrân* (ThA 16; Berlin, 1961), p. 136; Holm-Nielsen, *Hodayot*, p. 138; Dupont-Sommer, *Essene Writings*, p. 224.

126 Thus Morawe, *op. cit.*, p. 139. Cf. Holm-Nielsen, *Hodayot*, pp. 17ff.

127 Holm-Nielsen, *Hodayot*, pp. 28, 140.

128 The occurrences of the noun *tsedaqah* in 1QH 8:2 and 18:17 have not been discussed since there are too many lacunae in these passages.

129 1QH 6:29, 7:30, 9:35, 10:27, 11:11.

130 1QH 14:2 and according to Lohse, *Texte*, p. 116, also in 2:14, [*'anshe*] *'emet*.

131 Morawe, *Aufbau und Abgrenzung der Loblieder von Qumrân*, p. 161, shows that only 6 out of a total of 33 hymns are preserved in their entirety.

132 1QM 1:8; 3:6; 13:3, 10; 17:8; but the reading in 1:8 is not certain. The lacuna is completed as follows by various scholars: [*'emet watsede*]*q* by Habermann, *The Scrolls*, p. 95; [*da'at watsede*]*q* by Lohse, *Texte*, p. 180; *d*-[*'-t w-ts-*]*d-q* by Y. Yadin, *The Scroll of the War of the Sons of Light against the Sons of Darkness*, ET by Batya and Chaim Rabin (Oxford, 1962), p. 259; 'Then [the sons of righteou]sness' by Dupont-Sommer, *Essene Writings*, p. 170. The reading in 13:10 is also uncertain. While Yadin, *Scroll of the War*, p. 323, Lohse, *Texte*, p. 210, and Habermann, *The Scrolls*, p. 104, all fill the lacuna as *bene tsede*]*q*, Dupont-Sommer, *Essene Writings*, p. 189, has '[all the angels of justi]ce' and Gaster, *Dead Sea Scriptures*, p. 298, has 'all works of righteousness'.

133   Cf. Ziesler, *Righteousness*, p. 88.

134   So Yadin, *Scroll of the War*, p. 274 n. 6.

135   *Righteousness*, p. 88.

136   1QM 1:16; 4:6; 11:14; 13:1, 2, 9, 10 (twice), 12, 15; 14:12; 17:8.

137   See n. 132 above.

138   The expression *bene 'or* occurs in 1QM 1:1, 3, 9, 11, 13 and perhaps also
        in the lacunae in 13:16 (cf. Lohse, *Texte*, p. 210) and 1:16 (cf. Habermann,
        The Scrolls, p. 96).

139   The expression *bene hoshek* occurs in 1QM 1:1, 7, 10, 16; 3:6, 9; 13:16;
        14:17; 16:11 and possibly in the lacuna in 1:15 (cf. Habermann, *The
        Scrolls*, p. 95).

140   1QM 17:8 and possibly in 1:16 where Habermann, *The Scrolls*, p. 96, fills
        the lacuna as *'anshe ha-] 'emet.*

141   1QpHab 1:13, 5:10, 7:4, 8:3, 9:10, 11:5.

142   1QpHab 2:2, Habermann, *The Scrolls*, p. 43, has the reading *moreh
        ha-tsedeq.* Burrows (ed.), *The Dead Sea Scrolls of St. Mark's Monastery*, I,
        pl. LV, shows the necessity for a letter following the *q, m-w-r-h h-ts-. -q-.,*
        and the following scholars have suggested the reading *h-ts-d-q-h:* Lohse,
        Texte, p. 228; Kuhn, *Konkordanz*, p. 186; K. Elliger, *Studien zum Habakuk-
        Kommentar vom Toten Meer* (Tübingen, 1953), Beilage, p. 4.

143   Hab 1:4 is quoted in 1QpHab 1:12, and Hab 1:13 in 1QpHab 5:9. Possibly
        there is another occurrence of the adjective *tsaddiq* in 1QpHab 7:17, for the
        lacuna should be filled with Hab 2:4.

144   It should be noted that in 1QpHab the title *moreh ha-tsedeq is written* with
        the definite article while in CD it is not. It is generally agreed that the refer-
        ences in 1QpHab and CD refer to the same title. Cf. G. Jeremias, *Lehrer*,
        pp. 308ff.

145   Thus Elliger, *Studien zum Habakuk-Kommentar vom Toten Meer*, p. 168
        n. d, suggests that in 1QpHab 2:2, just as in 1:13, 5:10 and 7:4, there origi-
        nally was the reading *moreh ha-tsedeq.* The reading in 2:2 resulted because
        of a confusion with the definite article; 'Vermutlich erklärt sie sich aus dem
        Versehen eines Abschreibers, der das vor das Wort gehörende *h* (des Artikels)
        hinten setzte, so dass die Nachtragung des Artikels über der Zeile nötig
        wurde' (*ibid.*, p. 14).

146   Cf. Lohse, *Texte*, p. 236.

147   4QpPs37 2:26, 4:8.

148   Ps 37:12 is quoted in 4QpPs37 2:12; Ps 37:16 in 2:21; Ps 37:21 in 3:9; Ps
        37:29 in 4:2; Ps 37:32 in 4:7. It is also probable that Ps 37:17 is quoted in
        the lacuna in 4QpPs37 2:23; Ps 37:25 in 3:17; Ps 37:30 in 4:3; Ps 37:39
        in 4:19.

149   So K. G. Kuhn, 'Nachträge zur "Konkordanz zu den Qumrantexten"', *RQ*
        4 (1963), 221; H. Stegemann, 'Der Pešer Psalm 37 aus Höhle 4 von Qumran',
        RQ 4 (1963), 250.

150   Lohse, *Texte*, p. 276.

151   Ps 37:12 and 16 are quoted in 4QpPs37 2:12 and 21 respectively and the
        doers of Torah are mentioned in 4QpPs37 2:14 and 22.

152   Ps 37:21 is quoted in 4QpPs37 3:9 and the *'adat ha-'ebyonim* are mentioned
        in 3:10. The term *tsaddiqi[m* of Ps 37:29 is quoted in 4QpPs37 4:2; how-
        ever, in this instance the lacuna in the text prevents a determination of
        how this term is interpreted.

153 Ps 37:17 is quoted in the lacuna in 4QpPs37 2:23 and the *'anshe*] *retson*[*o*
      are mentioned in 2:24f.

154 Ps 37:25 is quoted in the lacuna in 4QpPs37 3:17 and the *more*[*h* is men-
      tioned in 3:19.

155 Ps 37:39 is quoted in the lacuna in 4QpPs37 4:19 and the third person
      plural suffix of the verbs *yoshi'em* and [*ya*]*tstsilem* in 4:21 refers back to
      tsaddiqim of 4:19.

156 Ps 37:30 is quoted in the lacuna in 4QpPs37 4:3 and in 4:4 it is stated that
      the interpretation concerns the *ha-'emet 'asher dibber*.

157 *Texte,* pp. 272–9.

158 Cf. John M. Allegro, *DJD*, V: *Qumran Cave 4* (Oxford, 1968), p. 44.

159 *Ibid.*

160 *Ibid.*, V, p. 45.

161 J. M. Allegro, 'Further Light on the History of the Qumran Sect', *JBL* 75
      (1956), 94. It should be noted that the method of citing passages in 4QpPs37
      is that followed by Lohse, *Texte*, pp. 272–9. Allegro refers to 4QpPs37 4:8
      as pPs 37:32–3 line 2 or Fragment II, 2.

162 E.g. Dupont-Sommer, *Essene Writings*, p. 272; Vermes, *Dead Sea Scrolls*,
      p. 245.

163 J. Carmignac, *Christ and the Teacher of Righteousness*, ET by K. G. Pedley
      (Baltimore, 1962), pp. 68f.

164 *Texte*, p. 276; cf. *DJD*, V, p. 45.

165 G. Jeremias, *Lehrer*, p. 147, does not indicate in his translation of 4QpPs37
      3:15 that the term *Gerechtigkeit* is not found in the text.

166 Lohse, *Texte*, p. 276; cf. *DJD*, V, p. 44.

167 Lohse, *Texte*, p. 276; cf. *DJD*, V, p. 45.

168 See esp. CD 14:19ff. Dupont-Sommer, *Essene Writings*, p. 160, refers to
      this passage as 'the penal code'.

169 CD 20:20.

170 See esp. CD 2:14–16.

171 'Der Begriff', I, p. 75.

172 1QS 11:13f.

173 E.g. 1QH 4:37, 7:19, 11:31, 17:20.

174 The verb *ts-d-q* is used in 1QH (e.g. 13:17, 16:11) in the sense that man
      can become righteous only by means of God's grace. Since these passages
      deal with the concept of salvation and since *tsedaqah* rather than *tsedeq*
      generally refers to God's saving, gracious activity, it is undoubtedly the idea
      of *tsedaqah* rather than *tsedeq* that is involved in these instances.

175 Cf. Holm-Nielsen, *Hodayot*, p. 301.

176 E.g. out of a total of 5 occurrences in the Dead Sea Scrolls the plural noun
      tsedaqot occurs 4 times in hymnic material (1QS 10:23, 11:3; 1QH 7:17,
      17:17) and only once in non-hymnic material (1QS 1:21). As von Rad,
      Theology, I, p. 372, has pointed out, this plural noun is used in the OT to
      refer to Jahweh's righteous acts, meaning His saving acts in history.

177 CD 19:33–20:13.

178 G. Jeremias, *Lehrer*, p. 311.

179 *Ibid.*

180 See ch. 1, sect. 3.

181 CD 6:19, 8:21, 19:33f, 20:12.

182   1QS 5:8ff, 8:13-16.
183   Cf. G. Jeremias, *Lehrer*, p. 310; 'Lag schon in dem Begriff *ts-d-q* als solchem, dass recht und gerecht nur das ist, was den Satzungen Gottes entspricht, so ist dieser Zug in den Qumran-Texten noch besonders ausgeprägt worden.'

Chapter 3. *Tsedeq*, *Tsedaqah* and *Tsaddiq* in the Tannaitic Literature

1   See ch. 1, sect. 2.
2   Thus H. Danby, *The Mishnah* (1933; rpt London, 1967), pp. 799f; J. Z. Lauterbach, 'Tannaim and Amoraim', *The Jewish Encyclopedia*, 12 (1946), p. 49. Others give the end of this period as *c*. A.D. 200, the date of the compilation of the Mishnah by R. Judah ha-Nasi. Cf. D. Sperber, 'Tanna, Tannaim', *Encyclopaedia Judaica*, 15 (1972), p. 798. Since the death of R. Judah ha-Nasi is generally put as *c*. A.D. 220 (*ibid*., p. 801), it would seem to be natural to take A.D. 220 as the end of the Tannaitic period.
3   It should be noted that the title '*Rabbi*' is in actual fact applied only to the Tannaim after the fall of Jerusalem (A.D. 70). However, even after 70 there were some unordained Tannaim, e.g. Ben Azzai.
4   Technically this term refers to any Tannaitic tradition outside of the Mishnah.
5   J. Neusner, *Eliezer Ben Hyrcanus* (2 vols.; Studies in Judaism in Late Antiquity 4; Leiden, 1973), II, pp. 1-3; cf. II, pp. 225f. It should be noted, however, that Neusner's scale of reliability is derived on the basis of the traditions pertaining to Eliezer ben Hyrcanus.
6   Cf. Danby, *Mishnah*, p. xxi; M. Mielziner, *Introduction to the Talmud* (4th edn; New York, 1968), p. 5; H. L. Strack, *Introduction to the Talmud and Midrash* (1931; rpt New York, 1969), p. 20.
7   E.g. Sotah 9:15 reports the death of R. Judah ha-Nasi. Rather than dealing in detail with the problem of later additions at this point, we will postpone such discussions until they arise in passages dealing with the concept of righteousness.
8   *The Targums and Rabbinic Literature* (Cambridge, 1969), p. 61.
9   Strack, *Introduction to the Talmud and Midrash*, p. 75, agrees with the opinion of Gaon Sherira that Ḥiyya bar Aba, a disciple and friend of R. Judah ha-Nasi, was the author of the Tosefta. Strack also notes the opinion of Joḥanan that the Tosefta is based on the lectures of Nehemiah, a contemporary of R. Meir.
10   See discussion above on *Eliezer Ben Hyrcanus*, II, pp. 1-3.
11   'The Date of the Mekilta de-Rabbi Ishmael', *HUCA* 39 (1968), 143. For a more detailed discussion of the dating of Tannaitic literature see E. P. Sanders, *Paul and Palestinian Judaism. A Comparison of Patterns of Religion* (London, 1977), pp. 63-9.
12   'A Reply', *JBL* 92 (1973), 114f, refers to the 'halakic midrashim' in general, not just to the Mekilta on Exodus.
13   'On the Problem of Method in the Study of Rabbinic Literature', *JBL* 92 (1973), 113. Cf. J. Neusner, *Development of a Legend. Studies on the Traditions Concerning Yoḥanan ben Zakkai* (SPB 16; Leiden, 1970), p. xiii n. 2; W. S. Towner, *The Rabbinic 'Enumeration of Scriptural Examples'. A Study of a Rabbinic Pattern of Discourse with Special Reference to Mekhilta D'R. Ishmael* (Leiden, 1973), p. 48 n. 1.

14 For the consensus view see Wacholder, 'The Date of the Mekilta de-Rabbi Ishmael', p. 117 n. 1.

15 *The Relationship between the Halakhic Midrashim and Tosefta* (in Hebrew; Jerusalem, 1967), p. 181.

16 J. Neusner, *The Rabbinic Traditions about the Pharisees before 70* (3 vols.; Leiden, 1971), III, p. 303, states that 'The rabbinic traditions about the Pharisees before 70 A.D. consist of approximately 371 separate items – stories or sayings or allusions – which occur in approximately 655 different pericopae.' It should be noted, however, that Neusner deals only with named sayings.

17 See W. G. Kümmel, *Introduction to the New Testament*, ET by A. J. Mattill, jun. (14th rev. edn; Nashville, 1966), p. 84, for a discussion of the dating of the Gospel of Matthew.

18 Since the Tannaitic literature is generally used as a background for the Pauline epistles which were composed before the fall of Jerusalem, the use of the Tannaitic literature with regard to the time of the Matthaean redactional activity is based on a relatively sound premise.

19 *The Rise and Fall of the Judaean State* (2 vols.; Philadelphia, 1962–7), II, pp. 344–6. For the relationship between Pharisaic and Rabbinic thought see also Sanders, *Paul and Palestinian Judaism*, pp. 60–2, 426–8.

20 The following concordances have been used: C. J. Kasowski, *'Otsar Leshon Ha-Tosefta. Thesaurus Tosephthae*, ed. Moshe Kasovsky (6 vols.; Jerusalem, 1932–61); C. Y. Kasovsky, *'Otsar Leshon Ha-Mishna. Thesaurus Mishnae*, rev. edn by Moshe Kasovsky (4 vols.; Tel Aviv, 1967); B. Kosovsky, *Otzar Leshon Hatanna'im. Concordantiae verborum quae in Mechilta D'Rabbi Ismael* (4 vols.; Jerusalem, 1965–6), *Otzar Leshon Hatanna'im. Concordantiae verborum quae in Sifra aut Torat Kohanim* (4 vols.; Jerusalem, 1967–9) and *Otzar Leshon Hatanna'im. Concordantiae verborum quae in Sifrei Numeri et Deuteronomium* (5 vols.; Jerusalem, 1970–4). In the case of the Tosefta the concordance does not list the references to the righteousness terminology which occur in scriptural quotations. The count of the latter type of reference is based on the research of the author.

21 E.g. in Sifra Qedoshim pereq 4:4 on Lev 19:15 *tsedeq* and *zekut* are related as far as the meaning of mercy is concerned.

22 It should be noted that in Mek. Beshallah 6 on Ex 14:22; I, p. 235; p. 106, it is stated that the *zekut* of the righteous is of help to them. The help in this case relates to very mundane matters and there is no hint as to a doctrine of the transfer of merit. Cf. Sanders, *Paul and Palestinian Judaism*, p. 197 n. 76. As a matter of fact, on the basis of a study of the terms *zakah*, *zekut* and *zakka'i* (*ibid.*, pp. 183–98), Sanders concludes, 'There is nowhere in Tannaitic literature a reference to a treasury of merits which can be transferred at the judgment' (p. 197).

23 *Der Zaddik in Talmud und Midrasch* (Leiden, 1957). A shortcoming of this study is that Mach does not differentiate between Tannaitic and Amoraic materials.

24 'The Meaning and Significance of the Concept of Righteousness in the Gospel of Matthew. With Special Reference to the Use of this Concept in the Dead Sea Scrolls and the Tannaitic Literature' (Ph.D. dissertation, McMaster University, Hamilton, Ont., 1975).

25 On Ex 13:3; I, p. 138; p. 61.
26 R. Judah the Patriarch.
27 Tr. by Lauterbach, *Mekilta de-Rabbi Ishmael* (3 vols.; Philadelphia, 1933–5), I, p. 138.
28 On Ex 14:24; I, p. 238; p. 107.
29 On Ex 15:12; II, p. 67; p. 145.
30 Tr. by Lauterbach, *Mekilta*, I, p. 238.
31 Tr. by J. Goldin, *The Song at the Sea* (New Haven, 1971), pp. 208f.
32 Cf. Mach, *Der Zaddik*, p. 41.
33 Joel 3:5 in Hebrew Bible.
34 Thus RSV (1952). As is apparent from the ensuing discussion, the Tannaim presupposed a different translation.
35 Unless stated otherwise, all English translations of Sifre on Deuteronomy are those of the author.
36 On Ex 15:1; II, p. 6; p. 118.
37 Aboth 5:1.
38 Sanhedrin 8:5.
39 Sifre Deut 38 on 11:10 (p. 75).
40 Sifra Aḥare parasha 9:7 on Lev 18:3, pereq 13:8 on Lev 18:3. Cf. Mach, *Der Zaddik*, p. 121.
41 On Ex 14:31; I, p. 253; p. 115.
42 On Ex 14:31; I, p. 254; p. 115.
43 Sifre Num 138 on 27:15 (p. 184) and 157 on 31:1–2 (p. 209).
44 Sifre Deut 47 on 11:21 (p. 105).
45 G. Kittel, *Sifre zu Deuteronomium* (Rabbinische Texte; 1ste Lieferung; Stuttgart, 1922), p. 117 n. 1, explains that in Aramaic *yom* can have the meaning 'sun'. That this meaning is accurate appears from the reference to Judges 5:31, 'But thy friends be like the sun as he rises in his might.' The description of the righteous in terms of the sun also appears in Sifre Deut 10 on 1:10 (p. 18) where R. Simeon b. Yoḥai states that in the future the faces of the righteous can be compared to seven joys. One of the joys mentioned is that of the sun (*hammah*).
46 No attempt has been made to subdivide the discussion of the adjective *tsaddiq* according to number, for in fact no significant differences between the use of the singular and plural forms of the adjective were found. Even though it appears to be general Tannaitic usage to contrast the *tsaddiqim* with the *resha'im*, in Mek. Pisḥa 11 on Ex 12:22; I, p. 85; p. 38, the singular adjective is used in a general comparison of the righteous and the wicked. Cf. Negaim 12:5.
47 Sifra Aḥare parasha 9:7 on Lev 18:3, pereq 13:8 on Lev 18:3; T. Sotah 6:6.
48 Sifre Deut 352 on 33:12 (p. 413).
49 T. Berakoth 4:16.
50 T. Sotah 10:3.
51 T. Sotah 6:7; Nedarim 3:11.
52 Aboth 1:2, 3; Sifre Num 22 on 6:2 (p. 26); T. Sotah 13:6, 7.
53 The feminine of *tsaddiq* is *tseddeqet*.
54 On Ex 22:22; III, p. 142; p. 313.
55 On Ex 15:13; II, p. 69; p. 146.
56 Tr. by Goldin, *The Song at the Sea*, pp. 213f.

57 On Ex 18:3; II, pp. 169f; p. 192.
58 Tr. by Lauterbach, *Mekilta*, II, pp. 169f.
59 Cf. Mach, *Der Zaddik*, p. 154.
60 *Sheba' kitot shel tsaddiqim began 'eden zo lema'alah mizzo.*
61 Ps 140:14 in Hebrew Bible.
62 Cf. Sifre Deut 47 on 11:21 (p. 105). Here Ps 121:1, 'A song for steps', is seen as referring to the various class differences among the righteous in the world to come.
63 Unless otherwise indicated, the English translations of Sifra are those of the author.
64 Sanders, *Paul and Palestinian Judaism*, p. 204, has suggested that their suffering and death atoned for their transgression.
65 This expression definitely occurs in Sifre Deut 307 on 32:4 (p. 345). With respect to Sifre Deut 40 on 11:12 (p. 81), T. Kiddushin 1:15 and T. Sanhedrin 13:3 there is conflicting textual evidence.
66 Both Mach, *Der Zaddik*, p. 35, and Strack and Billerbeck, *Kommentar*, IV, p. 1041, translate this expression as 'der vollkommene Gerechte'.
67 Strack and Billerbeck, *Kommentar*, IV, p. 1041, suggest that this is the theory of R. Akiba. It is at least the theory of the School of R. Akiba.
68 In Sifre Num 135 on Deut 3:26 (p. 181) it is explicitly stated that God prevents the righteous from committing a major transgression.
69 Finkelstein, *Sifre on Deuteronomy*, p. 81, does not include this reading in the text but notes in the apparatus that MS. *d* reads *ts-d-y-q-y-m g-m-w-r-y-m*. G. Kittel, *Sifre zu Deuteronomium*, p. 87, gives the following translation: 'Siehe, wenn die Israeliten am Anfang des Jahres vollkommene Gerechte sind . . .' M. Friedmann in his edition of Sifre on Deuteronomy (*Sifre d'Be Rab*; 1864; rpt Jerusalem, 1968) has adopted the reading *ts-d-y-q-y-m g-m-w-r-y-m* into his text (f. 78b).
70 In 10 of these the adjectives are in the plural and in one case (Negaim 12:5) in the singular.
71 Aboth 5:1; cf. Sanhedrin 8:5.
72 Mek. Beshallah 6 on Ex 14:24; I, p. 237; p. 107. Concerning the prayers of the righteous see also Mek. Vayassa' 1 on Ex 15:25; II, p. 91; p. 155.
73 Sifre Deut 33 on 6:6 (pp. 59f).
74 E.g. Sifre Deut 53 on 11:26 (p. 120).
75 'R. Akiba's View of Suffering', *JQR* 63 (1972/3), 336ff.
76 Tr. by H. Danby, *Tractate Sanhedrin*, *Mishnah and Tosefta* (Translations of Early Documents, Ser. III, Rabbinic Texts; New York, 1919), p. 111.
77 *Ibid.*, p. 112.
78 Sifre Num 40 on 6:24 (p. 44), 42 on 6:25 (p. 47), 103 on 12:8 (p. 102), 139 on 27:16 (p. 185); Sanhedrin 10:3.
79 Sifre Num 106 on 12:15 (p. 105).
80 Sifre Deut 357 on 34:5 (p. 428).
81 *Lekol tsaddiq wetsaddiq.* So P. Blackman, *Mishnayoth* (6 vols.; 3rd rev. edn; New York, 1965), VI, p. 796 n. 1. Cf. Danby, *Mishnah*, p. 789; 'every saint'.
82 Uktzin 3:12.
83 Sifre Deut 354 on 33:19 (p. 416).
84 Sifre Deut 357 on 34:3 (p. 427); Sifra Behuqqotai pereq 3:3 on Lev 26:12.

85 Sifre Deut 10 on 1:10 (p. 18).

86 *Ibid.*, cf. Mach, *Der Zaddik*, p. 204.

87 On Ex 13:2; I, pp. 134f; p. 60.

88 Tr. by Lauterbach, *Mekilta*, I, pp. 134f.

89 On Ex 18:12; II, p. 178; p. 196.

90 *Ha-tsaddiqim*; Lauterbach, *Mekilta*, II, pp. 178, introduces this term only as a variant reading while H. S. Horovitz and I. A. Rabin, *Mechilta d'Rabbi Ismael* (1931; rpt Jerusalem, 1970), p. 196, and J. Winter and A. Wünsche, *Mechiltha: Ein tannaitischer Midrasch zu Exodus* (Leipzig, 1909), p. 185, adopt this reading into their texts.

91 Tr. by Lauterbach, *Mekilta*, II, p. 178; cf. Sanhedrin 6:5 and Sifra Qedoshim pereq 11:6 on Lev 20:16.

92 In B. Sanhedrin 59a, B. Baba Kamma 38a and B. Abodah Zarah 3a this passage is attributed to R. Meir.

93 Sifra Aḥare pereq 13:13 on Lev 18:5.

94 Unless otherwise indicated the English translations of Sifre on Numbers are those of the author.

95 In B. Sanhedrin 59a, B. Baba Kamma 38a and B. Abodah Zarah 3a this passage is attributed to R. Meir.

96 Sifre Num 68 on 9:7 (p. 63).

97 On Ex 23:7; III, pp. 169-72; pp. 327f.

98 The parallel in P. Sanhedrin 22b (top) has *tsadaq*.

99 Tr. by Lauterbach, *Mekilta*, III, pp. 171f.

100 Mach, *Der Zaddik*, p. 3, points out that these two terms are synonyms. K. G. Kuhn, *Der tannaitische Midrasch Sifre zu Numeri* (Stuttgart, 1959), p. 535 n. 11, makes a similar observation with respect to the use of these two terms in Sifre Num 133 on 27:1 (p. 176).

101 Cf. Lauterbach, *Mekilta*, III, p. 172 n. 10.

102 Mach, *Der Zaddik*, pp. 9-13; Ziesler, *Righteousness*, pp. 116f.

103 E.g. Kertelge, *'Rechtfertigung' bei Paulus*, p. 47; Ziesler, *Righteousness*, p. 122.

104 Thus S. Lieberman, *The Tosefta* (4 vols.; New York, 1955-73). According to the text of M. S. Zuckermandel, *Tosephta* (new edn; Jerusalem, 1970), who enumerates this passage as 1:14f, the contrast is between the *tsaddiq gamur* and *rasha' gamur* rather than simply between the *tsaddiq* and *rasha'*. It should be noted that unless indicated otherwise, all translations of the Tosefta are those of the author.

105 *Der Zaddik*, p. 124.

106 *Ibid.*, p. 38. Cf. C. G. Montefiore and H. Loewe (eds.), *A Rabbinic Anthology* (1938; rpt New York, 1974), p. 601; Neusner, *The Rabbinic Traditions about the Pharisees before 70*, II, p. 238. It should be noted that Zuckermandel, *Tosephta*, p. 434, refers to a variant in T. Sanhedrin 13:3 which reads *tsaddiqim gemurim*. A parallel passage in B. Rosh ha-Shanah 16b (end) also has this reading.

107 Sanders, *Paul and Palestinian Judaism*, pp. 128-47, has demonstrated that 'weighing' in fact does not constitute Rabbinic soteriology.

108 For a detailed analysis of the soteriology implicit in the Tannaitic literature see Sanders, *Paul and Palestinian Judaism*, pp. 147-82.

109 *Ibid.*, p. 205.

110 E.g. Mek. Bahodesh 7 on Ex 20:7; II, pp. 249ff; pp. 228f; Yoma 8:8f.

111   See esp. T. Yom Ha-Kippurim 4(5):5. For a discussion of the means of
       atonement see Sanders, *Paul and Palestinian Judaism*, pp. 157–74. For the
       special role of repentance, *ibid.*, pp. 174–80; G. F. Moore, *Judaism in the
       First Centuries of the Christian Era. The Age of the Tannaim* (3 vols.; 1927;
       rpt Cambridge, Mass., 1970), I, p. 500.

112   Sifre Num 105 on 12:10 (p. 103) and 137 on 27:14 (p. 184).

113   Mek. Vayassa' 1 on Ex 15:25; II, p. 91; p. 155. Lauterbach has 'From this
       you learn that the righteous are not hard to complain to' *(Mekilta*, II, p.
       91). Since the passage goes on to deal with the topic of prayer, it appears
       that the translation of Winter and Wünsche, *Mechiltha*, p. 148, is more
       accurate: 'Von hier (ist zu entnehmen), dass die Gerechten keine Schwierig-
       keit haben, dass ihr Gebet angenommen werde.'

114   Cf. Sifre Deut 16 on 1:16 (pp. 25ff); Sifra Emor parasha 1:13f on Lev
       21:3; Sifre Num 106 on 12:15 (p. 105); Sotah 1:9.

115   The passages in question are the quotation of Ps 119:164 in Sifre Deut 36
       on 6:9 (p. 68), Ps 15:2 in Sifre Deut 286 on 25:3 (p. 305) and Ps 50:6 in
       Sifre Deut 306 on 32:1 (p. 330).

116   Is 42:21 is quoted in Mek. Pisha 16 on Ex 13:2; I, p. 132; p. 59 and in Mek.
       Nezikin 18 on Ex 22:20 (21); III, p. 140; p. 312. Is 41:2 is quoted in Mek.
       Shirata 6 on Ex 15:7; II, p. 45; p. 135. It should be noted that Lauterbach
       does not carry the quotation of Is 41:2 far enough, so that the term *tsedeq*
       does not appear in his text.

117   The first number in the bracket refers to the independent and the second
       to the dependent occurrences.

118   The independent use of the term *tsedeq* is restricted to the expression *ger
       tsedeq*.

119   Since the concordance to the Tosefta does not list the occurrences in biblical
       quotations, this count is based on the research of the author.

120   Cf. Stuhlmacher, *Gerechtigkeit Gottes bei Paulus*, p. 181; Fiedler, 'Der
       Begriff', I, p. 81.

121   Sifre Deut 144 on 16:19 (p. 199), Sifre Deut 334 on 32:44 (p. 384) (6
       times), Sifre Num 133 on 27:1 (p. 176).

122   E.g. Sifre Deut 294 on 25:15 (p. 313).

123   Lev 19:15, 36.

124   Sifra Qedoshim pereq 4.4 on Lev 19:15 and pereq 8:7 on Lev 19:36.

125   Sifra Emor parasha 1.14 on Lev 21:3.

126   Sifra Behar parasha 5.1 on Lev 25:35 and pereq 8.1 on Lev 25:47.

127   Deut 1:16; 16:18, 20 (twice); 25:15; 33:19.

128   Sifre Deut 16 on 1:16 (pp. 25ff), 144 on 16:18 (p. 198), 144 on 16:20 (pp.
       199f), 294 on 25:15 (p. 313), 354 on 33:19 (p. 416).

129   Sifre Deut 144 on 16:19 (p. 199), 334 on 32:44 (p. 384).

130   Sifre Deut 278 on 24:14 (p. 296).

131   Eight in Sifre on Deuteronomy and one in each of the other Tannaitic
       midrashim.

132   Both Lauterbach, *Mekilta*, III, p. 178, and Horovitz and Rabin, *Mechilta*,
       p. 331, have adopted the reading *ger tsedeq* into their texts.

133   Cf. Lauterbach, *Mekilta*, I, p. 121 n. 5.

134   *Ibid.*, II, p. 255. Cf. Strack and Billerbeck, *Kommentar*, II, p. 717. On the
       other hand, Winter and Wünsche, *Mechiltha*, p. 216, use the translation
       'Proselyt/Fremdling der Gerechtigkeit'.

135 On Ex 23:12; III, p. 178; p. 331.
136 On Ex 20:10; II, p. 255; p. 230.
137 Winter and Wünsche, *Mechiltha*, p. 216 n. 4.
138 Lauterbach, *Mekilta*, I, p. 121 n. 5.
139 On Ex 22:20(21); III, p. 141; p. 312.
140 Tr. by Lauterbach, *Mekilta*, III, p. 141.
141 *Ibid.*
142 Cf. C. Westermann, *Das Buch Jesaja* (Das Alte Testament Deutsch 19; Göttingen, 1966), pp. 111f; C. R. North, *The Second Isaiah* (Oxford, 1964), p. 134.
143 It appears that this discussion is based on the fact that Lev 25:47 can be read either as *leger wetoshab* or as *leger toshab*. The former reading is adopted in Sifra Behar pereq 8.1 where *ger* is said to refer to the *ger tsedeq* and *toshab* is said to refer to *ger toshab*. The latter reading is preferred by T. Arakin 5:9.
144 The verb *ts-d-q* is used.
145 Moore, *Judaism*, II, p. 189, explains that this is 'R. Jose ben Judah (ben Ila'i)'.
146 For the last part of the translation cf. Moore, *Judaism*, II, p. 189, 'Let your *Yes* be righteous and your *No* be righteous.' J. Winter, *Sifra. Halachischer Midrasch zu Leviticus* (Breslau, 1938), p. 518; 'Dein Nein sei richtig und dein Ja sei richtig.'
147 Cf. B. Baba Metzia 49a; I. Epstein (ed.), *The Babylonian Talmud* (London, 1935–48; rpt 1961), p. 291 n. 7; 'This is a play on words, "*hin*", a measure being connected with *hen*, Aramaic for "yes".'
148 Cf. B. Baba Metzia 49a, *ibid.*, p. 291; 'Abaye said: That means that one must not speak one thing with the mouth and another with the heart.'
149 M. Jastrow, *A Dictionary of the Targumim, the Talmud Babli and Jerushalmi, and the Midrashic Literature* (2 vols.; 1903; rpt Tel Aviv, 1972), I, p. 341, gives the following meanings for *hora'ah:* 'decision, instruction; teacher's or judge's office'. Cf. CD 6:11, *yoreh ha-tsedeq*.
150 On Ex 19:2; II, p. 199; p. 206.
151 On Ex 20:2; II, p. 232; p. 220.
152 Tr. by Lauterbach, *Mekilta*, II, pp. 198f.
153 J. Winter, *Sifra*, p. 542, translates this passage as follows: 'R. Jose sagt: Ein Mensch darf sich nicht an dem Gebein von der Grösse eines Gerstenkorns von seinem Vater verunreinigen.' There are parallels to this story in P. Nazir 55d and Šĕmahot pereq 4:15. In the latter the passage begins as follows: 'A priest should defile himself for a piece of bone from his deceased father the size of a barley grain, but not for a limb from a living person, even in the case of his father' (ET by D. Zlotnick, *The Tractate 'Mourning' (Šĕmahot)* (Yale Judaica Series, 17; New Haven, 1966), p. 43). The example which now follows deals with Joseph b. Paksas; that is, Sifra has *y-w-s-p b-n p-k-s-s*; P. Nazir has *y-w-s-y b-n p-k-s-s* and Šĕmahot has *y-w-s-p b-n p-s-q-n*. Zlotnick, *ibid.*, p. 116, states that 'Joseph ben Piskan' was a priest. The interpretation and translation of this story are based largely on the work of Zlotnick.
154 J. Winter, *Sifra*, p. 542, translates this passage as follows: 'Von nun an gehe hinaus, denn man darf sich nicht an dem Gliede eines Lebenden von seinem

Vater verunreinigen.' Cf. B. Nazir 43b, 'For it has been taught: R. Judah said that he may defile himself for her, but not for her limbs; for he is forbidden to defile himself for limbs severed from his father whilst still alive; but he may defile himself for limbs severed from his father after death' (Epstein (ed.), *The Babylonian Talmud*, p. 159). Zlotnick, *The Tractate 'Mourning'*, p. 116, explains that Joseph ordered his son to leave the house, because a limb from a living person causes tent defilement. For the custom of not severing something completely so that both patient and doctor could remain ritually clean see Kerithoth 3:8.

155   Zlotnick, *The Tractate 'Mourning'*, p. 116.
156   *Ibid.*
157   Tr. by Danby, *Mishnah*, p. 294.
158   *Ibid.*
159   Blackman, *Mishnayoth*, III, p. 340.
160   According to T. Peah 4:19 it is clear that gathering someone's bones would qualify as an act of lovingkindness (*gemilut ḥasadim*).
161   Ps 85:14 in Hebrew Bible.
162   The question of the extent of overlap in meaning between *tsedeq* and *tsedaqah* will be discussed below.
163   Note that the argument is based on the occurrence of two different spellings of the name in question; *Hoshe'a* and *Yehoshu'a*.
164   MS. *d* reads *b-ts-d-q-w*. Finkelstein, however, has adopted the reading *b-ts-d-q-y* into the actual text.
165   On Ex 15:26; II, p. 95; p. 157.
166   Tr. by Lauterbach, *Mekilta*, II, p. 95. See also Aboth 4:2.
167   Aboth 1:1; tr. by Danby, *Mishnah*, p. 446.
168   Finkelstein, *Sifre on Deuteronomy*, p. 27.
169   Tr. by Jastrow, *Dictionary*, II, p. 1645.
170   *Tractate Sanhedrin*, p. 63.
171   Cf. Sanhedrin 4:1 where it is stated that this procedure applies to capital cases only.
172   On Ex 31:17; III, p. 205; p. 344.
173   Lauterbach includes this quotation in his text while Horovitz and Rabin have it in brackets.
174   The passages in question are Joel 2:23 in Sifre Deut 42 on 11:14 (p. 90); Ps 11:7 in Sifre Deut 49 on 11:22 (p. 114); Ps 11:7 in Sifre Deut 307 on 32:4 (p. 345); Ps 106:31 in Sifre Num 131 on 25:8f (p. 172); Is 45:23 in Sifre Num 134 on Deut 3:24 (p. 180); Is 48:18 in Sifra Beḥuqqotai parasha 1:1 on Lev 26:3; Is 59:17 in Mek. Shirata 4 on Ex 15:3; II, p. 30; p. 129; Mal 3:20 (4:2) in Mek. Baḥodesh 8 on Ex 20:12; II, p. 258; p. 232; Gen 15:6 in Mek. Beshallaḥ 4 on Ex 14:15; I, p. 220; p. 99, and in Mek. Beshallaḥ 7 on Ex 14:31; I, p. 253; p. 114. Ziesler, *Righteousness*, p. 125, indicates that the use of *tsedaqah* in the last passage is relevant. It is quite clear, however, that the stress in this case is on the fact that Abraham believed, and Gen 15:6 is quoted to support this fact. No stress is placed on the term *tsedaqah* in the discussion.
175   The first number refers to the independent and the second to the dependent occurrences. As noted previously, the concordance to the Tosefta does not list the dependent occurrences. That count is based on the research of the author.

176 This number does not take the independent reference to *tsedaqah* in Sifre Deut 116 on 15:7 (p. 175) into account. This occurrence does not have a good textual basis and is, for example, not included in the translations by Montefiore and Loewe (eds.), *A Rabbinic Anthology*, p. 422 or Strack and Billerbeck, *Kommentar*, I, p. 346. In this instance *tsedaqah* definitely refers to almsgiving.

177 This number does not take the reference in Aboth 6:6 into account. Since the sixth chapter of Aboth appears to be a late gloss, probably from the eleventh century, this chapter will not be included in this discussion.

178 The term *tsedaqah* also occurs in Deut 6:25; 9:4, 5, 6 but these verses are not covered by Sifre on Deuteronomy.

179 *Judaism*, II, pp. 171f.

180 Mach, *Der Zaddik*, p. 19, notes that *gemilut hasadim* are of a wider scope than almsgiving (*tsedaqah*) so that the former concept really includes the latter. Cf. B. Sukkah 49b.

181 T. Baba Batra 8:14; T. Baba Kamma 10:22, 11:6; T. Ketubot 6:10 (twice), 9:3; T. Megillah 1:5, 2:15(3:4) (3 times); T. Niddah 6:10 (twice); T. Peah 4:16, 19 (4 times), 20, 21 (3 times); T. Pesahim 7:16; T. Shabbat 16:22; T. Shebiit 7:9; T. Sotah 14:10; T. Terumot 1:10.

182 *Tsedaqot*; T. Arakin 3:17.

183 T. Baba Kamma 11:6; T. Baba Metzia 3:9 (twice); T. Demai 3:17.

184 T. Peah 4:19.

185 T. Peah 4:20.

186 T. Demai 3:17.

187 T. Peah 4:16.

188 Tr. by Danby, *Mishnah*, p. 457.

189 *Ibid.*, p. 448.

190 C. Taylor, *Sayings of the Jewish Fathers* (2nd edn; New York, 1969), p. 32, and A. David (tr.), *The Commentary to Mishnah Aboth*, by Moses Maimonides (New York, 1968), p. 34, translate *tsedaqah* as 'righteousness', while Herford, *The Ethics of the Talmud, Sayings of the Fathers* (New York, 1974), p. 48, translates it as 'charity'. Blackman, *Mishnayoth*, IV, p. 500, suggests two translations. In the actual text he uses 'charity' and in the explanation in n. 10 he states, 'or righteousness'.

191 *Wehayah ma'asheh ha-tsedaqah shalom.*

192 On Ex 18:27; II, p. 190; p. 201.

193 Cf. Winter and Wünsche, *Mechiltha*, pp. 190f; 'Desgleichen findest du es bei den Almosengebern.'

194 Some MSS. add at this point 'to receive charity (*tsedaqah*)'. Neither Lauterbach nor Horovitz and Rabin incorporate this reading into their texts.

195 Tr. by Lauterbach, *Mekilta*, II, p. 190.

196 On Ex 21:30; III, p. 86; p. 286.

197 Tr. by Lauterbach, *Mekilta*, III, p. 86.

198 Dan 4:24 in Hebrew Bible.

199 *Theology*, I, p. 383.

200 Since Moses is portrayed as doing the righteousness of God, this passage casts doubt on the conclusion of E. Käsemann, 'Gottesgerechtigkeit bei Paulus', *ZThK 58* (1961), 370f, that in late Judaism (Spätjudentum) the expression 'righteousness of God' was a well-defined technical term referring

to God's redemptive activity (*Heilshandeln*), an activity stressing God's power (*Macht*).

201 Finkelstein, *Sifre on Deuteronomy*, p. 418.

202 Strack and Billerbeck, *Kommentar*, III, p. 163 n. 1.

203 *Sifre zu Numeri*, p. 136. P. P. Levertoff, *Midrash Sifre on Numbers* (Translations of Early Documents, Series III, Rabbinic Texts; New York, 1926), p. 38, gives the following translation: 'Great is peace, for it is given as a gift to those who do righteousness.' Levertoff explains that 'do righteousness' means 'to give alms' (p. 38 n. 3).

204 Kuhn, *Sifre zu Numeri*, p. 136 n. 55. It should be noted that the text of Sifre Num 42 (p. 47) is not absolutely certain. Horovitz adopts the reading *l-' sh-y ts-d-q-h*, but indicates that MS. *l* has *l-'-w-sh-h*.

205 This biblical quotation is included in the text by Zuckermandel, *Tosephta*, but only referred to as a variant reading by Lieberman, *The Tosefta*.

206 Strack and Billerbeck, *Kommentar*, II, p. 562, have the translation 'Wohltätigkeit' for *tsedaqah*.

207 *Ibid.*, II, p. 561, R. Eliazar b. Jose, *c.* 180.

208 Tr. by Danby, *Tractate Sanhedrin*, p. 28, except for the substitution of 'mercy' for 'charity' as the translation of *tsedaqah*.

209 Dr E. P. Sanders has suggested that a kindness is done in punishing the crime, probably since the punishment atones.

210 On Ex 15:5; II, p. 39; p. 133.

211 Tr. by Goldin, *The Song at the Sea*, pp. 145f.

212 *Ibid.*, p. 146.

213 Montefiore and Loewe (eds.), *A Rabbinic Anthology*, p. 392, point out that *tsedaqah* is here used 'in its later Rabbinic sense of almsgiving or charity'. The context, however, points to a comparison of strict justice with mercy, not charity.

214 This term is translated as 'arbitration' by Danby, *Tractate Sanhedrin*, p. 28, and as 'Vermittelung' by Strack and Billerbeck, *Kommentar*, III, p. 210.

215 T. Sanhedrin 1:2–9.

216 On Ex 15:1; II, p. 5; p. 117.

217 *Tsidqat yy 'ashah*.

218 Tr. by Goldin, *The Song at the Sea*, p. 73.

219 On Ex 22:23(24); III, p. 145; p. 314.

220 Cf. Kuhn, *Sifre zu Numeri*, p. 280 n. 23.

221 *Ibid.*, p. 280 n. 24.

222 Tr. by Danby, *Mishnah*, pp. 447f.

223 Maimonides, *The Commentary to Mishnah Aboth*, pp. 30f.

224 Tr. by Danby, *Mishnah*, p. 458.

225 Taylor, *Sayings of the Jewish Fathers*, p. 94, and Blackman, *Mishnayoth*, IV, p. 535, translate *zekut* as 'righteousness', thereby indicating that these two terms are equivalent.

226 It should be noted that the foregoing investigation of the terms *tsedeq*, *tsedaqah* and *tsaddiq* in the Tannaitic literature does not support R. Bultmann's contention that the Jewish conception of the formal meaning of righteousness is 'forensic–eschatological'. See *Theology of the New Testament*, ET by K. Grobel (2 vols.; New York, 1951–5), I, p. 273.

227 See end of ch. 3, sect. 2.

Chapter 4. The meaning of *dikaiosynē*, *eleēmosynē* and *dikaios* in the Gospel of Matthew

1   As was stated in ch. 1, sect. 2, the fact that the Jewish-Palestinian writings, as represented by the Dead Sea Scrolls and the Tannaitic literature, provide an adequate background for an understanding of the Matthaean concept of righteousness must be taken into account in the continuing debate concerning the Jewish-Christian versus the Gentile-Christian character of the Gospel of Matthew.

2   J. W. Wevers, 'Septuagint', *IDB*, IV, p. 277. Cf. Ziesler, *Righteousness*, p. 52; the 'LXX was the OT Greek version which the Church made peculiarly its own'. K. Stendahl, *The School of St. Matthew and its Use of the Old Testament* (Acta Seminarii Neotestamentici Upsaliensis 20; Uppsala, 1954), p. 205, calls the LXX 'the accepted edition of the O.T. in everyday church life'.

3   In this study the designation 'Matthew' stands for the person or group of persons who carried out the final redaction of the Gospel of Matthew.

4   Thus Stendahl, *The School of St. Matthew*, pp. 150f. R. H. Gundry, *The Use of the Old Testament in St. Matthew's Gospel. With Special Reference to the Messianic Hope* (Suppl. *NovTest* 18; Leiden, 1967), does not agree with this conclusion (p. 148). Yet he nevertheless points to an influence of the LXX by stating that of 'the twenty formal quotations peculiar to Mt., seven are Septuagintal' (p. 149) and of 'the forty-two allusive quotations peculiar to Mt. fifteen are Septuagintal' (pp. 14f).

5   Thus Ziesler, *Righteousness*, p. 22 n. 2.

6   *Ibid.*, p. 59.

7   *Ibid.*

8   *Ibid.*, p. 60.

9   Deut 6:25, 24:13; Ps 23(24):5, 32(33):5, 102(103):6; Is 1:27, 28:17, 59:16; Dan 4:27(24).

10   Is 56:1; Ez 18:19, 21.

11   Cf. Ziesler, *Righteousness*, p. 59.

12   It should be noted that although *tsedeq* and *tsaddiq* are generally translated in the LXX by some form of δικαι-, conversely there are 28 cases where *dikaiosynē* and 35 cases where *dikaios* render words which are not based on the root *ts-d-q* (so Ziesler, *Righteousness*, pp. 60–6). Consequently, it is not a foregone conclusion that the term *dikaiosynē* in the Gospel of Matthew necessarily stands for *tsedeq*. For a discussion of the use of *dikaiosynē* in the LXX see also Fiedler, 'Der Begriff', I, pp. 49–54.

13   It was also noted that *eleos* is used 3 times to translate *tsedaqah*. Since the meaning of *eleos* does not form an integral part of the Matthaean concept of righteousness, this term will not be discussed separately but simply in conjunction with the term *eleēmosynē*.

14   E.g. B, ℵ, D.

15   E.g. Koine, Θ.

16   'Gerechtigkeit – oder Almosen? (Mt 6, 1)', *VigChr* 15 (1961), pp. 141–5.

17   M. Smith, *Tannaitic Parallels to the Gospels* (JBL Monograph Series, 6; corrected rpt Philadelphia, 1968), p. 161, notes that in Mt 6:1 'to do righteousness' means 'give alms'. This does not necessarily mean that Smith accepts the reading ἐλεημοσύνην. Rather, it probably means that Smith

thinks that in this case δικαιοσύνην refers to righteousness in the sense of alms. Cf. H. H. Hobbs, *The Gospel of Matthew* (Grand Rapids, 1963), p. 39, who explains with respect to his translation of Mt 6:1, '"Alms" translates the word for "righteousness".'

18 E.g. W. C. Allen, *A Critical and Exegetical Commentary on the Gospel According to S. Matthew* (ICC; 3rd edn; Edinburgh, 1912), p. 56; Fiedler, 'Der Begriff', II, p. 122 n. 172; D. Hill, *The Gospel of Matthew* (NCB; London, 1972), p. 132; E. Klostermann, *Das Matthäusevangelium* (HbzNT 4; 2nd rev. edn; Tübingen, 1927), p. 52; Schniewind, *Matthäus*, p. 76; Strecker, *Weg*, p. 152 n. 2; T. Zahn, *Das Evangelium des Matthäus* (Kommentar zum Neuen Testament 1; 3rd edn; Leipzig, 1910), p. 260 n. 42.

19 B. M. Metzger, *The Text of the New Testament* (2nd edn; Oxford, 1968), p. 207.

20 *Matthäus*, pp. 261f n. 42.

21 Lk 1:75.

22 E.g. Ziesler, *Righteousness*, p. 142; Banks, 'Matthew's Understanding of the Law', p. 241; T. W. Manson, *The Sayings of Jesus* (1937; rpt London, 1964), p. 151.

23 Thus Fiedler, 'Der Begriff', I, p. 102; Strecker, *Weg*, p. 153; H. Hübner, *Das Gesetz in der synoptischen Tradition. Studien zur These einer progressiven Qumranisierung und Judaisierung innerhalb der synoptischen Tradition* (Witten, 1973), p. 35; Stuhlmacher, *Gerechtigkeit Gottes bei Paulus*, p. 188. E. A. Abbott, '"Righteousness" in the Gospels', *Proceedings of the British Academy* 8 (1917/18), on the other hand, has proposed that Matthew did not interpolate but rather preserved the words of Jesus while Luke omitted all these traditions as being too technical (pp. 362f). Abbott's view is based primarily on the rather subjective argument that it is improbable 'that Matthew, without any authority, interpolated all of these in Christ's doctrine' (p. 363).

24 *Weg*, pp. 150–3.

25 'Der Begriff', I, pp. 97–103.

26 *Weg*, p. 153.

27 'Der Begriff', I, p. 103.

28 *Weg*, p. 153.

29 'Der Begriff', I, p. 103.

30 For documentation of this view see the discussion of the respective verses below.

31 Strecker and Fiedler disagree as to the degree of redactional activity inherent in Mt 3:15, 5:10 and 21:32. Strecker (*Weg*, p. 153) argues that the term *dikaiosynē* is interpolated into a *Vorlage* in Mt 3:15 while in 5:10 and 21:32 it occurs in contexts which originate with the redactor. Fiedler ('Der Begriff', I, p. 103), on the other hand, argues that in 3:15 *dikaiosynē* is used as a thematic element in an independently formulated passage while in 5:10 and 21:32 it is used in an interpretive way, although more independently than in 5:6 and 6:33. The disagreement between Strecker and Fiedler suggests that in 3:15, 5:10 and 21:32 it is simply impossible to be certain as to the extent of the redactional activity.

32 E.g. Strecker, *Weg*, p. 153; Fiedler, 'Der Begriff', I, p. 122; Ziesler, *Righteousness*, p. 134; G. Barth, 'Matthew's Understanding of the Law', in

G. Bornkamm, G. Barth and H. J. Held, *Tradition and Interpretation in Matthew*, ET by Percy Scott (NT Library; London, 1963), p. 73; G. Bornkamm, 'End-Expectation and Church in Matthew', in *ibid.*, pp. 16f; Sand, '"Gesetzlosigkeit"', p.116; G. Schmahl, 'Die Antithesen der Bergpredigt', *Trierer Theologische Zeitschrift* 83 (1974), 285.

33   *The Setting of the Sermon on the Mount* (Cambridge, 1963), p. 102.

34   *Ibid.*

35   'Law', pp. 93f.

36   *Ibid.*, p. 95.

37   *Ibid.*, p. 139.

38   'End-Expectation', p. 25.

39   Barth, 'Law', pp. 93ff.

40   'End-Expectation', p. 25.

41   *Ibid.*, p. 16.

42   Strecker, *Weg*, p. 146.

43   *Ibid.*, p. 180. Cf. S. Sandmel, *A Jewish Understanding of the New Testament* (Cincinnati, 1956), pp. 148f. He implies that there is a new law, for Matthew affirms the law of Jesus rather than the law of Moses.

44   'Der Begriff', I, p. 124.

45   *Ibid.*, I, p. 123. Fiedler quotes from the German edition, but this quotation is taken from H. Windisch, *The Meaning of the Sermon on the Mount*, ET by S. MacLean Gilmour (Philadelphia, 1951), p. 28.

46   'Der Begriff', I, p. 127.

47   *Judaism*, I, p. 259. In the Tannaitic literature the principle of fencing Torah is mentioned in Aboth 1:1: 'They said three things: Be deliberate in judgment, raise up many disciples, and make a fence around the Law (*seyag latorah*)' (ET by Danby, *Mishnah*, p. 446). Cf. Sifre Deut 16 on 1:16, p. 25; Sifre Num 78 on 10:29, p. 74. J. Goldin, 'The End of Ecclesiastes. Literal Exegesis and its Transformation', in A. Altmann (ed.), *Biblical Motifs* (Studies and Texts 3; Cambridge, Mass., 1966), p. 141, has suggested that the reference to making a fence around Torah in Aboth 1:1 refers to 'the proper protection and preservation of the *text* of the Torah (almost certainly the five books of Moses) lest it be corrupted by false or inferior readings'. It should be noted, however, that Goldin does not deny that the principle here described as making a fence around Torah existed. Goldin only denies that this principle is designated by the expression *seyag latorah*. Consequently, even if the minority opinion expressed by Goldin is correct, it does not negate the view that the Tannaitic literature and Matthew make use of the principle of setting up a barricade to keep a man far from sin.

48   *Judaism*, I, p. 33. Cf. Aboth 3:14 where R. Akiba states: 'The tradition is a fence around the Law; Tithes [*sic*] are a fence around riches; vows are a fence around abstinence; a fence around wisdom is silence' (tr. by Danby, *Mishnah*, p. 452).

49   *Sayings of Jesus*, p. 154.

50   Cf. H. Braun, 'Beobachtungen zur Tora-Verschärfung im häretischen Spätjudentum', *ThLZ* 79 (1954), 352, concerning the intensive observance of the law in the Damascus Document.

51   *Rule of Qumran*, p. 251.

52   It should be noted that this saying is directed to the disciples in the context

of a polemical discussion dealing with the relationship between Judaism and Jesus's own teaching.

53 E.g. Allen, *Matthew*, p. 46; Davies, *The Setting of the Sermon on the Mount*, p. 291; Banks, 'Matthew's Understanding of the Law', p. 242; P. Gaechter, *Das Matthäus Evangelium* (Innsbruck, 1963), p. 167; Hill, *Matthew*, p. 119; Manson, *Sayings of Jesus*, p. 155; R. S. McConnell, *Law and Prophecy in Matthew's Gospel. The Authority and Use of the Old Testament in the Gospel of St. Matthew* (Theologische Dissertationen 2; Basel, 1969), p. 35; Schniewind, *Matthäus*, p. 56; Strecker, *Weg*, pp. 153f; Trilling, *Israel*, p. 184; Zahn, *Matthäus*, pp. 223f.

54 'Der Begriff', I, pp. 124, 127. For the view that righteousness is the gift of God see also F. F. Bruce, 'Justification by Faith in the Non-Pauline Writings of the New Testament', *EQ* 24 (1952), 68: J. C. Fenton, *The Gospel of St Matthew* (Pelican Gospel Commentaries; Harmondsworth, 1963), pp. 85, 95; P. Schaff, *The Gospel According to Matthew* (International Revision Commentary 1; New York, 1882), p. 58; A. Schlatter, *Das Evangelium nach Matthäus* (rev. edn; Stuttgart, 1961), p. 64.

55 Cf. Barth, 'Law', p. 139, for the observation that in the Gospel of Matthew the term *dikaiosynē* occurs only in actual sayings of Jesus.

56 *Ibid.*, p. 140.

57 Ziesler, *Righteousness*, p. 133.

58 *Ibid.*, p. 134.

59 *Ibid.*, p. 142.

60 *Ibid.*, pp. 142f. Also Schrenk's viewpoint is not clear with respect to the point under discussion (*TDNT*, II, pp. 198f).

61 Cf. D. R. A. Hare, *The Theme of Jewish Persecution of Christians in the Gospel According to St Matthew* (SNTS Monograph Series, 6; Cambridge, 1967), p. 131 n. 2: 'The possibility of non-Christian righteousness is acknowledged in 5:20 and 21:32.'

62 'Matthew's Understanding of the Law', p. 242. Cf. Strecker, *Weg*, pp. 141f, who notes that πλεῖον is to be understood in the quantitative sense of 'more'.

63 E.g. Allen, *Matthew*, p. 56.

64 *Matthäus*, p. 259. Cf. W. Grundmann, *Das Evangelium nach Matthäus* (Theologischer Handkommentar zum Neuen Testament 1; Berlin, 1968), p. 151; Schmahl, 'Die Antithesen der Bergpredigt', p. 287.

65 Tr. by K. Lake, *The Apostolic Fathers* (2 vols., Loeb Classical Library; New York, 1914), I, pp. 309f.

66 Thus Barth, 'Law', p. 97 n. 1; 'Matt 5.48 = Luke 6.36 forms in Matthew the summary of the preceding section (οὖν). If the Matthaean form had stood in Q, Luke would have turned a good conclusion into a worse. But in the Luke-form it is the beginning of the next section; the alteration by Matthew, who made of it a concluding verse to what was said about loving enemies, or alternatively to the whole of 5.21–47, in this way becomes intelligible.'

67 E.g. G. Bornkamm, *Jesus of Nazareth*, ET by Irene and Fraser McLuskey with J. M. Robinson (New York, 1960), p. 108; H. Braun, *Qumran und das Neue Testament* (2 vols.; Tübingen, 1966), I, p. 18; R. Bultmann, *Jesus and the Word*, ET by L. P. Smith and E. H. Lantero (New York, 1958), p. 120.

68 Tr. by Lake, *The Apostolic Fathers*, I, p. 319.

69 '"Knowledge" in the Dead Sea Scrolls and Matthew 11:25–30', *HTR* 46 (1953), 115.

70   *Ibid.*

71   Thus Barth, 'Law', p. 71. Cf. Strecker, *Weg*, p. 141.

72   There are yet other indications that Matthew puts an emphasis not only on the qualitative but also on the quantitative aspects of conduct. E.g. Jesus came to fulfil the law and the prophets (5:17), 'Fill up, then, the measure of your fathers' (23:32).

73   R. Hummel, *Die Auseinandersetzung zwischen Kirche und Judentum im Matthäusevangelium* (BEvTh 33; München, 1966), p. 69, states that it was self-evident to Matthew that there could be no righteousness without the law.

74   Thus Allen, *Matthew*, p. 56; Fiedler, 'Der Begriff', I, pp. 127f; Zahn, *Matthäus*, p. 261.

75   Thus Barth, 'Law', p. 139 n. 2; Davies, *The Setting of the Sermon on the Mount*, pp. 307f; Fiedler, 'Der Begriff', I, p. 127; Gaechter, *Matthäus*, p. 201; Hill, *Matthew*, p. 132; Schaff, *Matthew*, p. 68; Strecker, *Weg*, p. 153; Strack and Billerbeck, *Kommentar*, I, p. 386.

76   Hill, *Matthew*, p. 132, suggests that these are the 'three fundamental acts of Jewish piety'. Cf. Zahn, *Matthäus*, p. 260; Schaff, *Matthew*, p. 68.

77   Cf. Allen, *Matthew*, p. 57; Hill, *Matthew*, p. 132; Ziesler, *Righteousness*, p. 57.

78   *The Setting of the Sermon on the Mount*, p. 307.

79   *Matthäus*, p. 76.

80   Strack and Billerbeck, *Kommentar*, I, p. 386.

81   The verb ποιέω occurs in 5:19 and 6:1.

82   This argument is reminiscent of a point of contention between the Shammaites and Hillelites over the relationship between studying and doing. For example, in Aboth 1:15 Shammai states, 'say little and do much', thus exalting doing over studying, while in Aboth 1:17 Simeon b. Gamaliel states that 'not the expounding [of the Law] is the chief thing but the doing [of it]' (tr. by Danby, *Mishnah*, p. 447).

83   For the importance of the balance between theory and practice see also Mt 7:24 and 23:3.

84   'Der Begriff', I, p. 133.

85   As Gaechter, *Matthäus*, p. 233, has pointed out, Mt 6:34 is simply an addendum.

86   Cf. Strecker, *Weg*, p. 155; Kertelge, *'Rechtfertigung' bei Paulus*, p. 46; Stuhlmacher, *Gerechtigkeit Gottes bei Paulus*, p. 189. An alternative view is proposed by H. Günther, 'Die Gerechtigkeit des Himmelreiches in der Bergpredigt', *KerDog* 17 (1971), 116; 'Doch kann man den Genetiv des Personalpronomens auch weniger stringent auffassen, fast adverbial: "... trachtet nach der Gerechtigkeit dort ...".'

87   E.g. F. V. Filson, *A Commentary on the Gospel According to St. Matthew* (BNTC; London, 1960), p. 102; A. H. McNeile, *The Gospel According to St. Matthew* (London, 1915), p. 89; Stuhlmacher, *Gerechtigkeit Gottes bei Paulus*, p. 189.

88   Hill, *Matthew*, p. 145.

89   E.g. Barth, 'Law', p. 140 n. 1; Grundmann, *Matthäus*, p. 217; Ziesler, *Righteousness*, pp. 142f.

90   E.g. Fiedler, 'Der Begriff', p. 139; Kertelge, *'Rechtfertigung' bei Paulus*, p. 47 n. 130; Schlatter, *Matthäus*, p. 106; Schrenk, *TDNT*, II, p. 199.

91 'Der Begriff', I, p. 140.

92 Ziesler, *Righteousness*, p. 135. Cf. Barth, 'Law', p. 140 n. 1; Fiedler, 'Der Begriff', I, p. 140.

93 Cf. Barth, 'Law', p. 139; Kertelge, *'Rechtfertigung' bei Paulus*, p. 46; G. D. Kilpatrick, *The Origins of the Gospel According to St. Matthew* (Oxford, 1946), p. 16; Stuhlmacher, *Gerechtigkeit Gottes bei Paulus*, p. 188; Trilling, *Israel*, p. 146.

94 Lk 12:31 also reads προστεθήσεται.

95 Cf. Schaff, *Matthew*, p. 82; Mt 6:33 'contains the crowning thought of this chapter'.

96 For a discussion of the interconnection of Mt 5:20; 6:1, 33 see also Gaechter, *Matthäus*, p. 232; Trilling, *Israel*, pp. 146f.

97 For the suggestion that Mt 6:33 echoes 5:48 see Schaff, *Matthew*, p. 82; Stuhlmacher, *Gerechtigkeit Gottes bei Paulus*, p. 189.

98 Trilling, *Israel*, pp. 146f.

99 Hill, *Matthew*, p. 145. Cf. A. Descamps, *Les Justes et la Justice dans les évangiles et le christianisme primitif* (Louvain, 1950), p. 178; Strecker, *Weg*, p. 155; Trilling, *Israel*, p. 145.

100 Thus Barth, 'Law', p. 139; M. Dibelius, *Der Brief des Jakobus* (Meyers Kommentar 15; 10th rev. edn; Göttingen, 1959), p. 105; Strecker, *Weg*, p. 155.

101 For a discussion of this passage see ch. 3, sect. 2.

102 See O. Eissfeldt, 'Πληρῶσαι πᾶσαν δικαιοσύνην in Matthäus 3:15', *ZNW* 61 (1970), 209–15, for a good summary of the history of interpretation of this text.

103 Barth, 'Law', p. 140.

104 *Ibid.*, pp. 140f.

105 *Ibid.*, p. 140 n. 3.

106 *Ibid.*

107 *Ibid.*, p. 141 n. 4.

108 *Ibid.*, p. 138 n. 4. Some commentators have treated ἡμῖν as a *pluralis maiestatis*. E.g. J. M. Gibson, *The Gospel of St. Matthew* (Expositor's Bible; Toronto, 1890), p. 33, claims that the 'us' refers strictly to Jesus himself and points to the fact that Jesus at this time reckons himself not as the Messiah but simply one of Israel. McNeile, *Matthew*, p. 31, states: 'By ἡμῖν the Lord associates Himself with the Jewish people.' C. G. Montefiore, *The Synoptic Gospels* (2 vols.; 2nd rev. edn; London, 1927), II, pp. 16f, sees ἡμῖν as referring to all Israelites, not just to Jesus and John. Strecker, *Weg*, p. 180, and B. Weiss, *Das Matthäusevangelium und seine Lucas-Parallelen* (Halle, 1876), p. 110, on the other hand, hold the same view as Barth and this view appears to be the one which has the soundest grammatical basis.

109 Barth, 'Law', p. 138 n. 4.

110 For Pauline interpretations of Mt 3:15 see also H. Schlier, 'Zur kirchlichen Lehre von der Taufe', *ThLZ* 72 (1947), 326; Schniewind, *Matthäus*, p. 326; H. Ljungman, *Das Gesetz erfüllen, Matth. 5,17ff. und 3,15 untersucht* (Lund 1954), pp. 124f; 'Mit *Christus* wird die Schrift (das Gesetz) in Gerechtigkeit "gefüllt". Durch Christus kommt Gerechtigkeit. Der Akt, der die Gerechtigkeit mit Christus verbindet, ist sein Opfertod, Matth. 3,15–17. Auf diesen Tod wird gezielt, wenn es heisst, die Taufe Jesu geschehe, "um alle δικαιοσύνη zu 'füllen'".'

111   'Der Begriff', I, p. 109.
112   *Ibid.*, I, p. 111.
113   *Ibid.*, I, p. 112.
114   *Ibid.*, I, p. 113.
115   The data presented by Fiedler, 'Der Begriff', I, p. 111, and Schrenk, *TDNT*, II, pp. 186f, to substantiate the claim that the Messiah is designated as being righteous and as doing righteousness are taken primarily from the Old Testament. It should be noted that there is no scholarly consensus on the messianic interpretation of many Old Testament passages. However, even if this interpretation of the Old Testament were correct, it would still not prove that it was a generally accepted belief in Matthew's time that the task of the Messiah was to fulfil all righteousness in the sense that Fiedler attributes to Mt 3:15.
116   For example, in Sifre Deut 144 on 16:19 (p. 199) *tsedeq* refers to everything that is right (see ch. 3, sect. 3). *Tsedeq* embraces the total will of God which is to be taught by the sages. On the basis of the Damascus Document (see ch. 2, sect. 2) it is clear that the Teacher of Righteousness teaches righteousness in the sense of teaching the entire will of God. See esp. CD 1:1, 11f, 16; 6:11; 20:32f.
117   *Baptism in the New Testament*, ET by J. K. S. Reid (SBT 1; London, 1950), p. 18.
118   Hill, *Matthew*, p. 96. Cf. Ziesler, *Righteousness*, p. 133.
119   *Baptism*, p. 19.
120   *Ibid.*, p. 20.
121   *Ibid.*
122   So Zahn, *Matthäus*, p. 144. Cf. Klostermann, *Matthäusevangelium*, p. 25; Lohmeyer, *Matthäus*, p. 51; 'So ist also die Taufe die letzte und höchste Forderung, die Gott jetzt zu allen Geboten des Gesetzes noch auferlegt; mit ihr ist dann "alle Gerechtigkeit erfüllt".'
123   Attempts to translate πᾶσαν δικαιοσύνην as 'righteousness of all' or 'righteousness for all' do violence to Greek syntax and seem to be motivated by a desire to bring Mt 3:15 into harmony with Pauline theology. E.g. A. Descamps, *Les Justes et la Justice*, pp. 116-18.
124   Cf. Stuhlmacher, *Gerechtigkeit Gottes bei Paulus*, p. 191; 'In dem πληρῶσαι πᾶσαν δικαιοσύνην ist ja auch nicht, paulinisch, Jesu stellvertretende Gesetzeserfüllung, sondern sein urbildlicher Toragehorsam betont.'
125   Allen, *Matthew*, p. 28. For the view that in Mt 3:15 righteousness refers to right conduct see also A. W. Argyle, *The Gospel According to Matthew* (Cambridge Bible Commentary; Cambridge, 1963), p. 37; Grundmann, *Matthäus*, p. 97; Hill, *Matthew*, p. 96; Montefiore, *Synoptic Gospels*, II, p. 16; Schaff, *Matthew*, p. 33; D. M. Stanley, *The Gospel of St. Matthew* (New Testament Reading Guide; 2nd rev. edn; Collegeville, 1963), p. 33; Strecker, *Weg*, pp. 179f.
126   Windisch, *Sermon on the Mount*, p. 66, suggests that 'The phrase "to fulfill all righteousness" in ch. 3:15, also, means "to evince righteousness by means of a specific deed"'. Cf. Trilling, *Israel*, p. 176. This interpretation is unconvincing since πληρῶσαι here means fulfil in the sense of observe rather than evince.
127   E.g. Fiedler, 'Der Begriff', I, p. 149; Hill, *Matthew*, p. 96.

128 'The Baptism of John and the Qumran Community', *HTR* 50 (1957), 185.

129 'Der Begriff', I, p. 145.

130 *Ibid.*, I, pp. 141–4.

131 *Ibid.*, I, pp. 143f.

132 *Ibid.*, I, p. 149. Cf. H. Cremer, *Biblisch-theologisches Wörterbuch der Neutestamentlichen Gräcität* (5th edn; Gotha, 1888), p. 279; 'Es ist der Weg, auf dem Gerechtigkeit u. Heil zu Stande kommt, hier sich auf die Taufe Joh. beziehend.' Schlatter, *Matthäus*, p. 320; 'Allein die Priester und Lehrer verweigerten dem Propheten den Glauben und wandten sich damit von der Gnade und Gabe Gottes ab.'

133 'Der Begriff', I, p. 142.

134 Zahn, *Matthäus*, p. 626 n. 27, even claims that 'ἐν ὁδῷ δικαιοσύνης ist ein ungriechischer Ausdruck'.

135 It could also be that Mt 21:32 is meant in an ironical way. The opponents of Jesus are told that John came to them with their own teaching and they did not believe him.

136 *TDNT*, V, pp. 86f. Cf. Zahn, *Matthäus*, p. 626 n. 27.

137 *Righteousness*, p. 131. Cf. Argyle, *Matthew*, p. 161; Gaechter, *Matthäus*, p. 679; Manson, *Sayings of Jesus*, p. 223; McNeile, *Matthew*, p. 308; Schniewind, *Matthäus*, p. 217; Strack and Billerbeck, *Kommentar*, I, pp. 866f; C. H. H. Scobie, *John the Baptist* (Philadelphia, 1964), p. 85.

138 Such a view is proposed by Fiedler, 'Der Begriff', I, p. 148; Grundmann, *Matthäus*, pp. 458f; Hill, *Matthew*, p. 298; Strecker, *Weg*, p. 187.

139 'Law', p. 140.

140 'Der Begriff', I, p. 117. Cf. Ziesler, *Righteousness*, p. 144; 'It is probably no accident that 5.6 precedes 5.20; human righteousness is inadequate, and what is needed is not only a more thoroughgoing kind, but one which comes as God's gift to those who long for it.'

141 Fiedler, 'Der Begriff', I, p. 118. Cf. E. Fuchs, 'Jesu Selbstzeugnis nach Matthäus 5', *ZThK* 51 (1954), 27.

142 E.g. Grundmann, *Matthäus*, p. 127; Lohmeyer, *Matthäus*, pp. 87f; McNeile, *Matthew*, pp. 51f; Schaff, *Matthew*, p. 52; Schniewind, *Matthäus*, p. 44; Schrenk, *TDNT*, II, p. 198; Zahn, *Matthäus*, p. 189; Ziesler, *Righteousness*, p. 142.

143 Bultmann, *Theology of the New Testament*, I, p. 273. Cf. Bornkamm, 'End-Expectation', pp. 123f; Strack and Billerbeck, *Kommentar*, I, p. 201.

144 *The Bible and the Greeks* (London, 1935), p. 55.

145 Cf. Stuhlmacher, *Gerechtigkeit Gottes bei Paulus*, p. 190.

146 Manson, *Sayings of Jesus*, p. 48. Cf. Barth, 'Law', p. 140; Günther, 'Die Gerechtigkeit des Himmelreiches in der Bergpredigt', p. 123; Hill, *Matthew*, p. 112; Kertelge, *'Rechtfertigung' bei Paulus*, p. 47.

147 Hill, *Matthew*, p. 112. Cf. Grundmann, *Matthäus*, p. 126.

148 Weiss, *Matthäusevangelium*, p. 202.

149 The view that in Mt 5:6 righteousness refers to man's conduct rather than God's gift is supported by Strecker, *Weg*, p. 158; Allen, *Matthew*, p. 41; Fenton, *Matthew*, p. 81; Klostermann, *Matthäusevangelium*, p. 37; Weiss, *Matthäusevangelium*, p. 202.

150 Cf. Grundmann, *Matthäus*, p. 132. Although this appears to be the most log' explanation, the following suggestion by Hare, *Jewish Persecution of Christia*

p. 131, should not be ruled out completely: 'The phrase may be descriptive rather than interpretive; that is to say, ἕνεκεν δικαιοσύνης may serve simply to identify the persecuted ("Blessed are the persecuted righteous") rather than to indicate the cause of persecution.'

151 It has been suggested that the absence of the definite article in ἕνεκεν δικαιοσύνης indicates that this expression refers to human conduct. Thus Strecker, *Weg*, p. 154; Stuhlmacher, *Gerechtigkeit Gottes bei Paulus*, p. 190.

152 'Der Begriff', I, p. 118.

153 *Ibid.*, I, pp. 118f.

154 W. Michaelis, *Das Evangelium nach Matthäus* (2 vols.; Zürich, 1948–9) I, p. 225, as quoted by Fiedler, 'Der Begriff', I, p. 119.

155 'Der Begriff', I, p. 179.

156 *Ibid.*, I, pp. 120ff.

157 E.g. Barth, 'Law', p. 139; Strecker, *Weg*, p. 154; Ziesler, *Righteousness*, p. 142; Hill, *Matthew*, p. 113; McNeile, *Matthew*, p. 53; Stuhlmacher, *Gerechtigkeit Gottes bei Paulus*, p. 190; Schrenk, *TDNT*, II, p. 199.

158 *Righteousness*, p. 59.

159 *Ibid.*, p. 60.

160 *Ibid.*

161 *Ibid.*, p. 61; 'It 4 times renders *chesed* when referring to man's righteousness (Gen. 19.19; 20.13; 21.23; Prov. 20.28), and 5 times when referring to God's (Gen. 24.27; 32.11(10); Ex. 15.13; 34.7; Isa. 63.7 – where *chesed* occurs twice, the first case being rendered by ἔλεος).'

162 *Ibid.*, p. 61.

163 *Ibid.*, p. 61 n. 3. For support Ziesler cites E. Hatch, *Essays in Biblical Greek* (Oxford, 1889), p. 50, who states that the meanings of these two words had interpenetrated each other.

164 *The Bible and the Greeks*, p. 56.

165 *Ibid.*, pp. 45f.

166 *Ibid.*, pp. 55f.

167 *Essays in Biblical Greek*, p. 49.

168 *Righteousness*, p. 59. For the view that in the LXX *eleēmosynē* as a translation of *tsedaqah* reflects the specialized meaning of the latter as alms see also F. Rosenthal, 'Sedakah, Charity', *HUCA* 23 (1950–1), I, 429.

169 Dodd, *The Bible and the Greeks*, p. 56.

170 Ziesler, *Righteousness*, p. 60.

171 Thus Allen, *Matthew*, p. 56; Gaechter, *Matthäus*, p. 204; Hill, *Matthew*, p. 132.

172 Cf. Strack and Billerbeck, *Kommentar*, I, pp. 387f.

173 See Ziesler, *Righteousness*, p. 59.

174 If the variant readings in Mt 20:7; 27:4, 24 are taken into account then there are 20.

175 Mt 1:19 in 'The Birth of Jesus' (1:18–25); 13:43 in 'The Interpretation of the Parable of the Weeds' (13:36–43); 13:49 in 'The Parable of the Net' (13:47–50); 20:4 in 'The Parable of the Labourers in the Vineyard' (20: 1–16); 25:37, 46 in 'The Last Judgment' (25:31–46).

176 Mt 5:45, 10:41 (3 times), 23:28, 27:19.

177 Mt 13:17 = Lk 10:24; Mt 23:29 = Lk 11:47; Mt 23:35 (twice) = Lk 11:50f.

178 Thus RSV (London, 1952).

179 Thus American Standard Version (New York, 1929). Cf. Grundmann, *Matthäus*, p. 495, who refers to Heb 11:4.

180 Kilpatrick, 'A Theme of the Lucan Passion Story and Luke xxiii.47', *JThS* 43 (1942), p. 35, claims that in Mt 23:35, 'innocent' is at least as suitable a translation as 'righteous'. Ziesler, *Righteousness*, p. 138, states, 'but more probably Abel is righteous because, in contrast to his lawless contemporaries, he did God's will'.

181 *Righteousness*, p. 138. Cf. Grundmann, *Matthäus*, p. 342, with respect to Mt 13:17.

182 Some commentators claim that when *dikaios* is found in conjunction with 'prophet', it refers to a witnessing or teaching function. Thus D. Hill, 'Δίκαιοι as a Quasi-Technical Term', *NTS* 11 (1964), 296–302; Descamps, *Les Justes et la Justice*, pp. 135–8; Kilpatrick, *The Origins of the Gospel According to St. Matthew*, p. 126. The evidence for this view is very conjectural.

183 *Righteousness*, p. 138.

184 *Ibid.*, p. 140.

185 Cf. Allen, *Matthew*, p. 9; Hill, *Matthew*, p. 78, and *Greek Words and Hebrew Meanings. Studies in the Semantics of Soteriological Terms* (SNTS Monograph Series, 5; Cambridge, 1967), p. 124; McNeile, *Matthew*, p. 7. The view expressed by Hatch, *Essays in Biblical Greek*, p. 51, and C. Spicq, 'Joseph, son mari, étant juste . . . (Mt. I, 19)', *RB* 71 (1964), pp. 213f, that *dikaios* refers to Joseph's kindness toward Mary is not explicit in the text. As Ziesler, *Righteousness*, p. 140, points out, this adjective appears on the whole not to have such a meaning. On the other hand, insofar as the law is good, treatment according to the law is in fact compassionate.

186 *Righteousness*, p. 140.

187 Cf. Allen, *Matthew*, p. 91; Hill, *Matthew*, p. 175.

188 *Les Justes et la Justice*, pp. 201ff.

189 *Synoptic Gospels*, II, p. 154.

190 *Righteousness*, p. 141. Hill, *Matthew*, p. 196, suggests that this saying belongs to the period of Jewish Christianity.

191 For the view that *dikaios* = innocent in 27:19 see Grundmann, *Matthäus*, p. 554; Hill, *Matthew*, p. 350. For the view that *dikaios* has the double meaning of righteous and innocent in this case, see Ziesler, *Righteousness*, pp. 137f, Schrenk, *TDNT*, II, p. 187.

192 Barth, 'Law', p. 144 n. 5.

193 E.g. E. Schweizer, *Lordship and Discipleship* (SBT 28; London, 1960), p. 33, cites Mt 27:19 as proof that 'there is no doubt that the early Church has seen Jesus in the character of the Righteous One suffering in obedience'. However, L. Ruppert, *Jesus als der leidende Gerechte? Der Weg Jesu im Lichte eines alt- und zwischentestamentlichen Motivs* (Stuttgarter Bibelstudien 59; Stuttgart, 1972), p. 74, has shown that if Jesus attributed an atoning efficacy to his suffering, it was in his capacity as suffering prophet rather than as suffering Righteous One.

194 *Righteousness*, pp. 136, 138.

195 *Ibid.*, p. 141.

196 *The History of the Synoptic Tradition*, ET by J. Marsh (2nd edn; Oxford, 1968), p. 124.

197 *Righteousness*, p. 138.

198   *TDNT*, II, p. 188. Cf. Hill, *Matthew*. p. 286; 'There is no need to suggest a hint of Paulinism here.'

Chapter 5. The relative significance of the concept of righteousness in the Gospel of Matthew

1   Cf. Mt 5:17–18.
2   *Righteousness*, pp. 142–4.
3   *TDNT*, II, pp. 198–200.
4   'Der Begriff', I, p. 150.
5   'End-Expectation', p. 31.
6   *Righteousness*, p. 144.
7   *TDNT*, II, p. 200.
8   'Der Begriff', I, *passim*.
9   '*Rechtfertigung' bei Paulus*, p. 47. See ch. 1, sect. 1, for a discussion of Kertelge's view.
10   *Gerechtigkeit Gottes bei Paulus*, pp. 190f.
11   Cf. Ziesler, *Righteousness*, p. 144, who notes that if righteousness is not both demand and gift in Matthew then this is true.
12   See ch. 4, sect. 3.
13   Mt 20:28 = Mk 10:45.
14   *Weg*, pp. 157f, 179ff, 187. Trilling, *Israel*, p. 184 n. 91, agrees with Strecker.
15   *Weg*, p. 231.
16   *Ibid*., p. 181.
17   *Ibid*., p. 213.
18   E.g. Strecker, *Weg*, p. 191; W. F. Albright and C. S. Mann, *Matthew* (Anchor Bible; Garden City, 1971), p. lxxvii.
19   'Disciples and Discipleship in Matthew and Luke', *BThB* 3 (1973), 254.
20   *Ibid*., p. 254 n. 23.
21   *Weg*, p. 191: Mt 8:21; 10:24f, 42.
22   *Ibid*.
23   *Ibid*.
24   *Ibid*.
25   Cf. U. Luz, 'Die Jünger im Matthäusevangelium', *ZNW* 62 (1971), 145, who comments with respect to Mt 10:42: 'hier muss μαθητής eindeutig von der matthäischen Gemeinde her, also transparent verstanden werden'. It should also be noted that there are a number of passages which, while not actually providing proof that the term 'disciple' has an inclusive meaning, are best explained in terms of this meaning. E.g. Lk 24:9 states that the women 'told all this to the eleven and to all the rest'. Mt 28:8 simply states: 'and ran to tell his disciples.' It appears that the term 'disciples' could refer to 'the eleven and all the rest' in this case. The fact that the Gospel of Matthew does not contain the tradition found in Mk 5:18f is also note-worthy. Cf. Barth, 'Law', pp. 99f, 'In Mark not all who believe on Jesus enter into discipleship. The wish of the possessed man who was healed (Mark 5.18f.) to enter into discipleship is turned down. Matthew omits these verses.'
26   In the rest of the NT this verb occurs only in Acts 14:21. The 3 occurrences in Matthew appear to be redactional. Thus Luz, 'Die Jünger im Matthäus-evangelium', p. 157; G. Baumbach, 'Die Mission im Matthäus-Evangelium', *ThLZ* 92 (1967), 889.

27   H. Kasting, *Die Anfänge der urchristlichen Mission* (BEvTh 55; München, 1969), p. 36, notes that the emphasis in vv. 19–20 is on μαθητεύσατε.

28   Cf. Sheridan, 'Disciples and Discipleship', p. 242.

29   C. Rogers, 'The Great Commission', *BibSac* 130 (1973), 263, explains that the verb means 'to practise the duties of a μαθητής, that is, to be a disciple'. The verb can also have a 'causative meaning, "to make a disciple".'

30   Strecker, *Weg*, p. 192.

31   Albright and Mann, *Matthew*, p. lxxvii. Cf. Allen, *Matthew*, pp. 154f.

32   Albright and Mann, *Matthew*, p. lxxvii.

33   *Ibid.*

34   *Ibid.*

35   *Ibid.*, p. 361.

36   Cf. Luz, 'Die Jünger im Matthäusevangelium', p. 158: 'Vielmehr dient das Verb μαθητεύω gerade dazu, Jüngerschaft für die Gegenwart des Evangelisten transparent zu machen.'

37   *The Parables of Jesus*, ET by S. H. Hooke (rev. edn; New York, 1963), pp. 39f.

38   *Ibid.*, p. 40. Jeremias points out that the Johannine Shepherd parable is also addressed to opponents; John 10:6; cf. 9:40, 10:19ff (*ibid.*, p. 40 n. 65).

39   And Mk 15:43: 'a respected member of the council'.

40   'Law', p. 121.

41   *Ibid.*, p. 122.

42   *Weg*, p. 179.

43   'End-Expectation', p. 130.

44   *Righteousness*, p. 134.

45   See esp. Mt 7:16–20, 21:43.

46   Mt 16:27, Barth, 'Law', p. 95: 'Matthew has expanded Mark 8.38b to a description of the judgment, in which the Son of man will reward everyone according to his πρᾶξις.'

47   Thus O. Michel, 'Der Abschluss des Matthäusevangeliums', *EvTh* 10 (1951), 21. Cf. Trilling, *Israel*, p. 21.

48   J. D. Kingsbury, 'The Composition and Christology of Matt 28:16–20', *JBL* 93 (1974), 573, and Kilpatrick, *Matthew*, p. 49, have presented a good case for the view that vv. 16–20 are completely redactional. Others, e.g. Barth, 'Law', p. 131, and Kasting, *Die Anfänge der urchristlichen Mission*, pp. 37f, have argued that although redactional activity is prominent, these verses are based on traditional materials.

49   'Law', p. 102 n. 1.

50   The noun θέλημα is also found in Lk 12:47 (twice) and 23:25 but not used with direct reference to God.

51   In addition to these 5 references the noun θέλημα occurs in Mt 21:31, but in this case it is not used with direct reference to God.

52   Cf. Barth, 'Law', p. 58; Bacon, *Matthew*, pp. 412ff; Kilpatrick, *Matthew*, pp. 108ff.

53   *Jewish Persecution of Christians*, p. 131 n. 1.

54   Mt 16:18, 18:17; ἐκκλησία.

55   Fiedler, 'Der Begriff', I, pp. 96f.

56   See ch. 6 for a discussion of the fact that Mt 5:20, 6:1 and 21:32 do not deal with Christian righteousness *per se*. In these cases righteousness is a

provisional concept employed solely as a vehicle by which the teaching of Jesus could be explained to non-disciples.

57   See p. 110 above.

Chapter 6. The provisional function of the Matthaean concept of righteousness

1   See ch. 4, sect. 2.
2   For the discussion of the structure of Mt 5 see ch. 4, sect. 2.
3   It was suggested above that in 1QS 5:4 and 8:2, and possibly even in 1:5, the term *tsedaqah* may refer to almsgiving. But there is no definite proof that this is the case.
4   Cf. Mt 5:10.
5   This holds true even in those writings in which *tsedeq* is subordinated to *'emet*.
6   Possibly also in 1QS 10:26, 11:15 and 1QM 4:6.

BIBLIOGRAPHY AND SYSTEM OF REFERENCES

I Reference system for the major Tannaitic midrashim

1 Mekilta of R. Ishmael

The Mekilta is cited according to the tractate headings and chapter enumeration adopted in the edition by J. Z. Lauterbach, *Mekilta de-Rabbi Ishmael* (3 vols.; Philadelphia, 1933–5), and the first volume and page reference is to this edition. The second page reference is to the edition by H. S. Horovitz and I. A. Rabin, *Mechilta d'Rabbi Ismael* (1931; rpt Jerusalem, 1970). In addition, the chapter and verse number of the biblical passage being commented on is given.

2 Sifra (Torat Kohanim)

Sifra is cited by the biblical section, the relevant pereq or parasha and the number of the halakah according to the traditional text, *Sifra d'Be Rab. Hu' Sefer Torat Kohanim* (rpt Jerusalem, 1959). In addition the chapter and verse number of the biblical passage being commented on is given.

3 Sifre Numbers (Sifre Bemidbar)

Sifre Num is cited by paragraph (pisqa') and page number of the edition by H. S. Horovitz, *Siphre ad Numeros adjecto Siphre zutta* (1917; rpt Jerusalem, 1966). In addition, the biblical passage being commented upon is given.

4 Sifre Deuteronomy (Sifre Debarim)

Sifre Deut is cited by paragraph (pisqa'), biblical passage commented upon, and page number of the edition by L. Finkelstein, *Sifre on Deuteronomy* (1939; rpt New York, 1969).

II Texts and tools

Aland, Kurt *et al. The Greek New Testament.* Stuttgart: United Bible Societies, 1966.

Albeck, Hanok. *Mishnah.* 6 vols. Tel Aviv: Dvir, 1958.

Allegro, John M. *DJD*, V: *Qumran Cave 4.* Oxford: Clarendon Press, 1968.

Barthélemy, D., and J. T. Milik. *DJD, I: Qumran Cave I.* Oxford: Clarendon Press, 1955.

Blackman, Philip. *Mishnayoth.* 6 vols.; 3rd edn. New York: Judaica Press, 1965.

Burrows, Millar (ed.). *The Dead Sea Scrolls of St. Mark's Monastery.* Vol. I *The Isaiah Manuscript and the Habakkuk Commentary.* New Haven, Conn.: American Schools of Oriental Research, 1950.

Cremer, H. *Biblisch-theologisches Wörterbuch der Neutestamentlichen Gräcität.* 5th edn. Gotha: Friedrich Andreas Perthes, 1888.

Danby, Herbert. *The Mishnah.* 1933; rpt London: Oxford University Press, 1967.

Tractate Sanhedrin, Mishnah and Tosefta. Translations of Early Documents, Series III, Rabbinic Texts. New York: Macmillan, 1919.

Epstein, I. (ed.). *The Babylonian Talmud.* 35-vol. edn, 1935–48; rpt in 18 vols. London: Soncino Press, 1961.

Finkelstein, Louis. *Sifre on Deuteronomy.* 1939; rpt New York: Jewish Theological Seminary of America, 1969.

Habermann, A. M. *The Scrolls from the Judean Desert.* In Hebrew. Tel Aviv: Machbaroth Lesifruth Publishing House, 1959.

Horovitz, H. S. *Siphre ad Numeros adjecto Siphre zutta.* 1917; rpt Jerusalem: Wahrmann Books, 1966.

Horovitz, H. S., and I. A. Rabin. *Mechilta d'Rabbi Ismael.* 1931; rpt Jerusalem: Wahrmann Books, 1970.

Jastrow, Marcus. *A Dictionary of the Targumim, the Talmud Babli and Jerushalmi, and the Midrashic Literature.* 2 vols. 1903; rpt Tel Aviv, 1972.

Kasovsky, Chayim Yehoshua. *'Otsar Leshon Ha-Mishna. Thesaurus Mishnae.* Rev. edn, by Moshe Kasovsky, 4 vols. Tel Aviv, 1967.

Kasowski, Chaim Josua (same as above). *'Otsar Leshon Ha-Tosefta. Thesaurus Thosephthae.* Ed. by Moshe Kasovsky, 6 vols. Jerusalem, 1932–61.

Kautzsch, E. *Gesenius' Hebrew Grammar.* 2nd English edn, rev. and tr. according to 28th German edn by A. E. Cowley. Oxford: Clarendon Press, 1910.

Kittel, Gerhard, *Sifre zu Deuteronomium.* Rabbinische Texte; 1st Lieferung. Stuttgart: W. Kohlhammer, 1922.

Kittel, Gerhard (ed.), *Theological Dictionary of the New Testament.* ET by G. W. Bromiley; 9 vols. Grand Rapids, Mich.: Wm B. Eerdmans, 1964–74.

Kittel, Rudolf. *Biblia Hebraica.* 7th rev. edn. Stuttgart: Württembergische Bibelanstalt, 1968.

Kosovsky, Biniamin. *Otzar Leshon Hatanna'im. Concordantiae verborum quae in Mechilta D'Rabbi Ismael.* 4 vols. Jerusalem: Jewish Theological Seminary of America, 1965–6.

Otzar Leshon Hatanna'im. Concordantiae verborum quae in Sifra aut Torat Kohanim. 4 vols. Jerusalem: Jewish Theological Seminary of America, 1967–9.

Otzar Leshon Hatanna'im. Concordantiae verborum quae in Sifrei Numeri et Deuteronomium. 5 vols. Jerusalem: Jewish Theological Seminary of America, 1970–4.

Kuhn, K. G. *Der tannaitische Midrasch Sifre zu Numeri.* Stuttgart: W. Kohlhammer Verlag, 1959.

Konkordanz zu den Qumrantexten. Göttingen: Vandenhoeck & Ruprecht, 1960.

'Nachträge zur "Konkordanz zu den Qumrantexten"', *RQ* 4 (1963), 163–234.

Lake, Kirsopp. *The Apostolic Fathers.* 2 vols. Loeb Classical Library. New York: Macmillan, 1914.

Lauterbach, Jacob Z. *Mekilta de-Rabbi Ishmael.* 3 vols. Philadelphia: Jewish Publication Society of America, 1933-5.

Levertoff, Paul P. *Midrash Sifre on Numbers.* Translations of Early Documents, Series III, Rabbinic Texts. New York: Macmillan, 1926.

Lieberman, Saul. *The Tosefta.* 4 vols. New York: Jewish Theological Seminary of America, 1955-73.

Lohse, Eduard. *Die Texte aus Qumran. Hebräisch und Deutsch.* 2nd rev. edn. Darmstadt: Wissenschaftliche Buchgesellschaft, 1971.

Maier, Johann. *Die Texte vom Toten Meer.* 2 vols. München: Ernst Reinhardt Verlag, 1960.

Rahlfs, Alfred. *Septuaginta.* 2 vols. Stuttgart: Privilegierte Württembergische Bibelanstalt, 1935.

Schechter, S. *Fragments of a Zadokite Work.* Documents of Jewish Sectaries 1. 1910; rpt n.p.: Ktav, 1970.

Sifra d'Be Rab. Hu' Sefer Torat Kohanim. A reprinting of the traditional text. Jerusalem, 1959.

Vermes, G. *The Dead Sea Scrolls in English.* Rev. edn. Harmondsworth: Penguin Books, 1968.

Winter, Jakob. *Sifra. Halachischer Midrasch zu Leviticus.* Breslau: Stefan Münz, 1938.

Winter, Jakob, and Aug. Wünsche. *Mechiltha. Ein tannaitischer Midrasch zu Exodus.* Leipzig: J. C. Hinrichs'sche Buchhandlung, 1909.

Young, Robert. *Analytical Concordance to the Bible.* 22nd American edn. Grand Rapids, Mich.: Wm B. Eerdmans, n.d.

Zuckermandel, M. S. *Tosephta.* New edn. Jerusalem: Wahrmann Books, 1970.

III Books and articles

Abbott, Edwin A. '"Righteousness" in the Gospels', *Proceedings of the British Academy* 8 (1917-18), 351-63.

Albright, W. F., and C. S. Mann. *Matthew.* Anchor Bible. Garden City, N.Y.: Doubleday, 1971.

Allegro, J. M. 'Further Light on the History of the Qumran Sect', *JBL* 75 (1956), 89-95.

Allen, Willoughby C. *A Critical and Exegetical Commentary on the Gospel According to S. Matthew.* ICC; 3rd edn. Edinburgh: T. & T. Clark, 1912.

Argyle, A. W. *The Gospel According to Matthew.* Cambridge Bible Commentary. Cambridge: University Press, 1963.

Bacher, Wilhelm. *Die exegetische Terminologie der jüdischen Traditionsliteratur.* 2 vols. 1899-1905; rpt Hildesheim: Georg Olms, 1965.

Bacon, Benjamin W. *Studies in Matthew.* New York: Henry Holt, 1930.

Baillet, Maurice. 'Un recueil liturgique de Qumrân, Grotte 4. Les paroles des luminaires', *RB* 68 (1961), 195-250.

Banks, Robert. 'Matthew's Understanding of the Law. Authenticity and Interpretation in Matthew 5:17-20', *JBL* 93 (1974), 226-42.

Barth, Gerhard. 'Matthew's Understanding of the Law', in G. Bornkamm,

G. Barth and H. J. Held, *Tradition and Interpretation in Matthew.* ET by Percy Scott; The New Testament Library. London: SCM Press, 1963.

Baumbach, Günther. 'Die Mission im Matthäus-Evangelium', *ThLZ* 92 (1967), 889–93.

Becker, Jürgen. *Das Heil Gottes. Heils- und Sündenbegriffe in den Qumrantexten und im Neuen Testament.* StUNT 3. Göttingen: Vandenhoeck & Ruprecht, 1964.

Black, Matthew. *The Scrolls and Christian Origins.* London: Thomas Nelson, 1961.

Bornkamm, Günther. 'End-Expectation and Church in Matthew', in G. Bornkamm, G. Barth and H. J. Held, *Tradition and Interpretation in Matthew.* ET by Percy Scott; The New Testament Library. London: SCM Press, 1963.

Jesus of Nazareth. ET by Irene and Fraser McLuskey with James M. Robinson. New York: Harper & Brothers, 1960.

Bowker, John. *The Targums and Rabbinic Literature.* Cambridge: University Press, 1969.

Braun, Herbert. 'Beobachtungen zur Tora-Verschärfung im häretischen Spätjudentum', *ThLZ* 79 (1954), 347–52.

Qumran und das Neue Testament. 2 vols. Tübingen: J. C. B. Mohr, 1966.

Brownlee, W. H. 'A Comparison of the Covenanters of the Dead Sea Scrolls with Pre-Christian Jewish Sects', *BA* 13 (1950), 49–72.

'The Dead Sea Manual of Discipline', *BASOR*, Supplementary Studies 10–11 (1951).

Bruce, F. F. 'Justification by Faith in the Non-Pauline Writings of the New Testament', *EQ* 24 (1952), 66–77.

The Teacher of Righteousness in the Qumran Texts. London: Tyndale Press, 1956.

Bultmann, Rudolf. *Jesus and the Word.* ET by L. P. Smith and E. H. Lantero. New York: Charles Scribner's Sons, 1958.

The History of the Synoptic Tradition. ET by John Marsh; 2nd edn. Oxford: Basil Blackwell, 1968.

Theology of the New Testament. ET by Kendrick Grobel; 2 vols. New York: Charles Scribner's Sons, 1951–5.

Burrows, Millar. *More Light on the Dead Sea Scrolls.* New York: Viking Press, 1958.

The Dead Sea Scrolls. New York: Viking Press, 1955.

'The Discipline Manual of the Judean Covenanters', *OSt* 8 (1950), 156–92.

Butler, Harry A. 'The Chronological Sequence of the Scrolls of Qumran Cave One', *RQ* 2 (1960), 533–9.

Carmignac, Jean. *Christ and the Teacher of Righteousness.* ET by K. G. Pedley. Baltimore: Helicon Press, 1962.

Clark, K. W. 'The Gentile Bias in Saint Matthew', *JBL* 66 (1947) 165–72.

Cross, Frank Moore, jun. *The Ancient Library of Qumran and Modern Biblical Studies.* Garden City, N.Y.: Doubleday, 1958.

Cullmann, Oscar. *Baptism in the New Testament.* ET by J. K. S. Reid; SBT 1. London: SCM Press, 1950.

Culver, Robert D. 'What is the Church's Commission? Some Exegetical
Issues in Matthew 28:16-20', *BibSac* 125 (1968), 239-53.

Davies, W. D. '"Knowledge" in the Dead Sea Scrolls and Matthew 11:25-30',
HTR 46 (1953), 113-39.

The Setting of the Sermon on the Mount. Cambridge: University Press,
1963.

Descamps, Albert. *Les Justes et la Justice dans les évangiles et le christianisme primitif.* Louvain: Publications Universitaires de Louvain, 1950.

Dibelius, Martin. *Der Brief des Jakobus.* Meyers Kommentar 15; 10th rev.
edn. Göttingen: Vandenhoeck & Ruprecht, 1959.

Dodd, C. H. *The Bible and the Greeks.* London: Hodder & Stoughton, 1935.

Dupont-Sommer, A. *The Essene Writings from Qumran.* ET by G. Vermes.
Oxford: Basil Blackwell, 1961.

Eissfeldt, Otto. 'Πληρῶσαι πᾶσαν δικαιοσύνην in Matthäus 3:15', *ZNW*
61 (1970), 209-15.

Elliger, Karl. *Studien zum Habakuk-Kommentar vom Toten Meer.* Beiträge
zur historischen Theologie. Tübingen: J. C. B. Mohr, 1953.

Fenton, J. C. *The Gospel of St Matthew.* Pelican Gospel Commentaries.
Harmondsworth: Penguin Books, 1963.

Fiedler, Martin Johannes. 'Der Begriff δικαιοσύνη im Matthäus-Evangelium,
auf seine Grundlagen untersucht'. Vol. I, text; vol. II, notes. Ph.D.
dissertation, Martin-Luther-Universität, Halle-Wittenberg, 1957.

'Δικαιοσύνη in der diaspora-jüdischen und intertestamentarischen
Literatur', *JStJ* 1 (1970), 120-43.

Filson, Floyd V. *A Commentary on the Gospel According to St. Matthew.*
BNTC. London: Adam & Charles Black, 1960.

Frankemölle, Hubert. 'Die Makarismen (Mt 5,1-12; Lk 6,20-23). Motive
und Umfang der redaktionellen Komposition', *BZ* 15 (1971), 52-75.

Fuchs, Ernst. 'Jesu Selbstzeugnis nach Matthäus 5', *ZThK* 51 (1954), 14-34.

Gaechter, Paul. *Das Matthäus Evangelium.* Innsbruck: Tyrolia, 1963.

Gaster, Theodor H. *The Dead Sea Scriptures. In English Translation with
Introduction and Notes.* Garden City, N.Y.: Doubleday, 1956.

Gibson, John Monro. *The Gospel of St. Matthew.* Expositor's Bible.
Toronto, 1890.

Ginzberg, Louis. *An Unknown Jewish Sect.* New York: Jewish Theological
Seminary of America, 1976.

Goldin, Judah. 'The End of Ecclesiastes. Literal Exegesis and its Transformation', in Alexander Altmann (ed.), *Biblical Motifs. Studies and Texts*
3. Cambridge, Mass.: Harvard University Press, 1966.

The Song at the Sea. New Haven, Conn.: Yale University Press, 1971.

Goulder, M. D. *Midrash and Lection in Matthew.* London: SPCK, 1974.

Grundmann, Walter. *Das Evangelium nach Matthäus.* Theologischer Handkommentar zum Neuen Testament 1. Berlin: Evangelische Verlagsanstalt, 1968.

Gundry, Robert Horton. *The Use of the Old Testament in St. Matthew's
Gospel. With Special Reference to the Messianic Hope.* Suppl. to
NovTest, 18. Leiden: E. J. Brill, 1967.

Günther, Hartmut. 'Die Gerechtigkeit des Himmelreiches in der Bergpredigt',
KerDog 17 (1971) 113-26.

Hare, D. R. A. *The Theme of Jewish Persecution of Christians in the Gospel According to St Matthew.* SNTS Monograph Series, 6. Cambridge: University Press, 1967.

Hatch, Edwin. *Essays in Biblical Greek.* Oxford: Clarendon Press, 1889.

Herford, R. T. *The Ethics of the Talmud. Sayings of the Fathers.* New York: Schocken Books, 1974.

Hill, David. *Greek Words and Hebrew Meanings. Studies in the Semantics of Soteriological Terms.* SNTS Monograph Series, 5. Cambridge: University Press, 1967.

The Gospel of Matthew. NCB. London: Oliphants, 1972.

'Δίκαιοι as a Quasi-Technical Term', *NTS* 11 (1964), 296–302.

Hirsch, Emanuel. *Die Frühgeschichte des Evangeliums.* 2 vols.; 2nd enlarged edn. Tübingen: J. C. B. Mohr, 1941.

Hobbs, Herschel H. *The Gospel of Matthew.* Grand Rapids, Mich.: Baker Book House, 1963.

Holm-Nielsen, Svend. *Hodayot. Psalms from Qumran.* AThD 2. Aarhus: Universitetsforlaget, 1960.

Holtzmann, Heinrich J. *Die Synoptischen Evangelien. Ihr Ursprung und Geschichtlicher Charakter.* Leipzig, 1863.

Hübner, Hans. *Das Gesetz in der synoptischen Tradition. Studien zur These einer progressiven Qumranisierung und Judaisierung innerhalb der synoptischen Tradition.* Witten: Luther-Verlag, 1973.

Hummel, R. *Die Auseinandersetzung zwischen Kirche und Judentum im Matthäusevangelium.* BEvTh, Theologische Abhandlungen 33. München: Chr. Kaiser, 1966.

Hunzinger, Claus-Hunno. 'Beobachtungen zur Entwicklung der Disziplinarordnung der Gemeinde von Qumran', in H. Bardtke (ed.), *Qumran-Probleme.* Berlin: Akademie Verlag, 1963.

'Fragmente einer älteren Fassung des Buches Milḥamā aus Höhle 4 von Qumrān', *ZAW* 69 (1957), 131–51.

Huppenbauer, Hans Walter. 'Zur Eschatologie der Damaskusschrift', *RQ* 4 (1964), 567–73.

Jeremias, Gert. *Der Lehrer der Gerechtigkeit.* StUNT 2. Göttingen: Vandenhoeck & Ruprecht, 1963.

Jeremias, Joachim. *The Parables of Jesus.* ET by S. H. Hooke; rev. edn. New York: Charles Scribner's Sons, 1963.

Käsemann, Ernst. 'Gottesgerechtigkeit bei Paulus', *ZThK* 58 (1961), 367–78.

Kasting, Heinrich. *Die Anfänge der urchristlichen Mission.* BEvTh 55. München: Chr. Kaiser Verlag, 1969.

Kertelge, Karl. *'Rechtfertigung' bei Paulus.* NTAb, Neue Folge 3; 2nd edn. Münster: Verlag Aschendorff, 1971.

Kilpatrick, G. D. 'A Theme of the Lucan Passion Story and Luke xxiii. 47', *JThS* 43 (1942), 34–6.

The Origins of the Gospel According to St. Matthew. Oxford: Clarendon Press, 1946.

Kingsbury, Jack Dean. 'The Composition and Christology of Matt 28: 16–20', *JBL* 93 (1974), 573–84.

Klostermann, Erich. *Das Matthäusevangelium.* HbzNT 4; 2nd rev. edn. Tübingen: J. C. B. Mohr, 1927.

Knight, George, A. F. *A Christian Theology of the Old Testament.* London: SCM Press, 1959.

Kümmel, Werner Georg. *Introduction to the New Testament.* ET by A. J. Mattill, jun.; 14th rev. edn. Nashville, Tenn.: Abingdon Press, 1966.

La Rondelle, Hans K. *Perfection and Perfectionism. A Dogmatic-Ethical Study of Biblical Perfection and Phenomenal Perfectionism.* Kampen: J. H. Kok, 1971.

Lauterbach, Jakob Zallel. 'Tannaim and Amoraim', *The Jewish Encyclopedia* 12 (1946), 49–54.

Leaney, A. R. C. *The Rule of Qumran and its Meaning.* New Testament Library. London: SCM Press, 1966.

Licht, J. 'The Doctrine of the Thanksgiving Scroll', *IEJ* 6 (1956), 1–13, 89–101.

Ljungman, Hendrik. *Das Gesetz erfüllen, Matth. 5,17ff. und 3,15 untersucht.* Lund: C. W. K. Gleerup, 1954.

Lohmeyer, Ernst. *Das Evangelium des Matthäus.* Meyers Kommentar Sonderband. Göttingen: Vandenhoeck & Ruprecht, 1956.

Luz, Ulrich. 'Die Jünger im Matthäusevangelium', *ZNW* 62 (1971), 141–71.

McConnell, Richard S. *Law and Prophecy in Matthew's Gospel. The Authority and Use of the Old Testament in the Gospel of St. Matthew.* Theologische Dissertationen 2. Basel: Friedrich Reinhardt Kommissionsverlag, 1969.

Mach, R. *Der Zaddik in Talmud und Midrasch.* Leiden: E. J. Brill, 1957.

McNeile, A. H. *The Gospel According to St. Matthew.* London: Macmillan, 1915.

Maimonides, Moses. *The Commentary to Mishnah Aboth.* ET with an introduction and notes by Arthur David. New York: Bloch, 1968.

Malina, Bruce J. 'The Literary Structure and Form of Matt. XXVIII. 16–20', *NTS* 17 (1970), 87–103.

Manson, T. W. *The Sayings of Jesus.* 1937; rpt London: SCM Press, 1964.

Martin, James P. 'The Church in Matthew', *Interpretation* 29 (1975), 41–56.

Melamed, Ezra Z. *The Relationship between the Halakhic Midrashim and Tosefta.* In Hebrew. Jerusalem, 1967.

Metzger, Bruce M. *The Text of the New Testament.* 2nd edn. Oxford: Clarendon Press, 1968.

Michaelis, Wilhelm. 'ὁδός', *TDNT* V (1967), 42–96.

Michel, Otto. 'Der Abschluss des Matthäusevangeliums', *EvTh* 10 (1951), 16–26.

Mielziner, Moses. *Introduction to the Talmud.* 4th enlarged edn. New York: Bloch, 1968.

Milik, J. T. 'Fragments d'un midrash de Michée dans les manuscrits de Qumran', *RB* 59 (1952), 412–18.

'Recensions', *RB* 67 (1960), 410–16.

Minear, Paul S. 'The Disciples and the Crowds in the Gospel of Matthew', *ATR*, Supplementary Series 3 (1974), 28–44.

Montefiore, C. G. *The Synoptic Gospels.* 2 vols.; 2nd rev. edn. London: Macmillan, 1927.

Montefiore, C. G., and H. Loewe (eds.). *A Rabbinic Anthology.* 1938; rpt New York: Schocken Books, 1974.

Moore, George Foot. *Judaism in the First Centuries of the Christian Era. The Age of the Tannaim.* 3 vols. 1927; rpt Cambridge, Mass.: Harvard University Press, 1970.

Morawe, Günther. *Aufbau und Abgrenzung der Loblieder von Qumrân.* ThA 16. Berlin: Evangelische Verlagsanstalt, 1961.

Murphy-O'Connor, J. 'La genèse littéraire de la Régle de la Communauté', *RB* 76 (1969), 528–49.

Nagel, Walter. 'Gerechtigkeit – oder Almosen? (Mt 6,1)', *VigChr* 15 (1961), 141–5.

Nepper-Christensen, P. *Das Matthäusevangelium, ein judenchristliches Evangelium?* AThD 1. Aarhus, 1958.

Neusner, Jakob. *Development of a Legend. Studies on the Traditions Concerning Yohanan Ben Zakkai.* SPB 16. Leiden: E.J. Brill, 1970.

Eliezer Ben Hyrcanus. Studies in Judaism in Late Antiquity 4; 2 vols. Leiden: E. J. Brill, 1973.

The Rabbinic Traditions about the Pharisees before 70. 3 vols. Leiden: E. J. Brill, 1971.

North, Christopher R. *The Second Isaiah.* Oxford: Clarendon Press, 1964.

Osten-Sacken, Peter von der. *Gott und Belial. Traditionsgeschichtliche Untersuchungen zum Dualismus in den Texten aus Qumran.* StUNT 6. Göttingen: Vandenhoeck & Ruprecht, 1969.

Otzen, Benedikt. 'Die neugefundenen hebräischen Sektenschriften und die Testamente der zwölf Patriarchen', *StTh* 7 (1953), 125–57.

Ploeg, J. van der. *The Excavations at Qumran. A Survey of the Judean Brotherhood and its Ideas.* ET by K. Smyth. London: Longman, 1958.

'Zur literarischen Komposition der Kriegsrolle', in H. Bardtke (ed.), *Qumran-Probleme.* Berlin: Akademie Verlag, 1963.

Quell, Gottfried. 'The Concept of Law in the OT', *TDNT* II (1964), 174–8.

Rabin, Chaim. *The Zadokite Documents.* 2nd rev. edn. Oxford: Clarendon Press, 1958.

Rabinowitz, Isaac. 'Sequence and Dates of the Extra-Biblical Dead Sea Scroll Texts and "Damascus" Fragments', *VT* 3 (1953), 175–85.

Rad, Gerhard von. *Old Testament Theology.* ET by D. M. G. Stalker; 2 vols. Edinburgh: Oliver & Boyd, 1962.

Reicke, Bo. 'Die Ta'āmire-Schriften und die Damaskus-Fragmente', *StTh* 2 (1949), 45–70.

Ringgren, Helmer. *The Faith of Qumran.* ET by E. T. Sander. Philadelphia: Fortress Press, 1968.

Robinson, John A. T. 'The Baptism of John and the Qumran Community', *HTR* 50 (1957), 175–91.

Rogers, Cleon. 'The Great Commission', *BibSac* 130 (1973), 258–67.

Rohde, Joachim. *Rediscovering the Teaching of the Evangelists.* ET by Dorothea M. Barton. London: SCM Press, 1968.

Rosenthal, Franz. 'Sedakah, Charity', *HUCA* 23 (1950–1), I, 411–30.

Rowley, H. H. 'Some Traces of the History of the Qumran Sect', *ThZ* 13 (1957), 530–40.

Ruppert, Lothar. *Jesus als der leidende Gerechte? Der Weg Jesu im Lichte eines alt- und zwischentestamentlichen Motivs.* Stuttgarter Bibelstudien 59. Stuttgart: Verlag Katholisches Bibelwerk, 1972.

Sand, Alexander. 'Die Polemik gegen "Gesetzlosigkeit" im Evangelium nach Matthäus und bei Paulus', *BZ* 14 (1970), 112–25.

Sanders, E. P. *Paul and Palestinian Judaism. A Comparison of Patterns of Religion.* London: SCM Press, 1977.

'R. Akiba's View of Suffering', *JQR* 63 (1972–3), 332–51.

Sandmel, Samuel. *A Jewish Understanding of the New Testament.* Cincinnati, Ohio: Hebrew Union College Press, 1956.

Schaff, Philip. *The Gospel According to Matthew.* International Revision Commentary. New York: Charles Scribner's Sons, 1882.

Schlatter, Adolf. *Das Evangelium nach Matthäus.* Rev. edn. Stuttgart: Calwer Verlag, 1961.

Schlier, Heinrich. 'Zur kirchlichen Lehre von der Taufe', *ThLZ* 72 (1947), 321–36.

Schmahl, Günther. 'Die Antithesen der Bergpredigt', *Trierer Theologische Zeitschrift* 83 (1974), 284–97.

Schmid, Hans Heinrich. *Gerechtigkeit als Weltordnung.* Beiträge zur Historischen Theologie 40. Tübingen: J. C. B. Mohr, 1968.

Schnackenburg, R. 'Die Erwartung des "Propheten" nach dem Neuen Testament und den Qumran-Texten', *TU* 73 (1959), 622–39.

Schniewind, Julius. *Das Evangelium nach Matthäus.* NTD 2. Göttingen: Vandenhoeck & Ruprecht, 1950.

Schrenk, Gottlob. 'δίκαιος, δικαιοσύνη', *TDNT* II (1964), 182–210.

Schweizer, Eduard. *Lordship and Discipleship.* SBT 28. London: SCM Press, 1960.

'Observance of the Law and Charismatic Activity in Matthew', *NTS* 16 (1970), 213–30.

The Good News According to Matthew. ET by D. E. Green. London: SPCK, 1976.

Scobie, Charles H. H. *John the Baptist.* Philadelphia: Fortress Press, 1964.

Segal, M. H. 'The Habakkuk "Commentary" and the Damascus Fragments', *JBL* 70 (1951), 131–47.

Sheridan, Mark. 'Disciples and Discipleship in Matthew and Luke', *BThB* 3 (1973), 235–55.

Smith, Morton. 'On the Problem of Method in the Study of Rabbinic Literature', *JBL* 92 (1973), 112–13.

Tannaitic Parallels to the Gospels. JBL Monograph Series, 6; corrected rpt. Philadelphia, 1968.

Sperber, Daniel. 'Tanna, Tannaim', *Encyclopaedia Judaica* 15 (1972), 798–803.

Spicq, C. 'Joseph, son mari, étant juste . . . (Mt. I, 19)', *RB* 71 (1964), 206–14.

Stagg, Frank. 'Salvation in Synoptic Tradition', *RevExp* 69 (1972), 355–67.

Stanley, David M. *The Gospel of St. Matthew.* New Testament Reading Guide 4; 2nd rev. edn. Collegeville, Minn.: Liturgical Press, 1963.

Stegemann, Hartmut. 'Der Pešer Psalm 37 aus Höhle 4 von Qumran', *RQ* 4 (1963), 235–70.

Stendahl, Krister. *The School of St. Matthew and its Use of the Old Testament.* Acta Seminarii Neotestamentici Upsaliensis 20. Uppsala: C. W. K. Gleerup, 1954.

Strack, Hermann L. *Introduction to the Talmud and Midrash.* 1931; rpt New York: Atheneum, 1969.

Strack, Hermann L., and Paul Billerbeck. *Kommentar zum Neuen Testament aus Talmud und Midrasch.* 4 vols. 1926; rpt München: C. H. Beck'sche Verlagsbuchhandlung, 1974.

Strecker, Georg. *Der Weg der Gerechtigkeit. Untersuchungen zur Theologie des Matthäus.* FRLANT 82; 3rd rev. edn. Göttingen: Vandenhoeck & Ruprecht, 1971.

Strugnell, J. 'The Angelic Liturgy at Qumrân, 4Q Serek Šîrôt ʿÔlat Haššabbāt', *Suppl. to VT* 7 (1960), 318–45.

Stuhlmacher, Peter. *Gerechtigkeit Gottes bei Paulus.* FRLANT 87; 2nd rev. edn. Göttingen: Vandenhoeck & Ruprecht, 1966.

Sutcliffe, Edmund F. 'The First Fifteen Members of the Qumran Community. A Note on 1QS 8:1ff.', *JSS* 4 (1959), 134–8.

Tagawa, Kenzo. 'People and Community in the Gospel of Matthew', *NTS* 16 (1970), 149–62.

Taylor, Charles. *Sayings of the Jewish Fathers.* 2nd edn. New York: Ktav, 1969.

Teicher, J. L. 'The Damascus Fragments and the Origin of the Jewish Christian Sect', *JJS* 2 (1951), 115–43.

Towner, Wayne Sibley. *The Rabbinic 'Enumeration of Scriptural Examples'. A Study of a Rabbinic Pattern of Discourse with Special Reference to Mekhilta D'R. Ishmael.* Leiden: E. J. Brill, 1973.

Trilling, Wolfgang. *Das wahre Israel. Studien zur Theologie des Matthäus-Evangeliums.* StANT 10; 3rd rev. edn. München: Kösel Verlag, 1964.

Wacholder, Ben Zion. 'A Reply', *JBL* 92 (1973), 114–15.

'The Date of the Mekilta de-Rabbi Ishmael', *HUCA* 39 (1968), 117–44.

Weingreen, J. 'The Title Moreh Sedek', *JSS* 6 (1961), 162–74.

'The Construct-Genitive Relation in Hebrew Syntax', *VT* 4 (1954), 50–9.

Weiss, Bernhard. *Das Matthäusevangelium und seine Lucas-Parallelen.* Halle: Buchhandlung des Waisenhauses, 1876.

Wellhausen, J. *Das Evangelium Matthaei.* Berlin: Georg Reimer, 1904.

Wernberg-Møller, Preben. *The Manual of Discipline.* StTDJ 1. Leiden: E. J. Brill, 1957.

'*Tsedeq, Tsaddiq* and *Tsedaqah* in the Zadokite Fragments (CDC), the Manual of Discipline (DSD) and the Habakkuk-Commentary (DSH)', *VT* 3 (1953), 310–15.

Westermann, Claus. *Das Buch Jesaja.* Das Alte Testament Deutsch 19. Göttingen: Vandenhoeck & Ruprecht, 1966.

Wevers, J. W. 'Septuagint', *IDB* IV (1962), 273–8.

Windisch, Hans. *The Meaning of the Sermon on the Mount.* ET by S. MacLean Gilmour. Philadelphia: Westminster Press, 1951.

Woude, A. S. van der. *Die messianischen Vorstellungen der Gemeinde von Qumrân.* Studia Semitica Neerlandica. Assen: Van Gorcum, 1957.

Yadin, Yigael. *The Message of the Scrolls.* New York: Simon & Schuster, 1957.

The Scroll of the War of the Sons of Light against the Sons of Darkness. ET by Batya and Chaim Rabin. London: Oxford University Press, 1962.

Zahn, Theodor. *Das Evangelium des Matthäus.* Kommentar zum Neuen Testament 1; 3rd rev. edn. Leipzig: A. Deichert'sche Verlagsbuchhandlung, 1910.

Zeitlin, Solomon. *The Rise and Fall of the Judaean State.* 2 vols. Philadelphia: Jewish Publication Society of America, 1962–7.

Ziesler, J. A. *The Meaning of Righteousness in Paul.* SNTS Monograph Series, 20. Cambridge: University Press, 1972.

Zlotnick, Dov. *The Tractate 'Mourning' (Šěmahot).* Yale Judaica Series, 17. New Haven, Conn.: Yale University Press, 1966.

INDEX OF PASSAGES CITED

GENERAL INDEX

Aaron, 45, 48
Abel, 101, 156 n. 180
Abihu, 45f
Abraham, 44, 144 n. 174
Akiba, R., 44, 47, 140 n. 67, 149 n. 48;
  School of, 140 n. 67
almsgiving (*includes references to*
  almoners; alms; charity*): Dead Sea
  Scrolls, 25, 119, 133 n. 93, 159 n. 3;
  Mt, 77, 88, 100, 118–20, 147 n. 17;
  OT, 9, 11, 68, 100, 155 n. 168;
  Tannaitic literature, 25, 53, 66–71,
  73–6, 100, 118–20, 145 nn. 176, 180,
  190 and 193f, 146 nn. 203 and 213
antitheses, 80f, 83
Aramaic, 6, 57, 96, 139 n. 45, 143 n.
  147
atonement, 51f, 76, 91f, 140 n. 64, 142
  n. 111, 146 n. 209, 156 n. 193; Day
  of, 51

baptism, 91–4, 107, 153 n. 122, 154 n.
  132
Barabbas, 126 n. 1
baraitot, 39f
beatitudes, 97
Belial, 22
Ben Azzai, 137 n. 3
Benjamin, 44
Boaz, 44

Caiaphas, 126 n. 1
Canaanites, 44
charity *see* almsgiving
Chorazin, 126 n. 1
church, 80, 107, 113, 115, 147 n. 2, 156
  n. 193
circumcision, 45
congregation of the poor, 34
covenant, 9f, 21f, 24f, 31, 51, 76, 102,
  106, 122, 130 n. 51, 133 n. 93; New

Covenant in Land of Damascus, 20–2,
  35, 38, 119, 122, 130 n. 52; with
  Aaron, 48; with David, 49

Damascus Document, relationship to
  Dead Sea Scrolls, 14f, 128 nn. 16
  and 19
David, 49, 61, 72
Dead Sea Scrolls: chronological sequence,
  14f, 128 n. 21; dating, 5, 14, 127 nn.
  5f; homogeneity of, 13–16, 30–2,
  127 n. 3, 128 n. 24; relevance as
  background to Mt, 4–8, 13, 16f
Dead Sea Sect, 15
death: of the righteous, 45, 47, 140 n.
  64; of the wicked, 47
deeds *see* works
deeds of lovingkindness, 66f, 70, 144
  n. 160
dietary law, 56
disciple, 80, 84f, 87–9, 91, 102, 113–17,
  122, 149 n. 52, 157 n. 25, 158 n. 29;
  esp. as the properly religious in Mt,
  108–12; *see also* Twelve, the
doers of Torah, 33f, 135 n. 151
dualistic thought of Dead Sea Scrolls, 14

Egypt, Egyptians, 45, 48, 61
Eleazar, R., 64, 70
Eleazer of Modiim, R., 45
Eliezer, R., 48
Eliezer ben Hyrcanus, R., 137 n. 5
Elijah, 130 n. 44
Elisha, 44

faith, 44; justification by, 2f, 106.
fasting, 51, 88, 100
fence around Torah, 63, 81–4, 87, 149
  nn. 47f
foreknowledge of God, 48